FORT POWELL
AND THE CIVIL WAR

Western Approaches
to Mobile Bay

1861–1865

SIDNEY HENSON SCHELL

HERITAGE BOOKS
2012

HERITAGE BOOKS
AN IMPRINT OF HERITAGE BOOKS, INC.

Books, CDs, and more—Worldwide

For our listing of thousands of titles see our website
at
www.HeritageBooks.com

Published 2012 by
HERITAGE BOOKS, INC.
Publishing Division
100 Railroad Ave. #104
Westminster, Maryland 21157

Copyright © 2012 Sidney H. Schell

All rights reserved. No part of this book may be reproduced or transmitted in any form or by any means, electronic or mechanical, including photocopying, recording or by any information storage and retrieval system without written permission from the author, except for the inclusion of brief quotations in a review.

International Standard Book Numbers
Paperbound: 978-0-7884-5425-7
Clothbound: 978-0-7884-9130-6

To Roxie, It has been a grand adventure.

TABLE OF CONTENTS

Chapter		Page
	PREFACE	iii
1	NECESSITY FOR A FORT AND FEDERAL PLANS	1
2	FORT GRANT	23
3	THE GUNS ARE REMOVED	36
4	1863 AN ENGINEERS WORK IS NEVER DONE	49
5	JANUARY 1864-THE 21ST ALABAMA AT THE PASS	65
6	THE FIRST BATTLE OF MOBILE BAY	74
7	CEDAR POINT AND CHUGEE POINT	89
8	JULY-THE EAST FACE	105
9	THE STORM FROM THE EAST-THE *CHICKASAW*	118
10	FINAL DAYS OF THE WAR	133
11	POST WAR	144
12	CENTENNIAL	152
13	RESEARCHING POWELL	163
14	DESCRIPTION OF THE FORT	176
15	ARTIFACTS	186
	CONCLUSION	192
	APPENDIX 1 TIMELINE COL. WILLIAMS AND THE 21ST ALABAMA	193
	APPENDIX 2 GRANTS PASS POSSESSION TIMELINE	197
	BIBLIOGRAPHY	201
	INDEX	208

Preface

Fort Powell was a small Civil War fort built on an oyster reef on the north side of Grants Pass, a dredged channel connecting Mobile Bay with Mississippi Sound, between Dauphin Island and Cedar Point.

This book details the reasons the pass was fortified and the history of the fort and Grants Pass. The defense of the pass required that additional fortifications be built on Little Dauphin Island and Cedar Point. The construction of those supporting works is covered as well as post war activities that might have impacted the several sites.

I have included a great many illustrations including a number of my drawings, paintings, sketches and models.

Much of the Civil War history related here is from an engineering and construction perspective. This is not a history of the well-known August 5, 1864 battle of Mobile Bay (although Fort Powell was involved in and blown up as a part of the battle) but I have included a short description of the strategy and tactics of the combatants.

Most of this book is based upon documents, books, photographs, drawings and interviews accumulated over forty years. In keeping with the broad-brush approach that I have taken to the subject, I have included not only the researched history but my personal experiences in exploring the site. One editor referred to the accumulated material as "eclectic" and that description may be fitting.

Local Mobile historian Caldwell Delaney once wrote that he felt a pressure of responsibility to publish information that he had gathered which no one else had bothered to assemble in just the same fashion. I suppose I share Caldwell's feelings as to the need to transfer my research materials from file folders to what I hope are coherent writings.

A compulsion to organize and write materials in a publishable form does not automatically result in a manuscript. Before I retired from my law practice, the preparation of papers and articles on historical subjects was the same as the preparation of lengthy legal briefs or court filings. I had a dictating machine on my desk which created a cassette with which my experienced secretary, typist and editor in one, would take and shortly thereafter present to me a document for my signature. This post-retirement/post-secretary effort is the culmination of nearly a year of an often frustrating learning curve with my computer word processing program and my Dragon Naturally Speaking voice recognition software.

To my wife Roxie, my thanks for enduring with me my computer frustrations and tolerating the clutter produced by my stacks of notes and files. I am afraid my library will not be less cluttered for the foreseeable future in that I have rows of files lined up, somewhat organized, for my next projects.

Thank you Bill Armistead for introducing me to Fort Powell, which started me on forty years of off and on research of the place. Further thanks to David Smithweck, who accompanied me on many expeditions, gathered together surveys, documents and photographs of the 1960s activities, encouraged me to reduce my notes to writing and made helpful suggestions and useful editing notes.

As I was dictating this book I gave only slight regard to the rules of footnote etiquette or for that matter the proprieties of grammar. If it read well to me it was in, if Google could identify the cited book or paper and refer the reader to a seller on Amazon.com or a library computer can pull it up, then I considered that to be sufficient. The further edits have, I trust, given to the text at least some sense of grammatical propriety.

My nephew Fritz Schell reviewed an early draft and reminded me of the correct, accepted grammatical and footnote protocols, some of which I followed. Fritz unexpectedly passed away, at age 54, during the preparation of this book. I and all his family miss him.

Dr. David Alsobrook, Director of the History Museum of Mobile and former director of the William J. Clinton Presidential Library & Museum in Little Rock, Arkansas did a time consuming edit together with suggestions on shifting some sections of the book and adding to or reducing others, which suggestions I mostly followed, and for which I am grateful.

My twelve year old granddaughter and computer assistant Sarah Frances assisted with my word processor questions and helped lay out the cover. Thank you Sarah Frances.

The history of Fort Powell that I relate includes the building of the work in several stages, the temporary abandonment, its successful repulsion of Admiral Farragut's fleet in February 1864 and its role in the battle of Mobile Bay on August 5, 1864. I try to give some insight into the lives of the troops on the isolated island fort and the difficulties of the engineers in securing men and materials to build it. Particular attention is given to the engineers, who they were, and the problems they had in carrying out their orders in relation to the Fort and its dependencies.

The Fort Powell story extends beyond the Civil War. I have chronicled the early history of the lower bay forts and the pre-Civil War efforts to fortify the western approaches to the bay and the necessity for such a fort.

Since this is a history of the defense of the western approaches to Mobile Bay I discuss the works built on little Dauphin Island and Cedar Point and the Union occupation of Cedar Point. Also covered is the present status of the fort, post war activities in the area and construction projects that might have impacted the site as well as the storms that by the early 1900s had returned the site to a submerged oyster reef. The fort was substantially forgotten and because of some inaccuracies in postwar maps its location was obscure. With the Civil War Centennial came renewed interest in all things Civil War and led some locals to the site and resulted in the removal and display of a large cannon from the site of the fort. That story is also told here.

Included in this book are not just archival and history book history but hands on underwater surveys done over several years, beginning about 1972, and the construction of a picture of the remains of the fort. Involved were many trips to the archives in Washington, New Orleans, Chapel Hill, North Carolina and other locations. Because of the way the fort was built and the effect of post war storms piecing together a plausible description of the place was difficult but I hope that I have succeeded in doing so.

Thank you for allowing me to tell to you the story of Fort Powell.

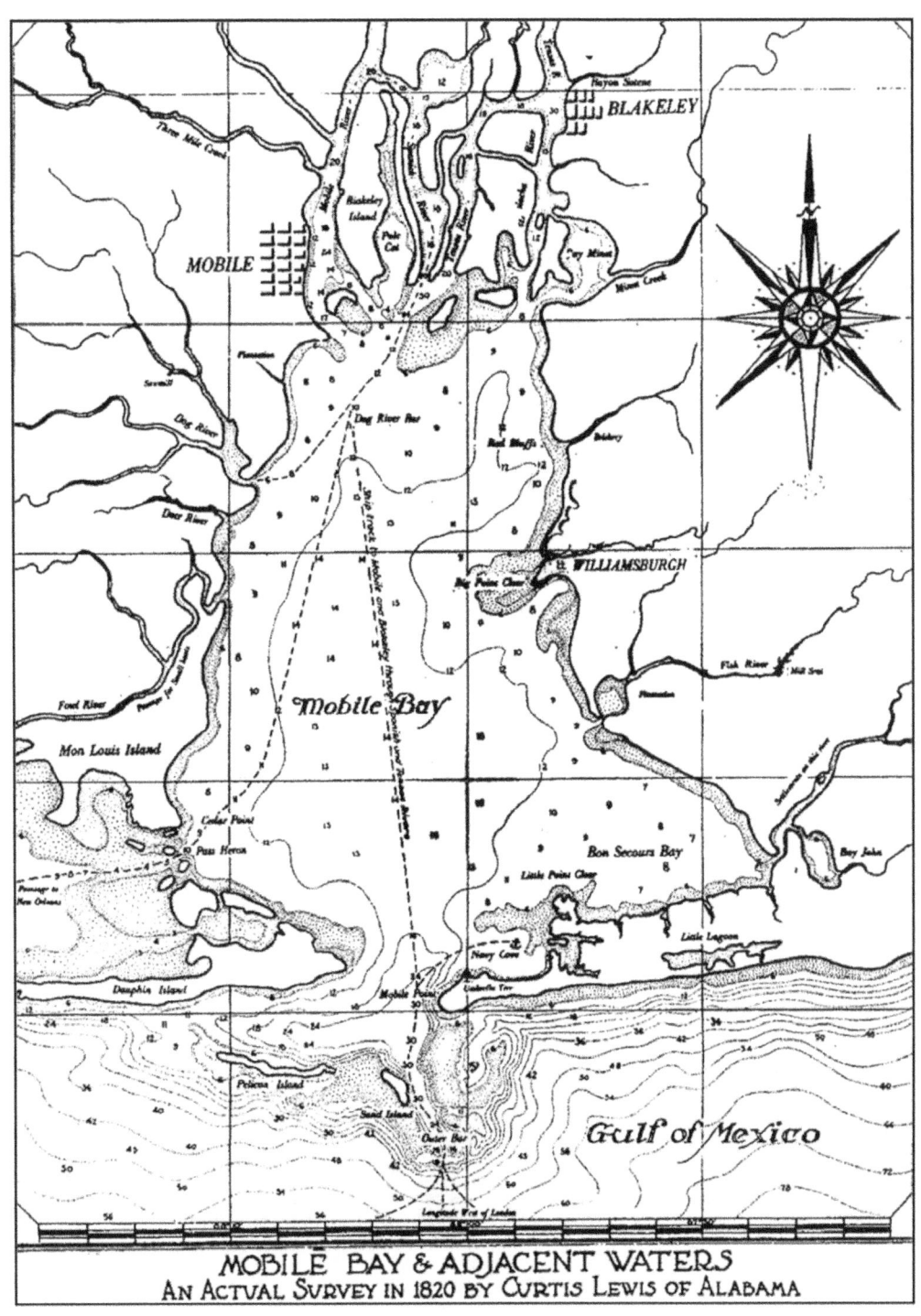

Entrance to Mobile Bay 1820

CHAPTER 1

Necessity for a Fort and Federal Plans

At the mouth of Mobile Bay stand Fort Morgan, at Mobile Point, and Fort Gaines on the east end of Dauphin Island. Both are relatively intact and are operated as tourist attraction museums. During the Civil War they stood, along with Fort Powell, as the first line of defense of Mobile Bay and the City of Mobile. Forts Morgan and Gaines are large brick structures built by the U.S. Government as a part of the "third system" of forts designed to protect the Atlantic and Gulf seaboards. Fort Powell was a smaller work of sand and oyster shells built by the Confederates during the Civil War. Another third system fort to protect the western entrance of Mobile Bay from Mississippi Sound was designed but never built

President James Madison initiated the third system of fortifications when in 1816 when he called for improved coastal defenses to prevent a repetition of the burning of Washington by a British amphibious landing force during the War of 1812. Madison asked the American representative in Paris to secure the services of a prominent military engineer to assist the U.S. Army Engineers with our coastal forts.

General Lafayette recommended Simon Bernard,[1] formerly aide-de-camp to and Field Marshal of the army of Napoleon Bonaparte then serving as Brigadier-General under the restored French Monarchy. Bernard designed, among other works, the great defensive system of fortifications around Antwerp. Bernard had gone to Napoleon's aid at Waterloo and stood beside his General in that battle. Such was to be expected of an old aide-de-camp, and Louis XVIII forgave him and again permitted him to enter the service of the Crown. At the time Paris was filled with unattached French officers because of the final downfall of Napoleon at Waterloo. Bernard was available for American service only because he had just been warned by the

---

[1] Bernard was made a Baron in 1834.

French Minister of War that for his personal safety he should leave France without delay.

Bernard's reputation as a military engineer was so high that he was eagerly recruited by several European governments. He declined their offers to follow the example of those eminent French nobles who had cast their lot with the American colonists during the Revolution. He gathered together his collection of engineering plans and data, unequaled in all Europe, and sailed for America. On November 16, 1816, the President commissioned Bernard to be "an assistant in the Corps of Engineers of the United States, with the rank of Brigadier-general by brevet and the compensation that is allowed to the chief of that corps."[2]

General Simon Bernard (1779-1839)

Bernard served as chairman of a board of five officers whose task was to recommend and to oversee the design and construction of fortifications along our entire coastline. Bernard resigned his post in 1831 and returned to France. Upon his arrival in France he was appointed to the grade of Lieutenant General and soon after was appointed as aide-de-camp to King Louis Philippe. The board continued its work. In 1816 there were no immediate threats of war or invasion so Bernard and the commission had time to carefully survey and consider before making proposals.

Until the commission was organized in 1816, specific plans and designs for forts had been prepared by engineers working independently of each other under general instructions issued by the Secretary of War and the Chief Engineer of the Army. Thus, each project and each fort was somewhat different and not part of an integrated defensive system. Notwithstanding,

---

[2] *Simon Bernard and America's Coastal Forts* by Thor Borresen, *The Regional Review*, February 1939, National Parks Service.

the first and particularly the second system included several substantial works.[3]

Bernard surveyed the Mobile area in 1817 and found two forts already constructed on Mobile Bay. Where Fort Morgan now stands was Fort Boyer, built in 1813. It was a circular sand battery partially open in the rear, elevated about 18 feet above water level. It more closely resembled Fort Powell than the larger regular brick Forts Morgan and Gaines.

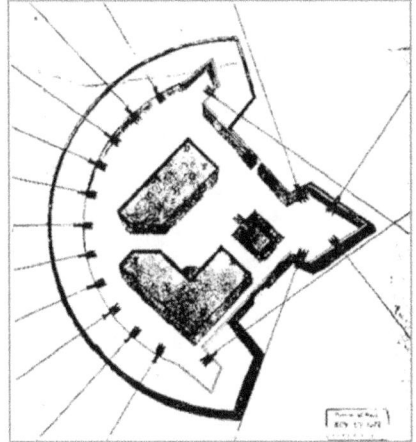
Fort Boyer (Library of Congress)

Fort Charlotte in Mobile was the old 1702 French Fort Condé renamed by the British when they took possession of Mobile at the close of the French and Indian War. It was the only regular brick fort built on the European model on the Gulf Coast during colonial times. It was quite adequate for the purpose of its construction, which was as a stronghold against the Indians and a refuge for the inhabitants of the community in the event of an Indian invasion.

The fort barely defended the west bank of the Mobile River and offered no protection against invasion by way of the several eastern branches of the waterways flowing into Mobile Bay. Bernard concluded that the fort should be retained; however, as an arsenal for the militia and as a place to rendezvous against Pensacola as long as that city remained under Spanish control. The fort was not to be retained, and was leveled and the property subdivided in the early 1820s.

Fort Conde (Adrien de Paug, 1725, University Of South Alabama Archives)

Fort Conde/Charlotte and Fort Boyer had both suffered siege and capture. Charlotte was taken from the British by Spanish General Galvez in

---

[3] For instance, Fort McHenry in Baltimore harbor that repulsed a British attack in the 1812 War and inspired Francis Scott Key to pen the *Star Spangled Banner*.

1780 and Boyer by the British on February 11, 1815, following their failed attack on New Orleans. Boyer had its moment earlier. On September 15, 1814, four British vessels attacked the sea face, and 600 Indians and 130 Royal Marines attacked from the land side. The attack was beaten back, resulting in the burning of the British Sloop of War *Hermes* on the sand spit later named Dixey Bar.[4]

H.M.S. *Hermes* approaching Fort Boyer on Mobile Point Sept. 15, 1815 (Painting by the Author on display at Fort Morgan Museum)

Bernard's survey found Fort Charlotte in good condition but Fort Boyer's timber components were rotten and the work was indefensible from the rear because of the sand dunes there. Bernard recommended that a new brick fort (Morgan) be built on the site at Mobile Point as well as a sister structure on the east end of Dauphin Island and a fort to cover the entrance into the Bay from Mississippi Sound. The forts proposed by the commission were all elaborate, expensive state of the art defense systems for the time.

---

[4] A number of years ago I located the builders plans of the *Hermes* in the British Naval Museum at Greenwich. The plans had been filed, with some slight indicated modifications, under the name of another vessel of the same class. With those plans in hand I painted the above picture of the *Hermes* approaching Fort Boyer which hangs in the Fort Morgan Museum. The sandbar off the southeast side of the mouth of Mobile Bay where the *Hermes* sank took its name from the clipper ship *Robert H. Dixey* that sank there in the hurricane of 1860.

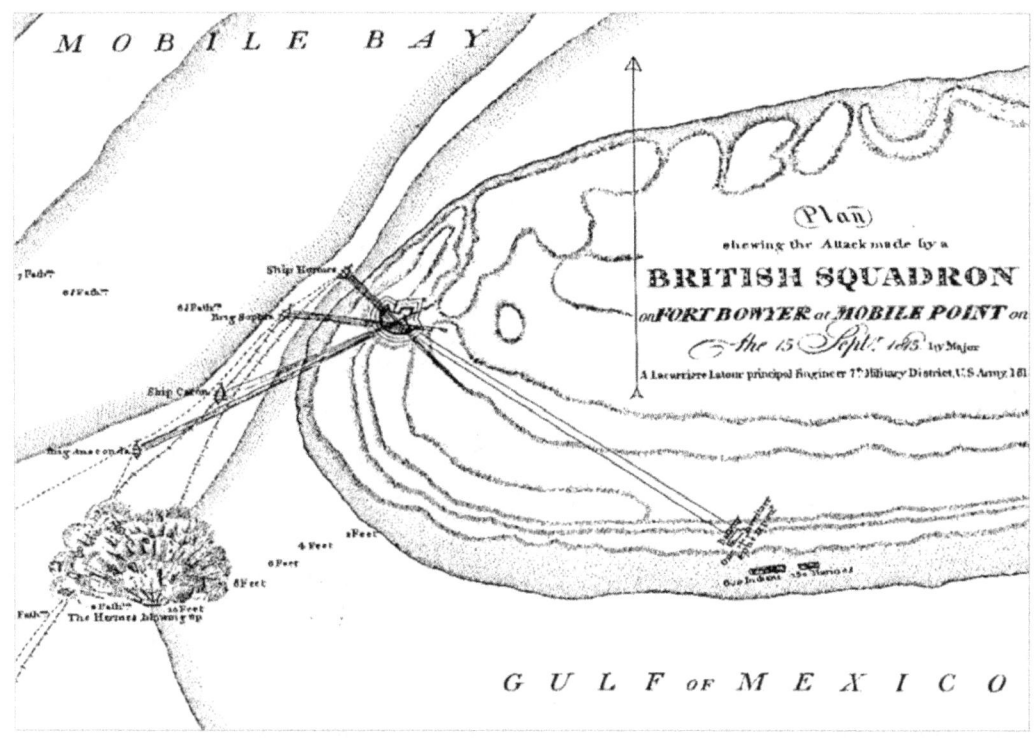

H.M.S. *Hermes* blowing up on Dixie Bar Sept. 15, 1815 (Latour, *Historical Memior*, 1816)

There were three considerations in justifying these expenditures. The first and most obvious was the necessity of protecting Mobile Bay. The second was protecting the area from an invasion from Spanish Pensacola by land. That requirement ceased when Florida passed into the hands of the United States. The third was the security of the Port of New Orleans, which had to be protected from an overland invasion from Alabama and also the coastal waterway which had to be to be kept open between Mobile and New Orleans by way of Mississippi Sound and Lake Pontchartrain. The Mobile Bay forts were not only intended to protect the Bay but also to provide a secure base for naval protection of Mississippi Sound.

With those considerations in mind and based upon surveys of 1816 – 1817,[5] plans were drawn for several forts in Louisiana and Forts Morgan and Gaines at the mouth of Mobile Bay. At a later date Fort Massachusetts on Ship Island was added. When Florida passed to the United States in 1819,

---

[5] The earliest known record of Corps of Engineers activity in the Mobile area was an order dated May 4, 1815, directing Lieutenant H. Dumas to examine the defenses of Mobile and New Orleans and to prepare a topographical map of the country from Pensacola to Lake Barataria, west of New Orleans. *A History of the Mobile District*, U.S. Army Corps of Engineers 1815 to 1971, Mobile District, page iiv.

the forts at Pensacola were also added. The final structure of the Mobile system of fortifications was to be a tower fort at Pass aux Heron to protect the entrance to Mobile Bay from Mississippi Sound.

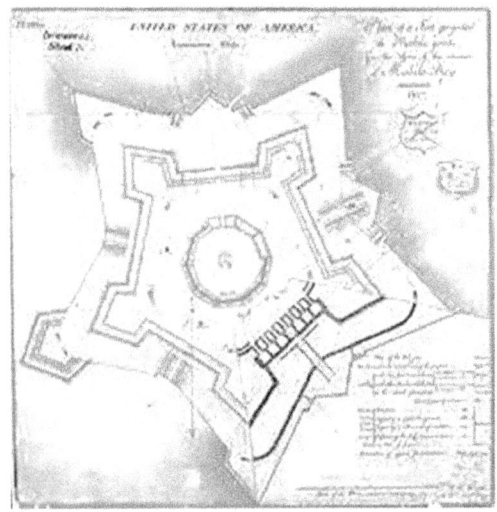
Fort Morgan (Auburn U. Digital Archives)

The free transit of Mississippi Sound for Mobile/New Orleans freight and passengers was of great importance to Mobile. Therefore, the protection of the sound by forts or naval vessels was an important part of Mobile's overall defensive position.

Not all agreed on fixed fortifications to protect Mississippi Sound. In 1836, while a fort on Ship Island was being discussed, Captain William H. Chase, the Corps Senior Engineer on the Gulf Coast, believed the best and most economical defense for the Sound and the protection of commerce there was a fleet of steam batteries to be based at Fort Morgan and Fort Pike. In 1846 the Senior Engineers called for construction of six shallow draft steam gunboats for that purpose. Fortified coaling depots were to be established at Fort Pike, Dauphin Island, and Ship Island.[6]

Bernard's report of 1817 projected a structure on a small shell island midway between Cedar Point and Dauphin Island on the north side of Pass aux Heron and south of the location of the yet to be dredged Grants Pass. He concluded that all that was needed was a Martello Tower[7] as the channel was narrow with a depth of only some four feet and practical only for boats or such small craft as then navigated the Inland Passage to New Orleans. Only a few pieces of ordnance would be necessary. The projected tower was to be 108 feet in diameter with six guns on the channel side of the island and six facing toward Dauphin Island. Thirty-six men would be a sufficient to

---

[6] *Historic Structure Report, Administrative Data Sections, Fort on Ship Island (Fort Massachusetts) 1857-1935* by Edwin C. Bearss, pages 10 and 14.

[7] Martello towers received their name from the small round fort at Martello Point in Corsica. In 1794 two British warships unsuccessfully attacked the tower.

man the fort in time of siege and only ten in time of peace. The estimated cost for the fort in 1817 was $16,677.41.

Fort Morgan was one of the first works of the third system to be started. Construction began in 1819 by private contractor. Because of the death by yellow fever of the first two contractors the project was taken over by Army Engineers in 1821. Because it was isolated on the tip of a peninsula it was built stronger than many of the other forts in the system and also had a decagonal citadel or defensive barracks in the middle of the work. The citadel was built first and completed in 1825. The fort was considered finished by 1834 with a total cost of $1,026,777.41. After December 1843, the fort was put on caretaker status commanded by an ordnance Sergeant.[8]

Fort Gaines on Dauphin Island was also begun in 1819 and was to have been the twin of Fort Morgan across the entrance of Mobile Bay. In 1821 Congress cut off funding for Fort Gaines after only a fraction of the work had been done on the citadel at a cost up to that point of $219,743.91. The majority in Congress believed such a large expensive work was not necessary since the channel covered by the fort was shallow and could not be navigated by the sailing ships of war of that period with their deep draft. Others argued that the original fort would be necessary to keep an enemy from using the Island for invasion as it had been used by the British in the war of 1812. The majority argument prevailed and the fort lay unfinished for decades.

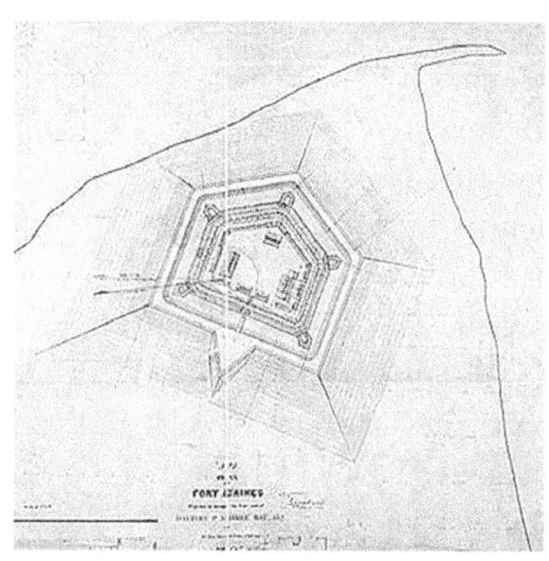

1854 plan of Fort Gaines (Library of Congress)

---

[8] *The Defenses of the Lower Mobile Bay* by Dale Manual, pages 18-19.

By 1840 war steamers had been developed with the requisite shallow draft to navigate the channel at the eastern end of Dauphin Island, which was some three miles from Fort Morgan and out of the range of the guns of that fort. Funds were therefore appropriated to resume construction on Fort Gaines in 1845. Because of title disputes[9] the work on the newly redesigned Fort Gaines was not begun until 1854. The old citadel in the northwest corner of the present parade was leveled when work began.

Plan for Martello Tower (National Archives)

The redesigned Fort Gaines was substantially smaller than the original plan but incorporated the latest technology. It is similar in design to Fort

---

[9] A private patent had previously been granted to the east end of Dauphin Island where Fort Gaines was built.

Clinch, Florida.[10] After Congress suspended work on the fort on Dauphin Island in 1821 nothing was said about the projected tower to protect Pass aux Heron for many years. The necessity for a fort to protect the western entrance was not forgotten for in 1842 the Government, at the direction of then Chief Engineer Totten, reserved all of the islands between Dauphin Island and Cedar Point for military purposes.[11] In the meantime John Grant completed his state licensed dredging of Grants Pass which allowed for the passage of vessels of seven foot draft.

The same new class of light draft steam warships that prompted the new work on Fort Gaines resulted in the redesign to then current standards of a smaller less expensive fort for Tower Island. Congress appropriated $100,000 for the construction of the fort on March 3, 1857, but the plans were not approved until September 5, 1860.[12] Given the perilous state of the Union at that time no contract was let and no work was done on the projected fort.

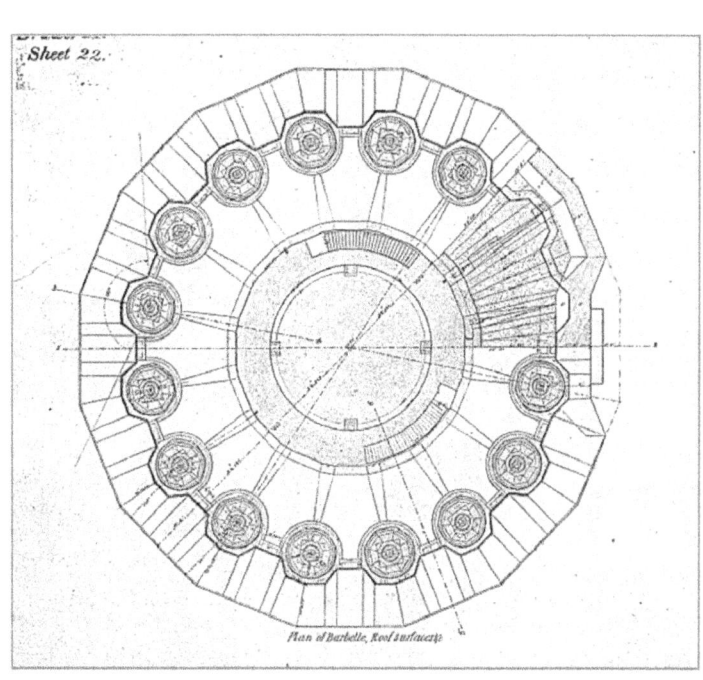

Barbette and rooftop level for proposed Martello Tower (National Archives)

---

[10] *The Defenses of the Lower Mobile Bay,* by Dale Manuel, pages 44 – 45.

[11] *History of the Mobile District, U.S. Army Corps of Engineers, 1815 to 1971*, Mobile District, 1975. Survey August 12, 1837 approved by James A. Weakley Surveyor General. Report of the Secretary of the Interior for the fiscal year ending June 30, 1880, volume 1, Washington, Government Printing office, page 36. *United States Military Reservations, National Cemeteries and Military Parks,* revised edition: 1910, Washington Government Printing Office, page 6. *Historic Structure Report, Administrative and Historical Data Sections, Fort on ship island (Fort Massachusetts) 1857 – 1935* by Edwin C. Bearss.

[12] National Archives Cartographic Section, *Modified Plan on Tower at Grants Pass & Pass Heron, Mobile Bay,* approved by John B. Floyd Secretary of War, September 5, 1860.

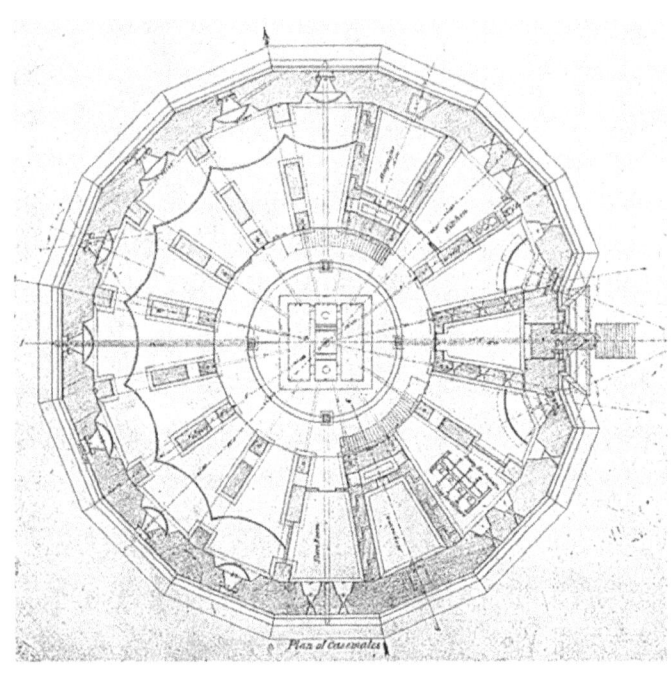
Casemate level of proposed Tower (National Archives)

Had the plans been carried forward the fort would have had two tiers with a casemate and a barbette level. The design was similar to but smaller than that of Fort Massachusetts on Ship Island. The original plan was for 12 guns while the new "smaller" work was to have 16 barbette guns, 8 casemate guns and 2 flank guns to guard the sally port. Entry was from a drawbridge connected to a wharf on the east side. The perimeter was to have been 400 feet and the estimated cost was $122,285.20.

A delay in letting the contract for the Tower was caused by concerns as to the rights of John Grant or to claims by him, under his state license, to the island upon which the fort was to be built.[13] Notwithstanding the reservation of all the islands between Dauphin Island and Cedar Point, the Corps of Engineers requested that the Alabama legislature cede jurisdiction of the island south of Grants Pass (Tower Island) to the United States for the site of the proposed fort. The dredge spoil oyster shell island that Grant's toll keeper's house was built upon was on the north side of the channel dredged by Grant.

---

[13] John Grant under an 1838 license from the Alabama Legislature had dredged a channel north of Pass aux Heron since known as Grants Pass. In connection with his operation of the channel he occupied a small dredge spoil dredge spoil shell island immediately north of his dredged channel subsequently known as Grants Pass.

Percy Walker, a member of the Alabama legislature was pressing for the construction of the tower and agreed to introduce and sponsor a bill ceding jurisdiction over the island. Walker believed that the 1839 act conveyed no title to Grant but rather only the right to take possession of so much of the shoal or shell reef as was necessary to excavate a channel. Walker's bill ceding title to and jurisdiction over the island was approved by the Alabama General Assembly on December 9, 1859. The act provided: "That for the purpose of enabling the United States to carry into effect an act of Congress of March 3, 1857, providing for fortifications for the defense of the inner passes into Mobile Bay (known as Grants Pass and Pass Aux Heron) by building and making such forts, magazines, arsenals, dock-yards, wharves and other structures, with their appendages, as may be necessary for the object aforesaid, jurisdiction is hereby ceded to the United States over the said 'Tower Island,' to include all the contiguous shores, flats, and waters within 1000 yards from the low water mark, and all the right, title and claim which this State may have in or to the said 'Tower Island' are hereby granted to the United States." Questions were to arise in the future over ownership of Grants Pass and the islands and water bottoms surrounding it.

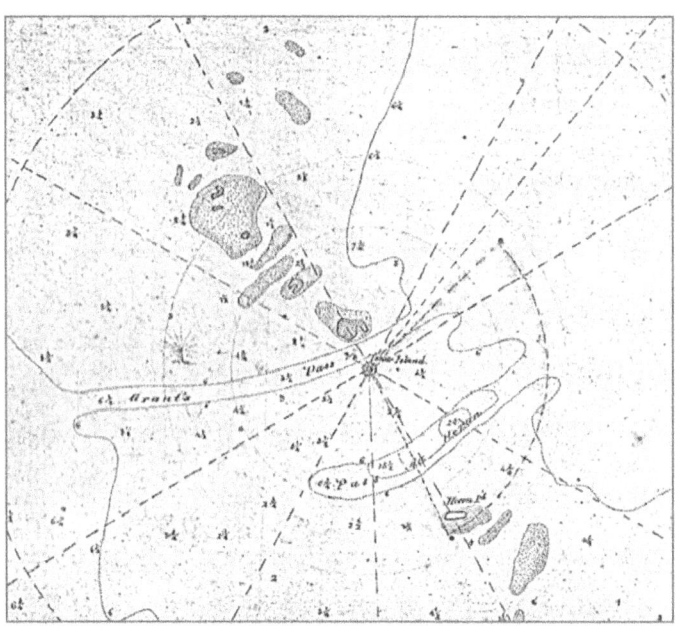

Corps of Engineers 1858 map of location of the proposed Tower (National Archives)

Compared to Forts Pickens, Morgan and Gaines, the tower at Pass Aux Heron/Grants Pass was to have been quite small, but still a substantial brick structure. It was to be constructed so that it could be easily demolished by explosives if there was danger that it might fall to an enemy. This of course was the fate of Fort Powell.[14] Grants Island or Fort Powell is often shown on period maps as being south of Grants Pass. The proposed Martello

---

[14]*A History of the Mobile District U.S. Army Corps of Engineers 1815 to 1971*, pages 30 – 31.

tower was intended to be built on the south side of the Pass. The oyster shell island upon which Fort Powell was built is on the north side of the pass but was often erroneously referred to as "Tower Island."

Captain Grant's License

The Gulf of Mexico is subject to severe and sudden storms, creating a real danger for small craft which venture into its open waters. River barges cannot survive in Gulf storms and tugs with such tows following the intra-coastal waterway have been known to break up in the passes between the barrier islands.

From N. Orleans.	MOBILE TO NEW ORLEANS.	Place to Place.	From Mobile.
	By Steamboat from		
166	MOBILE to......	0	0
136	Cedar Point, Ala..	30	30
124	Portersville........	12	42
111	Pascagoula, Miss..	13	55
83	Mississippi City...	28	83
72	Cat Island.........	11	94
61	East Marianne....	11	105
56	West Marianne....	5	110
51	St. Joseph's Island.	5	115
47	Grand Island......	4	119
38	Lake Borgne......	9	128
27	Fort Coquilles.....	11	139
20	Point Aux Herbes.	7	146
5	Lakeport (on L. Pontchartrain	15	161
	By Railroad to		
0	*NEW ORLEANS	5	166
From N. Orleans.	NEW ORLEANS TO MOBILE. (*Read up.*)	Place to Place.	From Mobile.
	Fare, $5 00. Time, 18 hours.		
	* See Routes from New Orleans.		

1851 Schedule Mobile to New Orleans (Traveler's and Tourist Guide, 1851)

The first regularly scheduled steamboat service from New Orleans to Mobile began in 1827. The shallow oyster reefs and sandbars stretching from Dauphin Island to the Alabama mainland barred passage of the new steamers. The upper Bay was also too shallow for the new boats. Cargo had to be shipped outside of Sand Island to be unloaded at Dauphin Island and ferried 30 miles to Mobile. Prior to 1840 passengers traveling from Mobile to New Orleans traveled from downtown Mobile by stagecoach to Portersville, which is now Bayou La Batre, and from there took a steamer through the Mississippi Sound to New Orleans.

John Grant was one of those self-educated engineers that gave impetus to this country's industrial revolution. He saw a need for dredged harbors and invented a machine to fill that need. The legislator, inventor and railroad man, was born November 25, 1796 in Chester County Pennsylvania. He moved to Baltimore as a child and at age 12 was the sole support of his family of 10 earning his living as a mechanic. At age 25 he invented the "Baltimore Harbor Dredge" and was operating the machine in Baltimore Harbor.[15] The government then hired him to construct dredges at Sackets Harbor, New York in 1825 and in 1827 at Mobile. Using his purpose built dredge he opened a channel 10 feet deep through Choctaw Point and Dog River bars just south of the harbor of Mobile which allowed coastal steamers from New Orleans to reach the city. But to do so they still had to go out into the open Gulf and around Dauphin Island to reach the Bay from the Mississippi Sound. In bad weather this was dangerous, and at all times it was risky because of the poorly marked shoals and sandbars at the mouth of the Bay.

John Grant (1796-1887) Jackson county Ms. Archives

Pontchartrain Railroad (La. State Library)

To assist in the navigation between Mobile and New Orleans, Congress appropriated $28,000 in 1828 for the improvement of Pass aux Heron connecting Mobile Bay with the Mississippi Sound, but after several years of effort the project was abandoned.[16] Grant did dredging work

---

[15] *Cruising Guide to the Northern Gulf Coast: Florida, Alabama and Mississippi*, by Claiborne S. Young, page 338.

[16] *A History of the Mobile District U.S. Corps of Engineers 1815 to 1971* by Virgil S. Davis page 61, published by the Mobile District 1975.

on the Pass Aux Heron project and later stated that it failed because storms filled it in with sand. In 1831 he was employed as builder and superintendent by the Pontchartrain Railroad Company of New Orleans, a line some 5 miles long connecting the Lake to the City and riverfront of New Orleans. This was first railroad in the South and in the process he invented the passing track and the raised station platform. He was superintendent on the road for several years. After which the city of New Orleans commissioned him to build wharfs on the riverfront for which he designed inclined ramps that allowed ships to be loaded and unloaded at any river stage or tide.[17]

Boat landing on Lake Pontchartrain for Mobile boats (G.W. Sully, 1836, from *New Orleans a Pictorial History*)

The Alabama Legislature took on the challenge of improving the Pass Aux Heron channel by providing in 1839 to Grant a charter for 25 years to dredge and collect tolls on a canal through the oyster reef between Mobile Bay and the Mississippi Sound. The channel had to be completed within 12 months and the charter would be revoked if the channel did not at any time have the required 7 foot depth for a period of six months. Grant did not repeat his efforts at Pass Aux Heron but moved north for his pass where he felt natural tidal currents would more effectively flush out the channel.[18]

---

[17] *Papers of Jefferson Davis*, Volume 2, June 1841-July 1846, pages 87-88.
[18] John Grant was not the only person to apply for and receive a grant to construct a canal in the area. The Alabama legislature in 1870 granted to Wilton L. Young a license to construct a toll ship canal from a point at or near the mouth of Fowl River, in Mobile Bay, to a point at or near the mouth of Fowl River in Mississippi sound. I've seen no records as to whether Mr. Young actually dredged such a canal. *Acts of Alabama* 1870, Act number 120, page 100.

1852 U.S. Coast Survey map. L.H. designates Grant's private lighthouse

By the fall of 1839 and at an expense of $100,000, Grant had completed a channel permitting the passage of vessels of 7 foot draft. The depth was afterwards increased to 8 1/2 feet and was kept open at that depth until 1869 by being dredged from time to time. After 1869 no work was done on the channel beyond staking it out with bush stakes.[19]

Grant later settled in Pascagoula and then in New Orleans. In 1848 he helped organize and manage the Mobile Steam Mail Line Company and just before the war operated smaller, low pressure vessels between New Orleans and Mandeville. During the War he lived in Covington, Louisiana and was reputed to be a strong Union man. After the War he moved to Mobile and in 1865 was elected to the Alabama Legislature. He served in the state legislatures of three different states. He also dredged the east branch of the Pascagoula River and was known as the "father of the Port of Pascagoula."[20]

By the fall of 1838, and after he had completed the pass thereafter known by his

Prewar view of Grants Pass (Manuel, The Defenses of Mobile Bay)

---

[19] *Annual Report of the Chief of Engineers, United States Army, to the Secretary of War for the year 1895, part two*. Washington: Government printing office, 1895 pages 1715 – 1724.

[20] *Pascagoula, Singing River City*, by Jay Higginbotham

Steamer *Cuba* thru the Pass (Ballou's Pictorial, June 27, 1857)

name, [21] he had built on the small dredge fill island on the north side of the channel a toll collector/lighthouse keeper's house and west of that the only private lighthouse ever built on the Gulf Coast.

Tolls were collected for each large vessel using the dredged channel. Grant was allowed to charge 15 cents per ton of cargo and could seize property for nonpayment of tolls. No effort was ever made to collect tolls from small oyster and fishing boats. He was further authorized to sell or convey any portions or all of the rights and privileges conferred upon him by the act. The license was a 25-year monopoly to excavate, maintain, and charge tolls on the use of the dredged channel.[22]

Grant may have been prepared to collect his tolls. It is reputed that he had 2 small cannon on the island for enforcement purposes. It is unlikely that Grant would have cannon for that purpose at the Pass since the pass keepers simply recorded the vessel transits and forwarded such information to Mobile for collection of the tolls. An entry in the Mobile Municipal Archives dated March 17, 1862 records that the Mayor received from a John Grant a gift to the City of a breech loading 6-pounder brass gun which was later loaned to Colonel J. B. Todd for aiding in the protection of the city. That gift would appear to be a patriotic Confederate gesture.

---

[21] *The Story of Mobile,* by Caldwell Delaney, page 89.
[22] *History of the Mobile District Corps of Engineers,* page 30

With the completion of Grants Pass, the Mobile to New Orleans mail vessels proceeded through it to the north shore of Lake Pontchartrain and thence by a short railroad trip to New Orleans.[23] The distance was about 166 miles.[24]

No railroad existed from Mobile to New Orleans at the time.[25] The Morgan Line had four steamers on a daily schedule from Mobile to the Mississippi Coast towns and New Orleans. A boat left their wharf at the foot of Conti Street every afternoon at 2 and reached New Orleans early the next morning. A boat from New Orleans arrived every evening in Mobile about 6 o'clock.[26] Grants' Mobile-New Orleans Mail line also had boats which with the Morgan Line combined to provide daily sailings. Weddings were planned around the steamers schedule so the wedding party could launch the newlyweds on their honeymoon cruise to New Orleans. The popular steamer *Cuba* was known as the "honeymoon boat."[27]

Steamer *Cuba* (James Bard 1815-1897)

The construction of the railroad from Mobile to New Orleans greatly reduced the value of Grant's license. Prior to the railroad's advent his revenues per year on the pass reached as much as $23,000 a year.

---

[23] Official Records Navy, Series 1, Volume 16, Page 630.

[24] *Early History of Steamboats in Alabama,* by Mell A. Frazer, Alabama Polytechnic Institute Historical Studies. The fare from Mobile to New Orleans in 1846 was five dollars. A typical steamer was the James L. Day, 185 feet long, drawing 5 1/2 feet water and only 7 feet when fully loaded.

[25] The railroad from Mobile to New Orleans was completed about 1872. My great grandmother was appointed post mistress of the new Post Office at Grand Bay, Alabama, a station on the new road.

[14] *The Mobile Register*, Mobilian Tells of This City in Civil War by B.B. Cox, Nov.1, 1915, page 5.

[27] Conversation with Caldwell Delaney, local historian and Director of The History Museum of Mobile, about 1985.

Afterwards it fell to $2500 and then again increased until in 1882 it reached $4500 and was rising.[28]

After the war Grant appealed to Union Army authorities for the restoration of the rights to his dredged channel, including collection of tolls based on his affidavit that he had always been a staunch Union man. His claim was granted, and he once again was in possession of the Pass. That possession is the basis of the University Of South Alabama's title to the water bottoms between Dauphin Island and Cedar Point and the oil and gas revenues generated therefrom.

Grants right to collect tolls following his being placed back in possession after the War did not go unchallenged. The vessel *Creole* made 41 trips through the pass between November 1865 and March 1866 generating a claim for tolls in the amount of $2416.95 which her owners refused to pay. Grant filed a suit to recover those tolls in New Orleans where he received a judgment which was appealed to the Supreme Court of Louisiana. The court's judgment on appeal in his favor was rendered on May, 1868.[29] The issue before the court was the right to collect tolls. Grant maintained that his grant from the State of Alabama was not revoked, and was one that could not be revoked without remuneration for the expenditure incurred by him, citing numerous authorities in support of that position. The court found that the legislature had given Grant: "a license coupled with an interest." There are numerous Alabama Supreme Court cases, mostly relating to timber, mining and oil and gas leases that delineate the rights under such an interest. Grant made no claim in that lawsuit that his license had morphed into a fee simple ownership.

---

[28] Statement of Captain John Grant contained in Chief Engineer's Report, 1895, page 1719.
[29] *Reports of the Supreme Court of Louisiana*, volume XX for the year 1868, page 329.

Jeffersonian Gunboat, Preble's third design 1805 (Model by Author)

The deepening of the channel by Grant also opened the Mississippi Sound entrance into the Bay to steam powered gunboats. The Jeffersonian gunboat fleet of Captain Thomas Ap R. Jones (uncle to Catesby Ap R. Jones)[30] apparently navigated the natural Pass aux Heron during the War of 1812. Now side wheel steam gunboats with heavy guns and nearly 300 feet long could pass through Grants Pass. Grant's dredging increased the necessity of a fort at the pass.

---

[30] Catesby Ap R. Jones was second in command of the *Virginia* (*Merrimack*) in the battle with the *Monitor*. He assumed command when Captain Buchanan was wounded. He was in command of the *Chattahoochee* and after that vessels boiler exploded was assigned as commander of the Naval Ordnance Foundry in Selma. Some of his Selma guns were used at Fort Powell.

1861

- January 11, 1861 Alabama Secedes from the Union.[31]

The State of Alabama Seizes the Forts

On January 3 or 4, 1861, the Governor of Alabama, ordered State militia to seize Forts Morgan and Gaines, the Arsenal at Mount Vernon and the U.S. Customs House at Mobile.[32] At the time of the seizure, the brickwork at Fort Morgan was essentially complete while Gaines was not and: "Not prepared for much defense."[33] Both forts were designed at a time when the 8-inch smoothbore cannon were the largest gun in or expected to be in service. The new heavy rifled cannon then coming into service would prove to be much more destructive to brick forts.

Fort Morgan had guns but considerable work was required to make them operational. Fort Gaines was unfinished and without guns. No State militia Force was left at Gaines at the time.[34]

- April 12, 1862 the bombardment of Fort Sumter initiates the Civil War.

The firing on Fort Sumter opened the Civil War. In May of 1861 the first blockading vessel appeared off Mobile,[35] soon to be followed by Admiral Farragut

Fort Sumter (engraving 1861, National Park Service)

---

[31] Timeline bullet points are used to place the local events in context.
[32] *Mobile Register and Advertiser*, April 25, 1861. Official Records Army, volume 1, pages 327 – 328, letter from Alabama Governor A. B. Moore to President James Buchanan stating his reasons for taking such action.
[33] Official Records Army, volume 122, page 51, report of Union Engineer General Joseph G. Totten.
[34] Department of Archives and History, Montgomery, Alabama, folder W- 31. Union Engineers who examined Fort Gaines after the war reported that the Confederates had completed the work essentially to the original plans, *A History of the Mobile District*, page 30.
[35] *Mobile Advertiser and Register* reported June 13, 1861 that the Frigate *Niagara* and the captured schooner *Aid* had been blockading the port.

and his fleet. Abraham Lincoln had declared the blockade of the southern States on April 19, 1861 and May 28 was the date assigned by the Union Navy to begin its "rigid" blockade off Mobile.[36] Fort Gaines was too distant from Grants Pass to prevent the passage of vessels through it. Since the tower had not been built some substitute battery was needed.

Confederate General Samuel Cooper was then in command of Fort Morgan. His responsibility extended to Fort Gaines, Grants Pass and the approaches generally to Mobile including Mississippi Sound to Ship Island.[37] He ordered Major Danville Leadbetter of the engineers to make a reconnaissance of the area and recommend needed fortifications.

Danville Leadbetter
(Delaney, Confederate Mobile)

Danville Leadbetter had a long association with the fortifications in the Mobile area. He was born in Leeds, Maine August 26, 1811. He graduated from West Point in 1836 and transferred to the Army Engineers. Leadbetter came to Mobile in 1853 to supervise construction at Fort Gaines and repairs to Fort Morgan. He resigned from the U.S. Army on the last day of 1857 and settled in Mobile, entering Confederate service in 1861 as a Major in the Engineer Corps. He designed the early Civil War works around Mobile. He was promoted to General on February 27, 1862. In May 1862 he was transferred to Tennessee and served as Chief Engineer of the Army of Tennessee until that Army under General Hood was driven out of the State, whereupon he returned to Mobile. After the war he fled to Mexico and then went to Canada where he died in 1866. His body was returned to Alabama and buried in the Magnolia Cemetery at Mobile.[38]

At this point in 1861 Southern leaders were hopeful that there would be no real war. Many Southerners believed that if war came, that Southern gallants each worth 10 Yankee shopkeepers would quickly make their way

---

[36] Official Records Navy, volume 4, page 157, David Porter to the British Counsel at Mobile.
[37] Official Records Army, Series 1, volume 52/2, General Samuel Cooper to Colonel W. J. Hardee April 17, 1861, and Cooper to Colonel W.J. Hardee April 17, 1861.
[38] A Yankee in Gray: Danville Ledbetter and the Defense of Mobile Bay, 1861-1863, *Civil War History*, Volume 37, number 3, September 1991, pages 197-218.

to Washington and force a settlement. Conversely, Union recruits expected to march into Richmond with only their bands leading the way. Coastal forts and a few steamers converted into gunboats were to hold the coastline until the lack of cotton brought British recognition and a forced or negotiated settlement.[39] Coastal forts were recognized as crucial to Southern war plans. The recognition that strong coastal forts and steam gunboats were necessary did not of itself translate into the capability of producing these necessaries in a timely manner.

Major Leadbetter recommended on April 23, 1861 placing a floating battery at Grants Pass to be in charge of the Navy.[40] The Navy at the time was commanded by Captain Lawrence Rousseau with headquarters in New Orleans who was justifiably preoccupied with the defense of the Mississippi River. In any event Rousseau had no floating battery available for that purpose. The army would have to build its own.

It was not a floating battery that the engineers constructed but a battery built around a lighthouse/toll keeper's house on a small oyster shell dredge spoil island known as Fort Grant and in its later variants as Fort Powell.

---

[39] Cotton was withheld at this point from Europe – cotton that would have built up valuable credits to purchase iron plate, steam engines, heavy guns, muskets and other war materials that would be desperately needed later on.

[40] Official Records Army, Series 1, Volume 52/2, page 65, D. Leadbetter to Colonel W. J. Hardee.

CHAPTER 2

Fort Grant

- July 21, 1861 the Battle of Bull Run brought home to both sides that a long and bloody war was in the offing.

Commencement of the Battle of Bull Run (Frank Leslie, *Famous Leaders and Battle Scenes of the Civil War*, 1896

In June and July 1861 a small battery with three 32-pounders was constructed on Grant's Island.[41] The battery was protected by sand and oyster shell parapets and had a small covered magazine. Brigadier General Danville Leadbetter recommended the addition of an 8-inch columbiad.[42] The battery was manned by a company of the 1st Alabama Artillery Battalion[43] housed in tents on the island. The battery was referred to as "Fort Grant."

---

[41] A 32-pounder cannon is a smoothbore gun that fires a 32 pound 6.4 inch diameter solid shot. It also fired fused explosive shells.

[42] Official Records Army, volume 52, page 125, Leadbetter to Hon. Robert H. Smith, M. C., August 4, 1861.

[43] Official Records Army, volume 52, Statement of Troops in Department Number One, C.S. Army, July 12, 1861, page 711. The 8-inch columbaid was developed in the 1830s with a heavier bottle shape and fired an 8-inch 64 pound solid shot as well as fused explosive shells.

32-pounder at Fort Morgan

The lower Bay forts had regular communication and mail with Mobile. The steamer *William Bagaley* was running as a packet from Mobile to Fort Morgan and the bay forts on Tuesday, Thursday, Saturday and Sunday. Supplies were easily sent down from Mobile. On June 10, 1861 in a letter to the editor of the *Mobile Advertiser and Register,* Lieutenant Colonel C. D. Anderson wrote from "Fort Grant" thanking the citizens of Mobile for a gift of fresh vegetables.[44]

Fort Grant (*Harpers Weekly*, March 26, 1864)-note the new lighthouse

At the time the Confederates controlled the North Shore of the Mississippi Sound and occupied Fort Massachusetts on Ship Island.[45] The gunboats *Florida* and *Pamlico* patrolled the area in an effort to keep open

---

[44] *Mobile Advertiser and Register,* July 1861.

[45] The fort was seized by the Confederates on January 20, 1861 but not garrisoned or permanently occupied and abandoned by the end of the month since Mississippi could provide no armament for the fort. *Historic Structure Report Administrative and Historical Data Sections Fort on Ship Island* (Fort *Massachusetts) 1857 – 1935* by Edwin C. Bearss, page 85 – 86. The fort was again occupied by the Confederates on July 6, 1861.The brick fort was only partially finished and not considered defensible by some engineers. It was ordered evacuated on Sept. 13, 1861 and Confederate evacuation was completed by the 17th. *Confederate Forts,* by Zed H. Burns pages, 47-48.

communications with New Orleans. The *Oregon* and *Arrow*[46] then operated by the Army took guns, troops, and supplies to and from Fort Massachusetts, occasionally coming into Mobile Bay. By September 17 the Confederates had withdrawn from Ship Island to prevent the possibility of the garrison being cut off by the Union Navy. The Confederates did not have the naval strength to contest the control of Mississippi Sound.

Guns

Samuel H. Lockett (Ala. Dept. Archives and History, Montgomery)

Cannon were in short supply. At the beginning of the war the only foundries in the South casting large seacoast cannon were the Tredegar Ironworks and the Bellona Foundry in Richmond, Virginia.[47] Fifty-three heavy guns were diverted to the Confederacy from stocks on hand at these works. When the Union evacuated the Southern forts, they left 429 pieces of seacoast ordnance and an additional 1202 were captured by Virginia at Gosport Naval Yard.[48] Given the number of forts on the Southern coastline and rivers this supply was soon exhausted.[49]

On September 2, 1861 the Engineer Bureau in Richmond advised engineer in charge Major Samuel H. Lockett[50] that there had been ordered

---

[46] Most of the Confederate vessels operating in Mississippi Sound were lost following the fall of New Orleans. The *Pamlico* and *Oregon* were burned by their officers on Lake Pontchartrain. The *Arrow* was lost up the Pearl River.

[47] Beginning in 1864 heavy guns were cast at Selma.

[48] *Ironmaker to the Confederacy,* by Charles B. Dew.

[49] The availability of Cannon or the lack thereof was from time to time reported by the press during the war. There was a curious piece in the *Mobile Advertiser and Register*, July 23, 1862 from the *Macon Telegraph* reporting that 22 pieces of artillery taken by the British from the Russians at the battle of Inkerman, and presented to the Confederacy by British merchants that were brought over in the blockade runner *Nashville*. "With some alterations, they will hereafter speak for themselves, in a manner highly credible." 38 more pieces from the same lot were expected.

[50] Samuel Lockett grew up in Marion, Alabama. He graduated from West Point in 1859. After secession he served in the Confederate Army as an engineer. Initially he replaced Leadbetter in August, 1861 in charge of Forts Morgan and Gaines. He saw action at Shilo and Vicksburg and rose to the rank of Colonel and Chief Engineer of the Army of Tennessee, then served as Chief Engineer, Department of Ala., Miss., and East La. After the war Lockett taught in Louisiana and Alabama and later at the University of Tennessee. He was a prolific writer and artist. From 1875 to 1877 he served in Egypt and Sudan as an

from North Carolina to Mobile thirty 32-pounders, some of which he was to add to the armament at Grants Pass as soon as possible, preferably reinforced with wrought iron bands.

Skates and Company Foundry of Mobile was rifling and banding 32-pounders and casting projectiles for those guns.[51] As a smoothbore they would fire a shot of 32 pounds, but the rifled shot weighed 42 to 45 pounds.[52] The North Carolina guns anticipated by Lockett never arrived forcing him to secure such from other sources.[53]

Engineer Leadbetter reported on September 23, 1861 that the battery at Grants Pass still mounted three 32-pounders "which will soon be rifled". Leadbetter believed that what was most needed in Mobile Bay at the time was an armed schooner to cope with any armed small craft which might steal into the Bay at night or be hauled overland. A single armed launch, he noted, could cut off communication between the City and the forts.[54]

Rifled and banded 32-pounder

---

engineer and explorer in the service of the King of Egypt. He served as the principal assistant engineer in the construction of the pedestal of the Statue of Liberty. He took an assignment to Chile in 1888 to work on a massive construction project. He died on October 12, 1891 in Bogota, Columbia. Biographical sketch and photograph courtesy of Alabama Department of Archives and History.

[51] Official Records Army, volume 52, page 131, letter Leadbetter to Lockett, August 22, 1861.

[52] Rifle projectiles are elongated, heavier and require more power and pressure to propel the projectile. Simply cutting rifling grooves in the barrel of a 32-pounder would not work. The gun aft of the trunnions was cut smooth on a lathe and iron reinforcing bands were heated and shrunk on. The gun could then be rifled and would withstand the pressure of the larger loads. 42-pounders and some 8-inch guns were also banded. The Brooke and Parrot guns were also made with such heat-shrunken reinforcements.

[53] Official Records Army, volume 6, chapter 16 page 726, Leadbetter (then in Engineers Bureau Richmond) to Lockett September 2, 1861.

[54] Official Records Army, series 1, volume 6, chapter 16, page 743, Leadbetter to Engineer Bureau Richmond, September 23, 1861.

On October 25, 1861, General Braxton Bragg commanding the Department of Alabama and West Florida, with headquarters at Pensacola gave a description of the then status of the work in a report to Richmond: "At Grants Pass a small earthwork has been erected, and furnished with three guns and a garrison of one company. This is probably sufficient for the purpose of keeping this pass open to our steamers still allowed to run to New Orleans. As the place is not susceptible of successful defense against any larger attacking force, I directed the hulk of an old vessel we own here to be heavily ballasted and anchored there, ready to close the pass at a moment's notice, and a practical ford to be staked out by which the garrison can reach the mainland."[55]

Bolt (solid shot) for rifled 32-pdr

The "practical staked out" ford to Cedar Point would prove to be useful some three years later when the fort was evacuated.

William Llewellyn Powell[56] was promoted to Colonel in the provisional Army and ordered to Mobile, where Bragg assigned him to overall command of Forts Morgan, Gaines and the fort at Grants Pass.[57] Powell died on September 25, 1863, and in October 1863 General Maury renamed the fort at Grants Pass in memory of its former brigade commander

Closing the Pass

The Confederate Naval presence in Mississippi Sound and around Ship Island was minimal. Union blockaders regularly patrolled those waters.

---

[55] Official Records Army, Series 1, Volume 6, chapter 16, page 755, Braxton Bragg to Adjutant General Richmond, October 25, 1861.

[56] Powell was a formerly in the federal Navy 1840 – 61. He joined the Confederate Navy in June 1861 then transferred to the Army. He had experience in seacoast artillery having previously commanded coastal batteries prior to being transferred to Fort Morgan. No photograph of Col. Powell Has been located.

[57] *Confederate Mobile,* by Arthur W Bergeron Jr., University Press of Mississippi, 1991, page 20. (Hereafter *Confederate Mobile*). Caldwell Delaney, former director of the History Museum of Mobile had previously written a pictorial history titled *Confederate Mobile* published by the Haunted Bookstore, Mobile. Delaney's name will be used when reference is made to his book.

According to General Jones M. Withers, commanding District of Alabama, a large trade of sugar, turpentine, molasses, rosin, lumber and cattle was carried out from Ship Island. A steamer to carry off such freight ran regularly between the Island and New York. The nearest coaling station for Farragut's blockaders was Key West and much of their provisions came from Baltimore, so local supplies were at the time a great benefit. It is not clear how the local traders with the Ship Island merchants secured passes through the Mississippi Sound blockade. Apparently there was some system of passes in place for this activity although a portion of the trade was contraband carried to Ship Island by reverse blockade running locals.

To stop the smuggling Withers suggested closing Grants Pass as the most effective way of removing all pretext for a coastal trade "so advantageous to the enemy." He suggested that closing the pass would allow the battery's armament to be moved to Cedar Point where it would command those waters while not being isolated as was Grants Pass. Cedar Point was part of the mainland with a good road leading into the interior.

Gen. Jones M. Withers (Delaney, *Confederate Mobile*)

Withers said he was tormented hourly by applications from "selfish boat owners for permits through Grants Pass." He thought that the railroad communication and reduced charges on the railroad prevented the necessity for the undue risk of keeping the coast trade open. "We cannot therefore afford to furnish the enemy the low cost water transportation which they can only get by taking our boats as well is the produce of our country." [58] General Bragg in December 1861 ordered the closing of Grants Pass effectively and unconditionally.[59] The work of obstructing the Pass was underway. The guns were not removed until after the fall of New Orleans.

A description of Grants Pass fort at the time is provided by a contraband who escaped to the Union Navy. He seemed to be quite

---

[58] Official Records Army, volume 6, page 780, Withers to Major George G. Garner, Assistant Adjutant General Pensacola, Florida, December 9, 1861.

[59] Official Records Army, volume 6, chapter 16, page 779, Braxton Bragg to J.P. Benjamin Secretary of War December 11, 1861.

knowledgeable of military construction matters around Mobile. He stated that a company or more of troops was stationed at the fort: "which is small and thoroughly sheltered by sandbags, thickly piled over sloping timber casemates. Another company, perhaps about 80 or 90 men are stationed at Portersville." [60]

1862- The Lower Bay Defense Line

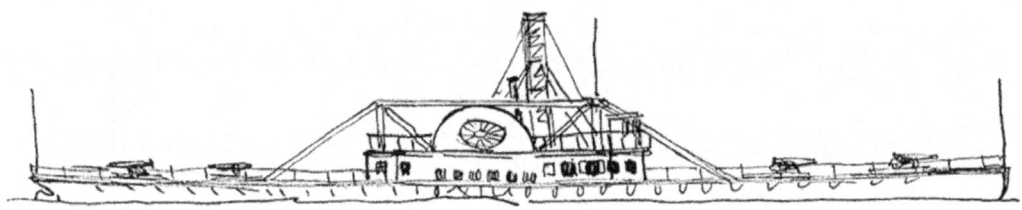

C.S.S. *Selma* ex. *Florida* (Drawing by Author)

On January 4, 1862 General Bragg reported that the condition of Forts Morgan and Gaines had improved to the point that with sufficient ammunition they would be in condition to prevent any entrance into the Bay. He was, however, not happy with the efforts of the Navy to support the lower Bay forts. "The services of a good gunboat, in conjunction with Forts Morgan and Gaines, would be of great service, but they are utterly useless at the City of Mobile, where they are now." [61] As a result of this Army insistence, the Navy began to routinely station a gunboat in the lower Bay, first the *Florida*[62] and later the *Morgan* or *Gaines*. The gunboats generally returned to the City each evening.

The building of the forts at the mouth of the Bay, including Fort Powell, the fortifications around Mobile, the upper Bay line and the upriver forts all required cash to pay for materials, ordnance, boats, barges, and labor, all of which were expensive. By the end of the war more Confederate

---

[60] Official Records Navy, volume 17, page 27.
[61] Official Records Army, volume 6, chapter 16, Braxton Bragg to Adjutant General at Richmond, January 4, 1862
[62] *The Mobile Advertiser and Register*, April 10, 1862 stated that the gunboat *Florida* was stationed at Grants Pass. The *Florida* was later renamed *Selma*.

dollars had been appropriated for the defense of Mobile than any other point in the South.

The Forts Would be Needed.

On January 20, 1862, Union Secretary of the Navy Gideon Welles, ordered then Flag-Officer David G. Farragut to proceed, as soon as his flagship *Hartford* was ready for sea, to the Gulf of Mexico. Farragut was there to take command of the Western Gulf blockading squadron of 26 vessels. In addition, there would be attached to his squadron a fleet of 21 bomb vessels together with armed steamers enough to manage them, all under the command of Commander David D. Porter.[63] When those vessels arrived and he was completely ready he was to collect such vessels as could be

C.S.S. *Gaines* (Painting by Author)

---

[63] Admiral Farragut had a very close relationship with David D. Porter and considered him something of a surrogate son. That relationship began when Farragut joined Capt. David Porter, father of Civil War David D. Porter as a 12-year-old midshipman in 1813 on the frigate *Essex* and was with him on that ships epic voyage to the South Pacific. David Porter was one of 10 children of the seafaring Porter family. *Perilous Fight, America's Intrepid War with Britain on the High Seas, 1812 – 1815*, by Stephen Budiansky (2010).

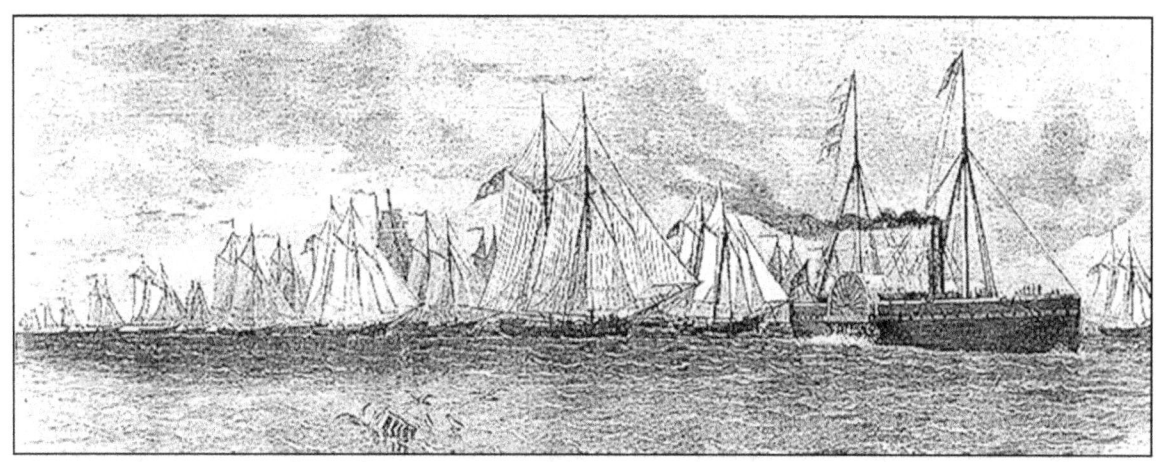

Porter's mortar fleet departing New York for the Gulf (Harpers Weekly May 10, 1862)

spared from the blockade and proceed up the Mississippi River, reduce the defenses which guarded the approach to New Orleans and take possession of that City. "You will also reduce the fortifications which defend Mobile Bay and turn them over to the Army to hold." [64] It was just a matter of time before he would attempt to do so.

- o February 6 Fort Henry falls followed by Fort Donaldson on the 12th opening the Tennessee and Cumberland Rivers to Union gunboats.

The 21st at the Pass

The 21st Alabama Infantry Regiment stationed at Fort Gaines sent working parties to assist in the closing of Grants Pass. On February 17, 1862 First Sergeant of Company A, James W. Williams (later Lt. Colonel and Commander of Fort Powell) wrote to his wife that he was a part of a detail of 100 that forded the shallows for that purpose. Because of heavy rain they got little work done, but on the way back he said they collected and ate some fine oysters.[65] The Confederate Navy was not happy with the closing of the

---

[64] Official Records Navy, volume 18, page 7, January 20, 1862.
[65] *From That Terrible Field, Civil War letters of James W. Williams*, 21st Alabama Infantry Volunteers, edited by John Kent Folmer, page 36. Hereinafter, *Williams,* letters. From the introduction of

Pass. Since June of 1861, the Army and then the Navy had been operating the gunboats *Oregon* and *Arrow* through Grants Pass and en route to Ship Island and New Orleans. Some privately owned steamships were still operating on that route.[66] The Mobile Advertiser and Register reported on March 4, 1862 that the gunboat *Arrow* arrived the previous day from Ship Island where she was keeping watch. Apparently the Pass was not fully closed at that time.

Flag officer Randolph of the Navy at Mobile was pressing for the removal of the Grants Pass obstructions and stated that if such was done, he would convoy vessels bound from Mobile to New Orleans and vice versa.[67] The Army countered that since the guns had been removed it would not be advisable to open the Pass until they were replaced. The battery at Cedar Point and obstructions were to provide the defense of the Pass.[68]

Fortifying Cedar Point

In February, 1862 two companies of the 21st Alabama were at Powell and two at Cedar Point and to the westward along the coast in small detachments. Deserters reported two 24-pounders on the southwest side of Cedar Point, and from there to the south point were breastworks for musketry and fieldpieces.

Folmer's book we find that James Madison Williams was born October 5, 1837 in St. Clairsville, Ohio. James moved to Augusta, Georgia in 1858 and then in November 1860 to Mobile to work with silversmith and sword maker James Conning. Williams enlisted with the 21st Alabama Regiment October 4, 1861 and served with that regiment throughout the war as related herein. On April 12, 1865, after the fall of Mobile, the 21st with Williams retreated up the M&O railroad. His wife had evacuated to Prattville, Alabama. Postwar times were hard. He and a partner tried a steam laundry business, and then he became a book keeper for retail dry goods stores. He was a clerk with the M&O railroad and worked finally as a clerk and deputy clerk with the Mobile County Probate Court. Williams died at Mobile January 21, 1903.

[66] National Archives, Mobile Squadron Papers. *Mobile Advertiser and Register* June 20, 1861.

[67] The Naval Commander at Mobile was feeling more confident as the gunboats *Morgan* and *Gaines* were ready. Each of these boats was armed with 10 heavy guns and were ready for service as soon as Flag Officer Randolph could find powder for them. Confederate Naval Records Mobile Squadron, Minor to Mallory, March 19, 1862. In early 1864 they were converted to 6 gun vessels with Brooke pivots fore and aft.

[68] Official Records Army, volume 18, page 842, March 19, 1862, Randolph to C. J. McRae April 6, 1862.

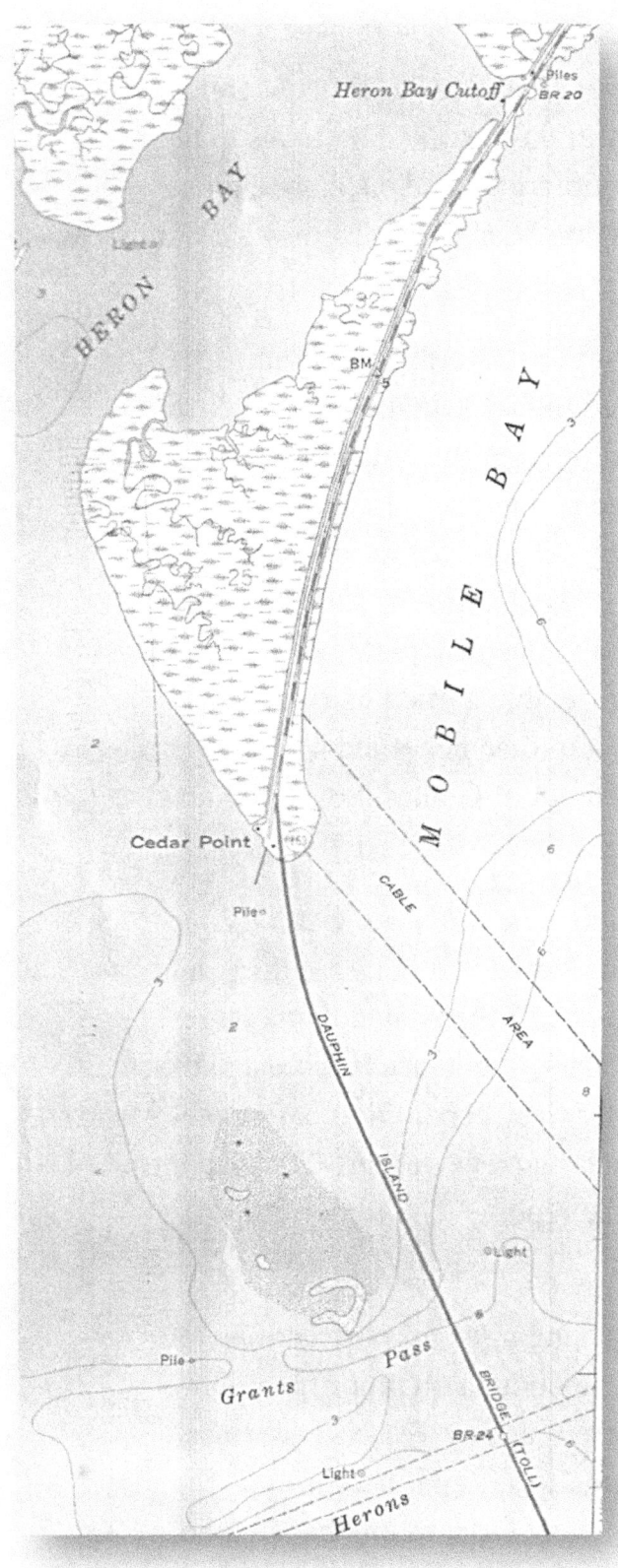

Cedar Point (U.S. Geological Survey)

Engineer Samuel H. Lockett had staked out positions for additional guns at Cedar Point. Henry B. Warren, a civilian engineer, was given responsibility for the battery. He found an infantry company at the Point (21st Alabama), but they were ordered to go to Corinth before he could put them to work mounting guns. Mounting guns was soldiers' work. At this time in the war the actual construction of the batteries was done by hired laborers. Warren laid foundations for the three guns, but had to await the arrival of laborers to complete the construction. By April, Warren had finished his task, and a company of the 1st Alabama Artillery Battalion occupied the earthwork. The lack of laborers already was hampering the work of fortifying the pass.[69]

The First Alabama Voluntary Infantry Regiment was brought to Mobile from Meridian to augment the defenses when it was thought that Sherman was a threat to the City. They left Meridian February 14, 1862 and marched to

---

[69] Bergeron, *Confederate Mobile*, page 52.

the Tombigbee River, embarked on a steamer and were landed at Mobile on February 24. After two weeks garrison duty at the forts and batteries in the line of land defenses at Mobile, they were withdrawn and encamped on a vacant square in the "residence part of the City." On March 13 they set out for Cedar Point.

After a two days march through what they described as a flat, lonesome piney woods country, they reached their destination and pitched their tents on the Bay front. Detachments of the Regiment did garrison duty at Cedar Point and Powell, while the rest did picket duty along the beach. There they captured and hung a "Yankee spy." Those not needed at Cedar Point and Fort Powell proceeded to Fort Gaines on April 5, 1862 and were assigned to guns. "We remained here a month, enjoying plenty of fish and oysters. The Garrison (Gaines) also had a vegetable garden of 10 acres, cultivated by daily details, but we left too soon to be benefited by this." About May 1, 1862 the Regiment was pulled out of Gaines, Powell and Cedar Point and assigned to the Army of Tennessee.[70]

The federal mortar fleet was in the Gulf. *The Mobile Press Register* reported April 6, 1862: "Reports last evening stated that between thirty and forty sail of vessels were off Ship Island. It was further stated that a large proportion of these new arrivals were schooners, and hence it is reasonable to conclude that they are Porter's Gulf mortar fleet, reported to have sailed from Key West sometimes since for an attack on New Orleans. We give the above as rumor, knowing no authority for the report." The rumor was correct.

Contractor Henry Warren was also driving piles for obstructions into the waters of Grants Pass. He drove some 250 about a quarter of a mile west of Grants Island. To protect the pile driver from enemy vessels a steamer was stationed nearby so it could pull the barge to safety if necessary.[71] Small vessels could go through the obstructions to New Orleans and back without any difficulty, but the larger vessels, including gunboats, could not.

---

[70] *History of the First Regiment Alabama Volunteer Infantry C. S. A.*, By Edward Young McMorries Ph. D., the Brown Printing Company, Montgomery, Alabama, 1904, page 72.

[71] Bergeron, *Confederate Mobile*, page 52.

Although there were no guns at Grants Pass the battery at Cedar Point covered it so as to prevent any Union effort to clear the obstructions and enter the Bay.[72]

Small vessels were indeed running through the obstructed Grants Pass. On June 19, 1862, the sloop *Venture* of Mobile made its way through the Pass and was captured west of Fort Powell. The Sloop's cargo consisted of 25 barrels of flour, 20 sacks of flour, 26 bushels of corn meal, four sacks of corn, 349 pounds of corn, one tierce of rice (657 pounds), and one barrel of rice (223 pounds). The cargo was sent to New Orleans.[73]

The Union Navy maintained a blockade in Mississippi Sound with occasional shore excursions. To combat such excursions and as sentries small units were stationed along the coast. Captain Hagan's company of dragoons had a camp at Bayou La Batre where they patrolled the Alabama north shore of the Sound.[74] The Mobile Dragoons (Captain Marshall) were in the same service at Pascagoula.

A letter from Pascagoula, dated April 11, 1862, stated that at about 11:00 A.M. on April 9 two gunboats steamed up to the Pascagoula wharf and deposited about 600 Union troops who raised their flag over the hotel. The Mobile Dragoons had five pickets under Lieutenant G. G. Gazzam who observed the arrival and alerted the company's camp about 2 miles distant. Captain Marshall with about 30 men (the others were on picket duty at various places) proceeded to mount up and ride to town. Marshall and his troopers there charged a large body of Federal troops, fired a volley from their carbines and received 400 mine' balls in return. The gunboats, some 200 yards off, opened up and three of the dragoons were slightly wounded. The Union troops withdrew with the loss of three guns leaving about dark for Ship Island.[75]

---

[72] Official Records Navy, series 1, volume 18, page 841, Flag Officer V. M. Randolph to Hon. C. J. McRae, April 6, 1862.
[73] Official Records Navy, volume 18, page 566, July 10, 1862.
[74] *Mobile Advertiser and Register*, August 16, 1861.
[75] *Mobile Advertiser and Register*, April 14, 1863.

CHAPTER 3

The Guns Are Removed

o April 25, 1862 Fall of New Orleans

Panic

When New Orleans fell to Union forces, the Mobile Advertiser and Register,[76] putting the best face on the situation and no doubt trying to calm the inhabitants, wrote that Mobile Bay was different from New Orleans. It was shallow and only small boats could reach the City, which would have to be taken by land and that the forts at the mouth of the Bay were formidable.[77] Notwithstanding the calming words of the press, there was a general panic.[78] Many people evacuated Mobile to the interior.[79] When it became apparent that Farragut was not going to immediately advance on Mobile the wives and families evacuated from Mobile started to trickle back. At the same time, and throughout the following year, refugees were arriving daily from New Orleans.[80]

Even before the fall of New Orleans, there was grave concern that Mobile could not be held without ironclad gunboats to defend it. On February 14th 1862, the editor of the Mobile Advertiser and Register wrote:

---

[76] *The Advertiser and Register* and the public accepted the loss of New Orleans fairly calmly. It considered that the place had simply been overwhelmed by the Federal Fleet. But an attack was expected momentarily on Mobile and if even that came and all the coastal ports were lost it was thought that the South would still win in the field.

[77] *Mobile Advertiser and Register,* April 29, 1862.

[78] Even General Robert E. Lee thought that Mobile would soon be taken. On April 27th 1862 he wrote to General Samuel Jones (commanding Mobile) advising that he should send 14 recently received 10-inch columbiads inland to a safe place and prepare to abandon Mobile. Official Records Army, volume 6, page 884.

[79] *The Eutaw Whig,* edition of May 18, 1862 reported that the town was about filled with females from Mobile. Every vacant house had been taken and the same was true of every town and village on the rivers in the State.

[80] *Mobile Register and Advertiser,* June 5, 1863.

"a Yankee gunboat is altogether an abominable contrivance." *** "They are of light draft and great speed and can have its way on most parts of the southern coast." And on another occasion: "the Yankee gunboat is a powerful and dangerous thing" that carries long-range guns. The editor concluded that fixed forts could not guard channels and for that purpose the Navy must have movable floating batteries. The local Army and Naval officers concurred with the press.

The packet *Florida* had been converted to a gunboat and the *Morgan* and *Gaines* were launched at Mobile by February 1862. All these were wooden vessels. The tug/lighter *Baltic* was converted to an ironclad by the State of Alabama and turned over to the Navy in May 1862. The *Baltic* was slow but heavily armored with heavy guns. She was not highly regarded by either the Confederate or the Union Navy but she was an ironclad and a deterrent. Notwithstanding, if Farragut could have forced his way into the lower Bay before the *Tennessee* arrived in May of 1864, he was prepared to do so and to take his chances with the *Baltic* even with his wooden vessels.

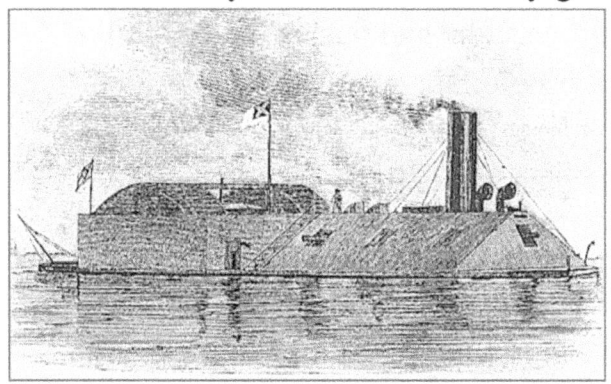

C.S.S. *Baltic* (Engraving published in *The Soldiers of Our Civil War*)

The fear that the Union Navy could force its way into Mobile Bay and up the rivers resulted in powerful batteries being constructed at Oven and Choctaw Bluff on the Tombigbee and Alabama Rivers in Clarke County.[81] Those forts were considered to be the first line of defense for the interior.[82] The guns were removed from the Cedar Point Battery and sent upriver to these forts, as were many guns from Morgan and Gaines.[83]

---

[81] I published the history of these forts in three volumes of the *Clarke County Historical Society Quarterly* in 1995-96.
[82] Official Records Army, volume 44, page 600.
[83] Official Records Navy, volume 18, page 847, Flag Officer Randolph to John Gill Shorter, Governor of Alabama.

The Navy was not immune from the panic. Flag Officer Randolph at Mobile was pleased to learn that the guns from Cedar Point had been sent up river. He wrote to Governor Shorter that the impression at Mobile was that Fort Gaines was useless for the protection of the harbor and City. In his opinion at least 40 cannon, some of large caliber, could be spared for the protection of the rivers above.

Adm. David G. Farragut, 1863 (Mathew Brady, National Archives)

The concern over Farragut's possible immediate movement into Mobile Bay was not unreasonable. Naval Commander Randolph's forces and the guns of Fort Morgan would not likely have been able to slow Farragut's fleet if he had pushed into Mobile Bay at that time.[84] A few heavy guns bearing on the relatively shallow and obstructed Grants Pass together with the three wooden gunboats then available, was another story.

On March 18, 1862, there was news in Mobile that the Union fleet then at Ship Island had sailed east. This turned out to be a rumor only, but the gunboats *Selma, Morgan,* and *Gaines* were sent to the lower Bay to back up the Cedar Point battery then covering Grants Pass.[85] On April 10 the *Florida*[86] was still stationed at the Pass.[87] A deserter reported that "the gunboats go up to Mobile every night."[88]

Adm. David D. Porter (Naval Historical Center)

Admiral Farragut wanted to move immediately from New Orleans to Mobile, but it was decided in Washington to open the Mississippi River, which required his forces and all

---

[84] Official Records Navy, volume 18, page 847.
[85] *Mobile Advertiser and Register*, March 18, 1862.
[86] The *Florida* was a packet converted to a gunboat in 1861. When the commerce raider *Florida* under Captain Maffitt ran into Mobile Bay on September 4, 1862, the Navy had two *Florida's* in Mobile Bay. The name of a converted packet was changed to *Selma*. The raider *Florida* ran back out of Mobile Bay on January 16, 1863 never to return.
[87] *Mobile Advertiser and Register*, May 24, 1862.
[88] Official Records Army, volume 18, page 549.

available troops. He thought General Butler did not have enough troops. He was correct. He wrote, "Mobile is so ripe now that it will fall to us like a mellow pear, while we, I fear, will fall like a mellow pear before the difficulties above in the river. We are not prepared for it and will fail. ***While we are 'up river' Pensacola will fall into the hands of the rebels again. *** It is of more value to us now than a dozen Vicksburg's. If we miss taking Mobile now, we won't get it."[89]

David D. Porter, Commander of Farragut's mortar flotilla, wrote Farragut in June 1862 criticizing the decision to move the fleet and General Butler's troops up the Mississippi River for an attack on Vicksburg. He also thought the effort should have been directed toward Mobile.

U.S.S. *Susquehanna* (Naval Historical Center)

Farragut continued to press for Mobile, writing to Secretary of the Navy Gideon Welles on September 30, 1862: "If the department can spare me two more steam sloops of the Housatonic class I think that, in

---

[89] Official Records Navy, series 1, volume 18, page 577, June 3, 1862.

conjunction with the Army, I can take Fort Gaines and Morgan. If an ironclad can be spared, so much the better. I must have the assistance of the Army to take Fort Gaines, as the ships cannot get sufficiently close to it, and it must be taken to secure our entrance for our supplies, as we have no vessels of light draft to get up Grants Pass to take Cedar Point, and get our supplies that way." [90]

The Union Navy did maintain a watch over the situation at Mobile and on June 20, 1862, the *U.S.S. Susquehanna* reported that the Confederates appeared to be "getting up a battery" at Cedar Point and had been strengthening the obstructions at Grants Pass.[91]

The Guns are Back

Pensacola Evacuated

In May 1862, the Confederate forces evacuated neighboring Pensacola.[92] The garrison of Pensacola was about 3500 strong, about half unarmed with no field artillery. It was correctly thought that Pensacola surely would fall with the loss of large quantities of ordnance and material and possibly loss of the garrison. Farragut's original orders were to proceed to New Orleans but Pensacola was useful as a base for his coastal blockade. Mobile was thought to be but little, if at all, more secure than Pensacola.[93]

---

[90] Official Records Navy, volume 19, page 242.

[91] Official Records Navy, Series one, volume 18, page 568, report of Commander Hitchcock of the *U.S.S. Susquehanna,* June 20, 1862. *Mobile Advertiser and Register,* May 24, 1862.

[92] The Confederates did not just walk away from Pensacola. The *Mobile Advertiser and Register* reported on May 13, 1862 that at about 11:30 PM, May 10, 1862, Brig. General Thomas Jones gave the signal, and the torch was applied to every point. The woodwork, gun carriages, etc. at Barrancas, McRae, hospitals and Navy Yard, the villages of Woolsey and Warrington were in flames. Fire was set to the oil factory and all government buildings in Pensacola and to the steamers at the wharf. Everything was dismantled and removed, "Even to small bits of copper and lead." The city was generally deserted. The track of the railroad was torn up and removed, and the telegraph office was closed and the wire removed.

[93] Official Records Army, volume 6, pages 874-75.

Short term the decision to withdraw made the Pensacola garrison available to contest Grant's offense in Tennessee and released seacoast cannon for the defense of Mobile. The downside was that the Port of Pensacola, the finest harbor in the Gulf, was made available to Farragut. The blockade of, or assault on, Mobile was made much easier by the availability of the protected anchorage and repair shops at Pensacola. The Confederates had to maintain a substantial force north of Pensacola at Pollard and on the Perdido River to prevent inland incursions from the Federal garrison.

Farragut reported from New Orleans on August 11, 1862 that the Rebels appeared to be clearing out Grants Pass to get their gunboats into Mississippi Sound where they would be a great annoyance. He was fearful that when in the Sound they could proceed into Lake Pontchartrain and fire on New Orleans unless the forts there had heavier guns.[94]

On August 31, 1862 the Admiral was in Pensacola repairing his vessels preparatory for an attack on Mobile. He wrote to General Banks at New Orleans that he hoped to be ready "in less than a fortnight." He told Banks that as soon as he was ready he would send him word and that he (Banks) can then decide as to what assistance would be available. Farragut was concerned that Banks had evacuated Baton Rouge and wrote "You must be expecting an attack, but I cannot think it possible that it would be made upon you. What will we do for troops when the attack comes off on Mobile?"[95]

Farragut still had few light draft vessels that could pursue the Confederate ships in the shallow waters of Mississippi Sound and Lake Pontchartrain. But he was still confident that if he could catch them out of Mobile Bay they would have trouble getting back in.[96]

By November, Franklin Buchanan[97] former commander of the *Merrimack/Virginia* had assumed command of the Confederate naval forces

---

[94] Official Records Navy, volume 19, page 147.
[95] Official Records Navy, volume 19, page 172.
[96] Official Records Navy, 19, page 147, Farragut to Major General Butler at New Orleans, August 11, 1862.
[97] Three U.S. Navy destroyers have been named in honor of Admiral Franklin Buchanan, the DD-131, DD-484 and DDG-14.

at Mobile. In a report to Navy Secretary Mallory, dated November 26, 1862 he stated that the guns at Grants Island Battery, removed some months since are to be replaced. He felt the battery was necessary to keep light draft boats out of the bay even though there were always one or two gunboats to protect it.[98]

His opponents were aware of the lack of guns at the Pass. In early December deserters from the gunboat *Morgan* had confirmed that the guns had been removed. That was about to change.[99]

A Union Navy report of December 12 stated that the rebels had brought to Grants Pass a floating battery and established tents on the small island there. We do not know what vessel was referred to here. It could have been the ironclad *Baltic,* but any vessel anchored in a defensive position seemed to be referred to as a "floating battery." Whatever vessel it was the *Hatteras*[100] and *Jackson* were sent to drive it and the troops off.[101]

Engineer General Danville Leadbetter had indeed decided to erect a strong earthwork at the Pass. The few guns placed there early in the war had been removed, pilings had been driven in the channel, and one or more gunboats stationed there, but a permanent battery was needed.

Building a Fort

Thomas H. Millington, a civilian engineer, took charge of the construction of an earthwork battery at Grants Pass designed to mount at least three guns. Millington's description of the work survives but no plans of these earthworks have been located.

---

[98] Buchanan Letter Book, Southern Historical Society Collection, University of North Carolina, Chapel Hill.
[99] Official Records Navy, volume 19, page 400.
[100] The *Hatteras* was sunk by the C.S.S *Alabama* off Galveston January 11, 1863.
[101] Official Records Navy, volume 19, page 733, December 12, 1862.

Millington began work at the island on December 7, 1862. He was instructed to transport dirt from Dauphin Island or Mobile Point near Fort Morgan for use in the construction, but he found it more expedient to use oyster shells and sand from the immediate vicinity. By December 13th the battery was ready for guns to be mounted.

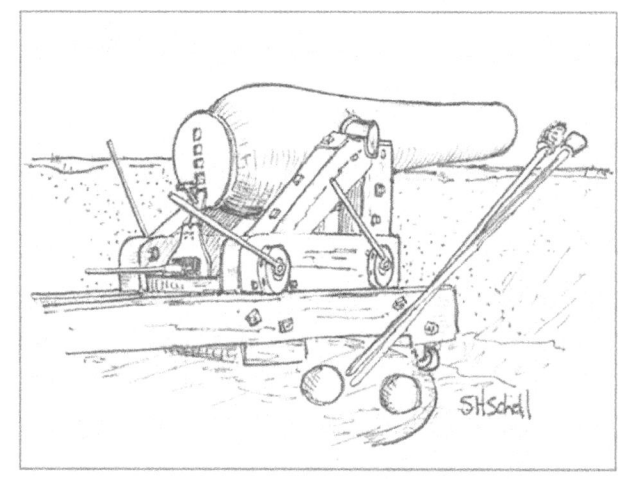

10-inch columbiad (drawing by Author)

The Chief of Artillery for the District of the Gulf had selected one 10-inch columbiad, one 8-inch columbiad and a 32-pounder rifled piece as armament for the work. Millington and his engineers worked unmolested until the construction was completed on December 17, 1862.[102]

Millington's report to Engineer Captain Charles T. Liernur[103] from Grants Pass December 12, 1862 details the work being done:

"The 10-inch and 32-pounder are mounted, the 8-inch will be in the same fix by noon - I have no further use for the *Ingomar*, please send for her by the next steamboat.

"If you sanction the alteration of the covered way and magazine, I shall not need the schooner *Smith*, longer than tomorrow. I shall need no more timber, and will have everything complete and be ready to leave here

---

[102] Bergeron, *Confederate Mobile*, page 62.

[103] Hermann Carl Anton Liernur was born in the city of Haarlen (Holland) on May 14, 1828. In 1855 he was living in Mobile and listed in the *City Directory* as a civil engineer. We have no records as to where he received his engineering training but likely he received a military education in Europe. At one time he resided in Whistler, Alabama where the M&O Railroad shops were located and probably was employed as an engineer with that railroad. He received his commission in the Confederate Army as an engineer and early in the war was involved in designing and building floating batteries at Mobile. On May 3, 1862 Capt. Liernur was ordered to Oven and Choctaw Bluffs in Clark County to lay out batteries there indicating a military education. After the war he returned to Europe and practiced his civil engineering trade there. He died in Berlin in 1893. See *Captain Charles T. Liernur 1828-1893*, a genealogy compilation by descendant Cyril William Ray.

on Wednesday. It will be a very complete little battery, as strong as the armament can make it.

"I wish you could lend me a circle plate for a 32. The one I have is too small in radius, and is as thin as a piece of tin, send some spikes for it also.

"The barge will not answer the place of a wharf here, and if you think it necessary to have one – send a pile driver, with 40 piles fourteen feet long – 250 linear feet 10 in" x 12" timber (or flatted sticks 10" thick) and 1500 feet board measure 2" plank, and one keg 4" spikes. It may answer without a wharf, but it will be awkward landing provisions, water, etc. as a boat cannot get nearer than 125 feet.

"Please reply my letter of yesterday's date. I am in a hurry for several reasons. – Very respectfully, Thomas H. Millington."[104]

Farragut still saw Grants Pass as the lightly guarded (compared to Fort Morgan) back door to Mobile Bay. The Pass was under almost constant surveillance. For instance, pile drivers had been working between Forts Gaines and Morgan. On December 1 the watching vessels logged that the pile driver at 4 p.m. went over to Grants Pass. On Dec 4 Pass aux Heron was reported to be closed with piles.[105]

Everyone did not agree with the building of the fort. Confederate Engineer John W. Glenn thought that a battery at Grants Pass would be untenable in the best of times as it could be cut off from supplies by shallow draft steamers outside. Glenn wanted a permanent closure of the pass with pilings, rocks and oyster shells. Glenn contended that they did not have the guns or men to lose at Grants Pass in the event Farragut passed Fort Morgan which he felt would surely happen.[106] Glenn's superiors would have been well served to have heeded his warning.

---

[104] Caldwell Delaney's book *Confederate Mobile a Pictorial History*; published by The Haunted Book shop Mobile, Alabama, 1971, page 96.
[105] Private Diary of Captain H. H. Bell, Official Records Navy, volume 19, page 732.
[106] McMillan Collection, History Museum of Mobile, John Glenn Letters, November 29 and December 4, 1862.

Captain J. M. Cary's Company C, 1st Alabama Artillery Battalion, was transferred from Fort Morgan to man the guns at the Pass.[107]

Victor Von Sheliha[108]

In October 1862, General Simon Bolivar Buckner of Kentucky assumed command of the Army at Mobile. He brought with him as a member of his staff, Major Victor Von Sheliha as his chief of artillery, who was to serve as Chief Engineer of the district, having transferred to the Engineers in the spring of 1863 having been promoted to Lieutenant Colonel. He technically served as chief assistant until Leadbetter left Mobile on October 18, 1863 to report to General Bragg in Tennessee but he was during that time effectively in charge of the designing, or redesigning, of several upper Bay line batteries and the works up river. He then served as Chief Engineer at Mobile until the Battle of Mobile Bay. He redesigned Fort Powell and the Mobile defensive works.[109]

Gen. Simon B. Buckner
(Library of Congress)

Victor Von Sheliha appears in the narrative of Fort Powell shortly after he came to Mobile in October 1862. Von Sheliha was a Prussian nobleman educated as an engineer with military experience in Europe. In an age where firstborn sons inherited family wealth and titles the younger siblings received an education then were often on their own. Von Sheliha was not a soldier of fortune that came to the South after the war had begun seeking military rank. Southerners were skeptical of foreigners and did not give high rank to distinguished foreigners or give commissions at all to undistinguished foreigners. Von Sheliha was obviously recognized as an

---

[107] Bergeron, *Confederate Mobile*, page 128.
[108] Full name from Baptism Records Christ Episcopal Church Mobile, Alabama, February 18, 1865 of Fanny Amelia daughter of Victor E. R. W. E. Von Sheliha and Pauline W. Von Sheliha. An internet source gives his name as Viktor Ernst Karl Rudolf Von Scheliha.
[109] Official Records Army, volume 15, page 905, Special Order number 62, December 23, 1862.

educated immigrant. He received his promotions based upon his service and demonstrated abilities.

The 1860 New Orleans City Directory lists him as a teacher at Kennerville, Louisiana. He was then operating a private boarding school for German boys. He was commissioned as a Captain in the Confederate Corps of Engineers on May 18, 1861. Because there were no engineer Major vacancies he was promoted to Major of Artillery on July 16, 1862 and promoted to Lieutenant Colonel of Engineers on May 25, 1863.

Von Sheliha served in the Kentucky Campaign and was at the Battle of Fishing Creek in January 1862. He was on the staffs of Generals Polk, Zillicoffer, Crittenden, Mackall and Buckner.[110] He was captured along with General Buckner at Island Number 10 in April 1862. As chief engineer of the District of Mobile (later the Department of the Gulf) his jurisdiction extended from Fort Morgan to Oven and Choctaw Bluffs in Clark County. While in Mobile he married Pauline Williams, daughter of Price Williams a prominent local cotton merchant.

Von Sheliha was a tireless worker, constantly on his horse. It is said by his peers that he built beautiful, powerful forts but probably over designed them and they considered them to have been too big and too complicated.[111] But engineers only recommend projects. The general in charge decided what was to be built and when to build it and had to come up with the troops to man them. As a result Von Sheliha was constantly frustrated when he did not get approval for recommended projects or the labor to build in a timely manner those that were approved.

Some of Von Sheliha's frustrations were self-induced, brought on by what were likely unnecessary changes, modifications, experiments and his attempt to achieve perfection in his works. His frustrations were such that in June 1864 he asked to be transferred back to the field. His request was

---

[110] *Foreigners in the Confederacy,* by Ella Lonn.

[111] Samuel Lockett on January 12, 1865 to Colonel A. L. Rives Assistant Chief Engineer at Richmond stated in reference to Von Sheliha, without mentioning his name: "I have scrupulously avoided making any material alterations in the works at this point, as this policy has already been pursued almost to a ruinous extent, resulting in great increase of expense and retardation of operations that long since should have been completed." Official Records Army, volume 94, page 780.

denied.[112] After the Battle of Mobile Bay he resigned and asked for permission to return to Europe.[113] That request was also denied but Samuel Lockett was appointed Chief Engineer with Von Sheliha acting as assistant. In early 1865 he was ill and was furloughed to Bladon Springs in Choctaw County to recuperate. Engineer Samuel Lockett assumed the supervision of the district. When Von Sheliha recovered his health he returned and assisted Lockett until the end of the war.

He did not retreat to Demopolis with the Army after the surrender of Mobile in April 1865. He surprised everyone by claiming the rights of an alien and returning to Europe with wife Pauline and daughter Fanny. He wrote a *Treatise on Coast Defense* that was published in London in 1868. He served in the Prussian Army during the Franco-Prussian War (1869-70) and later spent several years in Russia.

Von Sheliha died in 1903 at the age of 77 a resident of the Confederate Soldiers' Home in New Orleans. No photograph of Von Sheliha has been located. He is probably included in a group of the Soldiers' Home residents published on the cover of the *Confederate Veteran* magazine, January, 1899 issue..

The job of Chief Engineer at Mobile was often frustrating. There were never enough laborers for the work to be done. Projects the engineers thought necessary were sometimes not approved and the engineers often had to concentrate on work they thought unnecessary or of secondary importance.

The commanding General at Mobile was responsible for the defense, he decided what works would be built and when. The engineers' responsibility for the planning ended when their views were made known officially to the Commanding General. Von Sheliha continually made his views known officially to Generals, Governors, Congressmen, and anyone

---

[112] National Archives, record group 109, chapter 3, volume 16.
[113] National Archives, record group 109, chapter 3, volume 16, August 23, 1864.

else who would listen, but he still never had the resources that he thought he needed to properly do his job.[114]

---

[114] Official Records Army, volume 6, page 750. Leadbetter to Lockett, October 7, 1861.

CHAPTER 4

1863 An Engineer's Work Is Never Done

By Early 1863 engineer Lieutenant John Glenn reported that two 8-inch guns and one 32-pounder rifle were mounted at Fort Powell.[115] The carriage of one of the 8-inch guns was replaced. The leaking roof of the magazine also was repaired.[116] The work of the engineer's was never done.

Glenn was somewhat of an eccentric although Leadbetter described him as an "intelligent, enthusiastic, and laborious officer." He was assigned early in the war to assist in the supervision of the construction of the lower bay line of defenses from Fort Morgan to Cedar Point. He loved to fish, and was reprimanded for overworking and wearing out his steamboat and its crew by requiring them to take him on off-hour fishing excursions.[117]

He drove pilings using City of Mobile steam fire engines on the *Dick Keys* to jet the piles in place. The piles were jetted into the bottom of the Bay in much the same manner as done today. A suction hose drew water from the Bay to a borrowed Mobile Fire Department engine, a hose from the engines water pump with a pipe attached was placed alongside the pile and the water stream displaced the sand and mud allowing the piling to work its way into the bottom.[118] He was ordered to stop working the crew of the *C. S. M.*[119] day and night. He was told the boat was to be used only for transportation and he was to use his yawl for reconnaissance, taking observations and other activities, which presumably included fishing.[120]

Steam fire engine of 1860, Silsby Model 3S-1

---

[115] National Archives, record group 109, chapter 3, volume 12 Engineer Department letters.
[116] Bergeron, *Confederate Mobile,* page 64.
[117] McMillan collection, History Museum of Mobile.
[118] Von Sheliha, A *Treatise on Coast Defense*, page 191.
[119] The vessel was always referred to by the three letters "C.S.M." only.
[120] Record Group 109, chapter 3, volume 12, Engineer Department Records.

He also blew up Sand Island Light and in doing so almost blew himself up with it. The Union Navy was sending in boats from the blockading squadron to Sand Island Lighthouse and using it as an observation point. In 1863 the lighthouse was 150 feet tall. The present structure is only 125 feet. Glenn packed the base of the structure with 70 pounds of gunpowder and with his boat crew standing by lit the fuse. He cut his fuse too short. The resulting explosion showered large pieces of lighthouse around him as he scrambled back to his boat and the concussion from the falling pieces knocked him flat. Miraculously neither he nor his crew was injured. The demolition was a success as the lighthouse was thereby rendered useless as an observation post. The gunners at Fort Morgan found the stump of the lighthouse useful for target practice at a distance of 2 ¾ miles.

During this time Glenn referred to what would later be called Fort Powell as the "Battery at Grants Island," or the "Grants Pass Battery" or "Grants Battery." In his inspection report of the magazine dated January 21, 1863, he stated that the bombproof/magazine floor was sunk below the level of the island and was damp. He was to place it in good order, his work never done.[121]

A Wharf

On February 14, 1863, a wharf was ordered built at Fort Powell.[122] Glenn started work on the wharf on February 20. The wharf extended eastward from the Island some 600 feet. The pier allowed vessels drawing 6 feet of water alongside at the lowest tides.[123] The pier and pier head at

---

[121] McMillan Collection, History Museum of Mobile.

[122] National Archives, record group 109, chapter 3, volume 12, Engineer Department Records.

[123] In the Diary of Lt. Mumford found at the History Museum of Mobile there is an entry dated June 1864 that says if the tide is very low you could not get to Fort Powell. The tide has one high and one low daily, generally ranging about 1 1/2 feet, but in the winter or with north winds the tide is much lower. However, Glenn stated that even at the lowest tides there was 6 feet of water along the pier head of Grants Battery wharf. History Museum of Mobile, McMillan collection, binder number two, Glenn letters, March 1863.

"Grants Battery" was completed in March.[124] Meanwhile the Union naval vessels *Clifton* and *Jackson* were assigned to maintain a watch on the Pass.[125]

More Boats

The engineers working in the lower Bay required shipping to transport their men and materials. The schooner *Marshall I. Smith* was one of the vessels used to transport lumber.[126] Several barges, including the barge *Ingomar* were also in that service. On March 5, 1863 the *Ingomar* was to land an 8-inch gun and receive a 10-inch gun at Powell.[127] Glenn was also using the steamer *Natchez,* but his principal steamboat was the *Dick Keys*.[128]

Steamboats and barges were essential tools for the engineers in constructing the lower Bay defenses. Until the channel from the lower Bay to the Mobile Harbor was deepened about 1910, large sailing vessels and steamships that carried Mobile's commerce to market anchored in the lower Bay. Lighters and barges transported the cargo down for loading. In baymen's terminology a "lighter" is a steamboat that transports cargo to and from Mobile to the anchorage north of Fort Morgan or a "lighter" can be a barge in that service. Barges in engineering service in the lower Bay were used for transporting sand, brick and other building materials, guns and ordnance, water and coal.

---

[124] McMillan collection, History Museum of Mobile.

[125] Official Records Navy, series 1, volume 19, page 635, order of Rear Adm. D.G, Farragut, New Orleans, February 27, 1863.

[126] The Engineering Department secured most of its lumber from Escatawba, Alabama on the M&O Railroad. It regularly sent trains of from 8 to 15 cars up the road with gangs of 30 men with two days rations to load. National Archives, record group 109, chapter 3, volume 10, Engineer Department letters, January 19, 1865. Cordwood for the use by engineer steamboats was also transported on the M & O railroad. On December 3, 1864, 10 loads of cord wood for such use was transported from B. Smith's station between Escatawba and Deer Park on the M&O. National Archives, record group 109 chapter 3, volume 13, December 3, 1864. On December 18, 1864, the Engineer Department had lumber at Buckatunna, Mississippi, at the mill of Turner and Leak, at Escatawaba, at the mill of James Leak, at 8 mile station, at the mill of Harman and Hall and at Citronelle at the mill of Griffin.

[127] National Archives, record group 109, chapter 3, volume 12 Engineer Department Records.

[128] McMillan Collection, binder number 2, History Museum of Mobile.

The *Tennessee* had assigned to it a covered barge or lighter that was known as the "*Tennessee's hospital*." We know the details of that vessel and some of the other barges used only because four of them were captured during the battle of Mobile Bay and surveyed or appraised for prize money application purposes.

The *Tennessee's hospital*[129] was 80 feet long with a beam of 22 feet 6 inches. The depth of hold (distance underside of deck to the planking forming a floor on the ribs) was seven feet. Her planking was yellow pine 4 inches thick. She had two anchors and chains and was fitted with a davit and falls for one boat.

There was a coal barge, 80 feet long with a beam of 21 feet 6 inches and a depth of hold of 5 feet. The third of the smaller barges captured was a water lighter. She was 60 feet long with a beam of 17 feet and a depth of hold of 4 feet. Such a vessel was used to transport water from the Eastern shore to Fort Powell. All were built of southern yellow pine.

Vessels like the schooner *Smith* were also used to transport water. Millington reported on December 12, 1862: "The schooner *Smith* was at Fort Morgan for water for the soldiers yesterday, but could not get any, she goes today for some from near the city."[130]

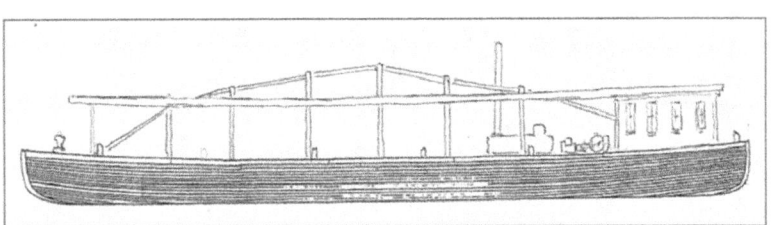
The *Ingomar* (drawing by Author)

The largest of the four barges or lighters captured was the *Ingomar*. She was a typical Alabama, Tombigbee or Mississippi River barge of the period. She was 138 feet long with a 29 foot 6 inch beam and 35 feet 6 inches over her guards (extensions on either side typical of steamboat design), with depth of hold of six feet four inches. She had 12" x 8" hog braces formed of four thicknesses of plank tying forward breast hook to stern frame, supported by seven stanchions 10" x 8" with turnbuckle and screw above the hog braces.

---

[129] Admiral Buchanan on July 18 ordered the naval constructor to equip a lighter as a hospital for the *Tennessee*. Official Records Navy, volume 21, page 907.
[130] Caldwell Delaney's book *Confederate Mobile,* page 96.

There was an anchor of 500 pounds and anchor chains and capstan forward with a light hurricane deck over all. On the lower deck aft was a house with the glazed windows containing bunks for the crew. Forward of the house was a steam engine with 9 inch diameter cylinders and a stroke of 15 inches with pumps and pipes and an Ashcroft's steam gauge. She had one boiler 12 feet long and 30 inch diameter of iron 5/16 thick. There was one counter shaft and pulley.

The above descriptions of the barges are from the Prize Court records of the U.S. District Court for the District of Massachusetts. The drawing included herein is based on plans of typical period vessels and the Prize Court surveys.[131]

Bigger Guns

Beginning in January 1863, the records show the local engineers submitting monthly reports to the Engineering Bureau in Richmond. These reports generally covered the work completed, the work being done, and status of the forts, obstructions, entrenchments, batteries ashore and floating and work to be done. These reports were first made by Daniel Leadbetter, then Victor Von Sheliha and finally by Samuel Lockett.

---

[131] National Archives, record group 21, Federal Archives and Records Center, Waltham, Massachusetts, being records of the U.S. District Court for the District of Massachusetts, December Term 1865. There were two cases, The U.S. versus Three Lighters and The U.S. versus Lighter *Ingomar*.

Fort Powell 1863 (artist E.B. Hough, *Frank Leslie's Illustrated Newspaper*, 2 April 1864)

The report for January states: "battery at Grants Pass: this battery mounts two 8-inch guns and one 32-pounder rifled. Magazine: some repairs of magazine have been made during the month, and a bombproof storehouse completed."[132] The February report shows that carpenters and laborers were engaged in building a wharf 600 feet long for receipt of supplies, etc. at the battery. The wharf was then available, but not yet finished. This work was to be completed in the month of March.[133] In the middle of March the battery still had its two 8-inch guns and one 32-pounder rifle in place. Repairs to the magazine and wharf were still in progress.[134]

- April 6, 1862 the Battle of Shiloh.

The engineers were constantly calling for more and bigger guns. That same call came from every corner of the South with the requests greatly exceeding the supply. In April Von Sheliha was sent to Richmond in an effort to secure more heavy pieces for Morgan, Gaines and Powell.[135]

The question of whether to open or close Grants Pass to shipping was still being debated into May 1863. On April 24 Grants Pass was ordered

---

[132] Official Records Army, volume 15, page 1010.
[133] Official Records Army, volume 15, page 1014.
[134] Official Records Army, volume 15, page 1011 and 1015.
[135] Bergeron, *Confederate Mobile*, page 67.

opened for steamers. On May 6 that work was suspended.[136] On May 8 Leadbetter advised Glenn that Brigadier General Slaughter gave the final order keeping the obstructions in place: "You will stop up the opening you have just made without delay."[137]

Torpedoes

The Ram (model of a "Bigbee Boat" by the author)

In the history of warfare until 1861, the only ship killing weapons were the ram and fire. Cannons battered and disabled ships but rarely sank them. The ram was still used, but the flame throwing fire weapons of the Greeks had long since been discontinued and was not adaptable in a time of explosive projectiles although fireships and shot heated in furnaces were used until the end of the age of sailing ships.

A third ship killing weapon was brought into service by the Confederates in 1861[138] in the form of floating mines then called "torpedoes."[139] That weapon could be free-floating, or floating tethered to an anchor, on fixed piles or sawyers or on a spar attached to the bow of a vessel. All of these delivery methods were used in the Mobile area although Admiral Buchanon adamantly refused to attach a spar torpedo to the

---

[136] National Archives, record group 109, chapter 3, volume 12 Engineer Department Records.
[137] National Archives, record group 109, chapter 3, volume 12 Engineer Department Records.
[138] July 8, 1861—the first Civil War use of a torpedo (mine) was in the Potomac River, *Civil War Naval Chronology*, Naval History Division, Washington, D.C. The contact mine was first tested, but not used, during the Napoleonic Wars. The first limited use of underpowered and generally unsuccessful mines was by the Russians during the Crimean war. The South during the Civil War made the first successful use of explosive mines then called "torpedoes." *19th Century Torpedoes and Their Inventors* by Edwyn Gray, pages 5-6.
[139] *Infernal Machines,* by Milton F. Perry, page 44.

Tennessee. The fixed defenses in the lower Bay all used the anchored floating torpedo.

Mr. B. A. Whitney contracted with the government to manufacture and place torpedoes of the Singer/Fretwell design. On May 16, 1863 Leadbetter directed Glenn to assist Whitney.[140] Whitney was using an extra wide rowboat to place the torpedoes in Grants Pass working from the Steamer *Natchez*.[141] By May 25 Admiral Buchanan reported that 10 or 12 torpedoes had been placed in the channel at Grants Pass, extending from the battery to gunshot range.[142] J.R. Fretwell & Company planted 6 torpedoes in Mississippi Sound west of Fort Powell in October, 1863.[143]

The servicing of torpedoes was a distinct branch of service handled privately by contract. The lower Bay was supplied with torpedoes by a seven man party stationed at Fort Morgan. They had a large and unusually broad launch which could be propelled by either oars or sails. The torpedoes were brought empty to Fort Morgan. Prior to being filled with powder they were stored in a wooden building once used as quarters and standing just outside of Fort Morgan. As needed they were filled then anchored as directed by the Engineers.[144]

The wharf being constructed at Fort Powell, which commenced in February, had been completed by the end of May and the battery was stated to be in good condition.[145] On June 5, piles were ordered driven along the wharf and the commanding officer ordered to construct quarters on them for the Garrison[146]

On June 28, 1863 the boat expedition of James Duke passed through Grants Pass. Duke left Mobile in command of a launch, proceeded to the

---

[140] Later Mr. J.R, McClintock was the representative of Singer and Company in Mobile. Singer had a contract to manufacture and place torpedoes at prices according to prevailing rates for wages and materials on of the direction of the local engineers. National Archives, record group 109 chapter 3, volume 13, letter Von Sheliha to George G. Garner, Chief of Staff, November 4, 1864.

[141] National Archives, record group 109, chapter 3, volume 12 Engineer Department Records.

[142] Official Records Navy, volume 20, page 828.

[143] Buchanan Letterbook, October 10, 1863.

[144] Official Records Navy, volume 21, page 373.

[145] Official Records Army, volume 26, page 27, report of operations for the month of May 1863.

[146] National Archives, record group 109, chapter 3, volume 12 Engineer Department records.

mouth of the Mississippi River, where he and his crew boarded and captured the Federal screw steamer and *Boston* and brought her back to Mobile.[147]

Incoming

In June 1863, the Federals shelled the battery. This, according to some Confederate officers, was not a bad thing.

Leadbetter wrote to Lieutenant Glenn on June 21, 1863: "Gratified to see a few shells thrown at Grants Pass. Such tends to steady the garrison and indicated the value of the bombproof." [148]

A Doctor Taylor[149] proposed chevaux-de-frise as boat obstructions, made of pointed wooden sticks, hoping to be able to eliminate the use of iron which was in short supply. These were placed around the battery. Apparently these were not satisfactory for railroad irons from Battery Gladden were later used for that purpose.[150] Lieutenant Glenn was transferred in June to field service. Leadbetter's letter of recommendation said: "In spite of some personal peculiarities, he is an excellent officer, and I shall lose him with regrets."

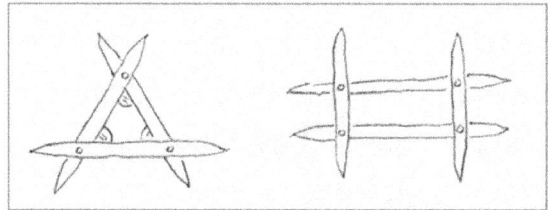
Doctor Taylor's chevaux-de-frise (sketch by Author from drawing in National Archives)

- July 1-3, 1863 battle of Gettysburg. July 4, 1863 Vicksburg falls. July 8, 1863 Port Hudson falls opening the Mississippi River to Federal troop transports.

---

[147] Official Records Navy, series 2, volume 2, page 53, report of Secretary Mallory, November 30, 1863.

[148] National Archives, record group 109, chapter 3, volume 10, Engineer Department Records.

[149] First name unknown.

[150] National Archives, record group 109, chapter 3, volume 10 Engineer Department Records.

The Red River

With the fall of Vicksburg and Port Hudson, two objectives were considered by the Union leadership for the next campaign in the Southwest – Mobile and Texas. Admiral Farragut and General Banks again expressed their desire to move immediately against Mobile.

General N.P. Banks (M. B. Brady, 1861)

Union Maj. General N.P. Banks, commanding Department of the Gulf, 19th Army Corps at Vicksburg, wrote to General H.W. Halleck, General in Chief U.S. Army on August 1, 1863: "The advantage of immediate operations against Mobile consists in the fact that its fortifications thus far are upon the Gulf and the Bay. The rear of the city is unprotected except by a line of incomplete works with few guns mounted, and is unprepared for an assault on the land side. In a short time these works will be completed, the guns mounted, the city provisioned, and garrison strengthened. The army and people are now in such panic from the fall of Vicksburg and Port Hudson, that if attacked on the land side, where assault is not anticipated, and reinforcements are not sent from the east at once, the place will probably be surrendered without serious contest. The approach by land from Portersville [now Bayou La Batre], on the Mississippi sound, is 25 miles, from Pascagoula, 65 miles. The country to Mobile is level and sandy. Roads can be made in any direction without labor for this."

General Richard Taylor (1826-1879) photo Library of Congress

Farragut believed that a march from the Mississippi River was not practical, and that movement against Mobile should be made by water to Pascagoula, which would require a march of only 65 miles. He thought the forts defending the water approaches would fall with the city.

He considered that 25,000 men, one corps of General Grant's Army, with the available forces at New Orleans, would be sufficient for the work.[151]

---

[151] Official Records Army, volume 26, page 666.

Fortunately for Mobile, Banks was ordered up the Red River to Texas, where the reverses he suffered at the hands of General Richard Taylor tied his forces up for a year.

The decision to operate up the Red River, rather than against Mobile was made in Washington. A French army had entered Mexico City on June 10, 1863. This movement by France was followed by an urgent order to Banks to occupy some point or points of Texas territory. This campaign was thought necessary to show the French that the U.S. would not permit their extension of control to lands over which the United States claimed authority though actually in revolt. The possibility that France might attempt to interfere was not lacking foundation and was shared with apprehension by the Confederate Government.[152]

Covert Construction

The Confederates did not want the Union Navy to know the scope, or lack thereof, of the defenses at Grants Pass. Unfortunately, there were numerous deserters that went over to the Union Navy in Mississippi Sound carrying with them knowledge of the forts.

When Colonel Robertson was ordered, on August 3, to proceed to Grants Pass in charge of the work there,[153] he was told that the work was to be carried on "with as little display as possible." Sand was to be loaded by day at Fort Morgan and delivered at Grants Pass at night. The steamer *C.S.M.* was placed at his disposal for that purpose.[154] The garrison at Grants Pass as of August 10, 1863, consisted of a unit of the 1st Alabama Artillery Battalion of 69 men effective total, 76 present with a total of 85 present and absent.[155]

---

[152] *The Gulf and Inland Waters, The Navy in the Civil War* by Alfred T. Mahan page 185.
[153] Robertson was transferred to Powell from Oven and Choctaw Bluffs. National Archives, record group 109, chapter 3, volume 12, July 22, 1863, letter from Leadbetter to Robertson.
[154] National Archives, record group 109, Chapter 3, Volume 12, Engineer Department Records.
[155] Official Records Army, volume 26, page 156, statement of regiments, batteries and attached companies in the Department of the Gulf August 10, 1863.

There was still some pressure to open Grants Pass or find some other route from Mobile Bay directly into Mississippi Sound. On August 21 three men captured in the Sound with passes from Admiral Buchanan stated that the steamer *Boston*, a captured tug then fitted out as a privateer, proposed to come out by some bayou at or near Grants Pass. The Union vessels then watched Fowl River, as well as Grants Pass.[156] The Pass remained closed.

On August 19 Lieutenant Colonel James M. Williams of Mobile, wrote to his wife that he had just been ordered to send a company of the 21st Alabama then at Fort Morgan to Grants Island. He was upset at his commander, Colonel Anderson, for not trying to secure a field assignment for the Regiment and having it divided and subdivided indefinitely for the smaller batteries. He did say, however, that Colonel Robinson was constructing a fine battery at Grants Pass which will not be completed for some time.[157] The Union Navy was doing its best to retard the progress of the work.

U.S.S. Genesee (Naval Historical Center)

The Union Navy Takes its Shots

On August 24, the Union vessels *Jackson*[158] and *Genesee* anchored three-and-one-half miles off Grants Pass and opened fire driving off a steamer that was inside.[159]

---

[156] Official Records Navy, volume 20, page 476.

[157] *From That Terrible Field, letters of James M. Williams*, page 121.

[158] The *John P. Jackson* (generally referred to as the *Jackson*) was a side wheel ferry steamer, built in Brooklyn, New York, in 1860. In November 1861 she was purchased by the Union navy and commissioned in February 1862. She was promptly sent to the Gulf of Mexico and played an active role in the campaign for New Orleans and the Mississippi River. At the end of September 1862, she took up station in Mississippi sound where she served for the rest of the conflict.

Williams reported the incident to his wife by letter on August 27, stating that the Yankees shelled our boys on Monday, treating us with 269 shells, of which some six or eight only took effect on the island with some narrow escapes reported.

U.S.S. J.P. Jackson (Naval Historical Center) Erik Heyl, 1888-1973, courtesy Bowling Green State University, Historical Collection of the Great Lakes

The narrowest escape was that of Lieutenant Savage of the 21st Alabama and his gun squad (members of the 1st Alabama Artillery Battalion).[160] The gun they were serving burst,[161] but only one man was wounded slightly by the explosion. The exploded gun was the only long range weapon they had, so, "after that accident they had to stand and take it until the Yanks were tired of the sport." The following day a "fine" gun was sent over from Fort Morgan.[162]

More Guns

Leadbetter's operations report for the month of September 1863 stated that the battery at Grants Pass was being enlarged by mounting six heavy guns. The battery would contain a bombproof shelter for the garrison and stores. A large quantity of sand had been transported to the site, and a part of the bombproof shelter had become available for use. Four of the gun

---

[159] Official Records Navy, volume 20, page 480, abstract log of the USS Genesee August 24, 1863.

[160] The 1st Alabama Artillery Battalion, Companies A – F was recruited in Mobile, Montgomery, Selma and Eufaula and organized about the first of February 1861 at Fort Morgan. The unit was stationed at the lower Bay throughout the war. During the battle of Mobile Bay they lost 150 killed or wounded out of about 500 engaged. The small detachment that evacuated Fort Powell continued to fight at Spanish Fort and Blakely and a small number moved to Choctaw Bluff in March 1865. Union General Granger pronounced the Regiment to be the most perfect body of troops in either Army.

[161] A rifled and banded 32-pounder.

[162] *Williams, Letters* from Fort Morgan, August 27, 1863. The exploded gun was most likely a rifled and banded 32-pounder, while the new gun from Fort Morgan was likely the 10-inch columbaid bored to 32-pounder and rifled now on display on Government Street downtown Mobile.

platforms had been laid. The work had been vigorously shelled on several occasions by Union gunboats in Mississippi Sound, but without effect. Near the end of September, 16 torpedoes were placed where the gunboats had been operating against the fort.

The battery was expected to be completed in October or November. Lieutenant Glenn, restored to his position on the Mobile defenses by General Johnston, was again in charge of the work.[163]

The attacks resumed on September 13, 1863. On this occasion, the *Genesee, Jackson,* and *Calhoun* fired on the battery. Their captains reported that a gunboat and a transport were forced to shift their berths and that their shells struck the middle of the island many times, silencing the battery. The *Genesee* fired 74 shells with her 100-pounder Parrott; the *Calhoun* fired 48 shells from a 30-pounder Sawyer and a 20-pounder Parrott. They reported that they struck the battery eight times and drove the steamer *Jeff Davis* from her anchorage.[164]

The Confederates returned fire, but the range was so great that none of their shots took effect. This exchange continued almost without interruption from 10 o'clock in the morning until 4 o'clock in the afternoon, when the Federal vessels disengaged and steamed back toward Ship Island. Of the 175 shells fired at the fort, 15 hit the island and only 9 did any damage. A soldier stationed at Fort Grant wrote, "The only loss on our side was a poor innocent rat that got killed in trying to make its escape out of the magazine."[165] Poor results indeed for so many projectiles.

In October six more torpedoes were planted in Mississippi Sound Southwest of Grants Pass. These were torpedoes designed by Dr. J. R. Fretwell and Company.[166]

Notwithstanding the torpedoes and obstructions on October 25, a boat from the "neighboring coast" ran the blockade to Grants Pass where it was

---

[163] Official Records Army, volume 26, page 275, report of operations for the defense of Mobile, Alabama, for the month of September 1863.
[164] Official Records Navy, volume 20, pages 584 – 585.
[165] *Confederate Mobile*, pages 129 – 30.
[166] *Buchanan Letter Book*, letter to Mallory, October 3, 1863.

chased by Federals. The boat ran aground, and its crew tried for 2 or 3 days to get through the Pass without success. A Captain Murphy came to their assistance with his pilot Mr. Walker and crew and assisted the boat through the pass. This report comes from a letter by James Edward Captain of the grounded blockade running boat published in the Mobile Advertiser and Register October 25, 1862.

Firing was resumed on December 19 by the *Hatteras* and *Jackson*. The "Shell Bank Island battery" returned fire from two heavy rifles. One shot passed over the *Jackson* and the other burst short. Two bombproofs and several tents were reported on the Island at the time. From the Bay on the east side of the battery the steamer *Selma* also returned fire. All the shot from the *Selma* fell short as did most of the Union's.[167]

Von Sheliha wrote on December 13, 1863, to Alabama Governor Watts that Fort Powell, with the battery projected for Cedar Point, would render the Pass safe against any attack by water. Fort Powell was not completed at the time and construction on the new battery not yet commenced because of a shortage of labor and transportation.

Slaves working on fortifications (Illustrated *London News*, April 18, 1863)

By this time the government had resorted to impressing Negro labor for 60-day periods of work on the fortifications. Planters had complained to Governor Watts about the engineers keeping the workers beyond the 60 days, the treatment of the laborers and the amount paid. Von Sheliha on December 13, 1863 wrote to Governor Watts explaining the reasons for the necessity of the impressment and responding to the planters' charges. He told the governor

---

[167] Official Records Navy, volume 19, page 734.

that with 4000 Negroes, 500 of them to be axmen, and 100 4-mule wagons, all of the defenses could be completed in three months.

Von Sheliha denied the impressed Negroes were being kept beyond the terms and as to the treatment he pointed to the fact that the planters sent the overseers who were in charge of their impressed hands. These overseers were "not always men who deserved the confidence of their employers…. The engineering department would be very thankful to any gentleman of standing who would come here and lend his assistance in this matter." By order of the War Department payment for impressed slaves was limited to $20 per month and he and General Maury had asked for authority to pay $30 per month.

Von Sheliha closed his letter with this suggestion: "Why not raise a corps of 5000 Negro laborers to serve during the war, and be paid, clothed, and subsisted alike with our common soldiers? The advantages of such an organization are too obvious for me to venture to tire your Excellency with that recapitulation."[168]

Engineering Office General Order No. 2 issued by Von Sheliha on December 9, 1863 provided that rations for Negroes employed on public works would consist of: "Beef – 1 lb. to the ration, daily issue. Pumpkins – 1 lb. to the ration, daily issue. Meal – 1 1/4 lb. to be ration, daily issue. Rice – 10 lb. per 100 rations, 8 days in 15. Pease – 15 lb. per 100 rations, 7 days in 15. Vinegar – 1/2 gallon per 100 rations, daily issue. Soap – 4 1/2 lb. per 100 rations, daily issue. Salt- 4 1/2 lb. per 100 rations, daily issue." Overseers were to see that the Negroes received not only full rations, but also that they were properly prepared and justly distributed.[169]

Still the confidence level in the lower Bay defenses was not high. Area commander General Dabney H. Maury on December 11 stated that he

---

[168] Official Records Army, volume 26, page 502.
[169] *Blackwood's Edinburgh Magazine*, American Edition – volume 16, New York 1865, A Visit to the Cities and Camps of the Confederate States, 1863 – 64 , Part 3.

expected the Federal fleets to be able to run past the forts at the mouth of the Bay.[170]

But not through Grants Pass.

---

[170] Official Records Army, volume 20, page 855.

CHAPTER 5

January 1864-The 21st Alabama at the Pass

Recruiting poster (Mobile Register)

A section of the 21st Alabama[171] consisting of two companies, the Mobile Cadets[172] and the Mobile Battle Guards, together with a part of Culpepper's South Carolina Battery,[173] under Lieutenant Colonel James M. Williams of Mobile still comprised the fort's garrison at the beginning of 1864. These Companies, along with a small detachment of the 1st Alabama Artillery Battalion, remained with Williams until the work was evacuated.[174]

The 21st Alabama had been mustered into service October 13, 1861 at Mobile. The Regiment was intended to be a carbon copy of the 3rd Alabama Infantry, the first Alabama command to be sent into the War in Virginia, which included several of the old volunteer militia companies from Mobile. Many of the younger brothers and relatives who didn't make it into the 3rd Alabama enlisted in the 21st Alabama and formed companies with the same names as those of the 3rd. Most of the young recruits shared the patriotic sentiments

---

[171] For abstracted compiled service records, rosters and a short history see Arthur E. Green's book, *Mobile Confederates from Shiloh to Spanish Fort, the Story of the 21st Alabama Infantry Volunteers CSA*, published March 2012.

[172] The original Mobile Cadets, organized as a militia company in 1845, departed Mobile April 23, 1861 for Montgomery, where they were to become a part of the Third Alabama Regiment, which was the first Regiment to leave for Virginia. The Third was in Virginia for the entire war. The Mobile Cadets, Company K of the 21st Alabama Regiment at Fort Powell, was sometimes known as the "Mobile Cadets number two". See The *Mobile Cadets* edited by William S. Coker.

[173] *The Alabama Review*, Lt. Col, James M. Williams and the Fort Powell Incident by John Kent Folmer page 125.

[174] *The Mobile Cadets 1845-1945*, an Anonymous Manuscript edited by William S. Coker, Patagonia Press, 1993.

James M. Williams (*From That Terrible Field*, Folmer, editor)

of James M. Williams, who wrote in December 1861: "my country calls me – and my own self-respect forces me to make the sacrifice."[175]

The 21st had been at Camp Halls Mill and at Fort Gaines until ordered to Fort Pillow in March 1862.[176] It remained there a few days, and then moved to Corinth and Tupelo where it was brigaded under General Gladden. The regiment took part in the bloody Battle of Shiloh on April 6, 1862 where it lost six color bearers in succession and 200 killed and wounded out of about 650 engaged. On the return to Corinth, the regiment was reorganized, and extended their enlistment from one year to "for the war." The 21st was at Farmington, Mississippi but its casualties were few. In the summer of 1862 the regiment was ordered to Mobile, and was on Garrison duty at Fort Morgan and at Oven and Choctaw Bluffs. It was at Pollard for a short time under General Cantey. It was then ordered to the lower Bay defenses with two companies stationed at Fort Powell.[177]

Heavy Artillery

As of January 11, 1864, the heavy battery at Fort Powell consisted of two 8-Inch columbiads and one 6.4-inch rifle based on a 10-inch columbiad rifled to 6.4 inch (this gun is now on display at the Admiral Semmes Monument in the median of Government Street, downtown Mobile).[178] The fort's armament also contained fieldpieces to repel boat attacks, but those were generally not listed in reports.

Catesby Ap R. Jones C.S.N (Naval Historical Center)

---

[175] Williams letters
[176] Attached as Addendum Number 1 is a timeline of the war record of the 21st Alabama.
[177] *Alabama, Her History, Resources, War Record, and Public Men* by Willis Brewer, page 623
[178] Official Records Army, volume 32, page 548.

Heavier 7-inch Brooke rifles from Selma were on the way. They would be needed. Admiral Farragut resumed command of his squadron on January 18, 1864. He wanted to attack the defenses of Mobile immediately before the Confederates had finished the ironclads they were building. But troops were needed for the reduction of the forts, and the Red River expedition had diverted those that might otherwise have been available.[179]

Catesby Ap R. Jones, former second-in-command of the *Virginia (Merrimac)* during her battle with the *Monitor*, cousin of Robert E. Lee and nephew of General Page (Commander at Fort Morgan) was beginning to ship guns from the Selma Naval Ordnance Foundry.[180] One of the first guns delivered was a 7-inch rifle marked S- 19 shipped to Admiral Buchanan on Timothy Maher's grand steamer *Southern Republic*, on January 22, 1864.[181]

7-inch Brooke rifle on naval carriage (Library of Congress)

Jones advised the Admiral that the gun had not been proof tested. Ordinarily to proof a gun it would have been fired with a charge of 16 pounds of powder and a cast-iron bolt (a solid projectile). Jones stated that because it had not been test fired he was requested by Commander Brooke, Chief of Ordnance and designer of the gun, to ask Buchanan to have it fired once with the above charge before placing it in battery. Jones did not think there was any danger in not testing the gun as the *Virginia's* guns had not been tested.[182] In any event, he said he had another gun ready that could be tested and shipped out the following week.

---

[179] *The Gulf and Inland Waters, The Navy in the Civil War* by Alfred T. Mahan, page 218.
[180] See *The Brooke Guns from Selma* by Stephen Crooms brother in law, Walter W. Stephen, *Alabama Historical Quarterly* volume 20, 1958.
[181] Official Records Navy, volume 21, page 867.
[182] Official Records Navy, volume 21, telegram Jones to Buchanan, January 14, 1864, page 865.

The gun S-19 was not tested by the Navy but was loaned to the Army and placed in battery at Fort Powell.

February – Ready for a Fight

February brought to Fort Powell Admiral Farragut and a fleet of mortar schooners and gunboats. That suited Williams, for after the bombardment started he wrote to his wife: "I have been longing for such a fight as I now have on my hands for a long time, and expect to have an interesting time of it."[183]

Since 1862 one or more Union Navy steam vessels were always on station off Grants Pass. On February 2, 1864 the *Calhoun* and *J.P. Jackson* were ordered to relieve each other in the performance of that duty. Should either of them break down or require repairs it was to signal across Dauphin Island to the vessel stationed nearest to Grants Pass on the other side, or by boat through Petit Bois or Horn Island Pass. The vessel not employed in watching Grants Pass would patrol the sound or be anchored at night close to Horn Island Pass to intercept vessels that might attempt to run in or out.[184]

U.S.S. *Calhoun* (Naval Historical Center)

---

[183] *Williams* Letters, page 126.
[184] Official Records Navy, volume 21, page 69, Captain Thornton A. Jenkins commanding blockade off Mobile to Commander *U.S.S. Calhoun*, February 2, 1864.

General Dabney H. Maury, Commander Department of the Gulf with headquarters at Mobile, had received reports that the Federals were planning a land expedition against Mobile. He wrote on February 2, 1864 to James A. Seddon, Secretary of War, that he found no evidence of an intention on the part of the enemy to immediately attack Mobile. He said it may be that his fleets will run past the outer forts and occupy the waters of the Bay. "I think 40,000 troops and three months' time should be devoted by the enemy to the enterprise if he expects success."

General Dabney H. Maury
(Recollections of a Virginian)

Maury had reason for confidence as it was thought that the mighty *Tennessee,* then fitting out in Mobile, would soon be ready. It was expected that she alone could defeat the blockading fleet.[185]

Ready or not Farragut was on his way.

Farragut on the Move

On February 8, 1864, Farragut ordered six mortar boats, then at Pensacola, prepared for immediate service and sent to the Mississippi Sound. There they were to move up as near as "prudence dictated" to the Lighthouse Island Battery, in Grants Pass, "for the purpose of shelling it."[186]

The attack was to be part of a "program" to assist General Sherman who was on the move east from Vicksburg toward Meridian, Mississippi from which point he would threaten either Mobile or central Alabama. Farragut asked General Banks to cut the railroad from Montgomery to Mobile north of Pensacola to slow any reinforcements coming through

---

[185] Official Records Army, volume 32/2, page 655-66, Maury to Seddon, February 2, 1864.
[186] Official Records Navy, volume 21, page 91, Farragut to Commander Gibson at Pensacola, February 8, 1864.

Mobile. He understood the defenders of Mobile expected an attack within the week, and with 2000 to 3000 troops he would accommodate them.[187]

Farragut appointed Lieutenant Commander W. W. Low of the double ender *Octorara* to command the bombardment flotilla. The attacking fleet consisted of the gunboats *Octorara, Port Royal* and *Jackson*, together with the Mortar Schooners, *Sea Foam* (actually a brigantine rigged vessel), *John Griffith, Orvetta, Sarah Bruen, Henry James* and *O. H. Lee*.[188]

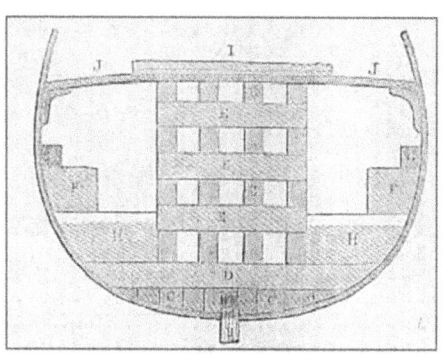

Frame work in schooners to support 13-inch mortars (*Harpers Weekly*, May 10, 1862)

Lieutenant Low's orders were simple. He was to proceed to Horn Island Pass and take charge of the gunboats and mortar schooners assembled in the sound and proceed toward Mobile Bay, place his vessels to the best advantage for shelling the Shell Bank Battery, and commence firing. The firing should be done slowly at first, until he got the range, and then he was to try to drive the troops out. If he succeeded in doing so, he was to move up and take possession of the fort and then commence upon the fort at Cedar Point.[189]

Mortar Schooners in the Sound

All of the above named Mortar Vessels and the *Octorara* and *Jackson* were with Admiral Farragut at New Orleans in March and April 1862. The bomb vessels had been placed under Commander Porter on February 10, 1862 while en route from New York to Key West. They sailed from Key West on March 6 and were towed across the bar at the mouth of the Mississippi River on March 18, 1862.

---

[187] Official Records Navy, volume 21, page 91-2, letter from Farragut to Maj. General Banks, U.S. Army, February 11, 1864.
[188] Official Records Navy, volume 21, page 94, February 12, 1864.
[189] Official Records Navy, volume 21, page 92-93, Farragut to Low, February 12, 1864.

Each of the bomb vessels had one 13-inch mortar that weighed some 17,300 pounds and threw a 212 pound explosive shell. The *Sea Foam, Sarah Bruen* and *Henry James* also were armed with two 32-pounders and two 12-pounder rifled howitzers. The *Oliver H. Lee* had, in addition to her mortar, two 32-pounders. The *Orvetta* had, in addition to her mortar, two 12-pounder rifled howitzers.[190] It was the vessels 13-inch mortars that Farragut expected to induce the garrison to abandon their fort.

Mortar Schooner (Peabody Museum of Salem)

These mortar schooners were part of a fleet of 21 schooners purchased in late 1861 by the U.S. Navy for conversion and sent from New York to the Gulf. A heavy framework of timbers strengthened the hull to provide support for the mortar. The schooners were 90 to 112 feet long and 150 to 285 tons. All were originally armed with one 13-inch mortar and two 32-pounder smoothbores, but later most added from two to four 12-pounder guns. These boats had crews of about 35.

Colonel Von Sheliha, in his usual energetic manner was gathering and mounting additional guns on the fort even as Farragut was issuing his orders. On February 13 Admiral Buchanan authorized a 7-inch Brooke gun with naval carriage, slide and ammunition intended for the ironclad *Nashville* to be turned over to the engineers for mounting that day at Fort Powell.[191]

About the same time as Buchanan was issuing his orders General Sherman was raiding east from Vicksburg toward Meridian. He entered Meridian on February 14 with more than 30,000 troops. It was unknown to the Confederates if his destination was Demopolis or Mobile.

---

[190] Official Records Navy, volume 18, page 25, Gideon Welles to Porter, February 10, 1862 (This was the armament in February 1862. A year later there probably were some additions or deletions).

[191] National Archives, record group 109, chapter 3, volume 12, Engineer Department Records, Von Sheliha to Lieutenant Eggleston Naval Ordnance Officer Mobile, February 13, 1864.

The Confederate Army facing Sherman stayed east of the Tombigbee River, having crossed over at Moscow some 15 miles south of Demopolis. On February 18 Sherman had moved down the M&O Railroad to a point 3 miles south of Quitman, Mississippi.[192] They got no closer to Mobile. The next day His troops left Quitman headed the other way.[193]

Union priorities were still focused on the Red River and Trans-Mississippi. But General Sherman had an army of 30,000 sitting idle and he did not want to wait for a spring campaign. General Ulysses S. Grant gave him permission to destroy the railroads at Meridian, and to do as much damage in the month of February as time allowed but to be prepared by the first of March to assist General Banks in a raid up the Red River in Louisiana. Three railroads intersected at Meridian and it was a Confederate strategic point. It served as an area storage and distribution center. By February 3, 1864 Sherman was ready and began his 150-mile march from Vicksburg to Meridian.

13-inch mortar on schooner (Ripley, Warren – *Artillery and Ammunition of the Civil War*)

Sherman's Meridian raid served as a practice operation for his later march to the sea from Atlanta. His troops were living off the land and if he was cut off from Vicksburg he could have fallen back to Pascagoula under the protection of Farragut's fleet. That was not necessary as he completed his objective and retraced his steps after destroying 115 miles of railroad track, 61 bridges, and 20 locomotives and assorted depots, buildings and structures.[194]

Sherman had written to General Banks on January 31 that he wanted to keep up the "delusion" of an attack on Mobile and the Alabama River. For this purpose he asked Banks, then at New Orleans, if he would initiate a

---

[192] Official Records Army, volume 32 – 2, page 753.
[193] Official Records Army, volume 32 – 2, page 764.
[194] For an interesting perspective on Sherman's raid see *Sherman's Meridian Campaign a Practice Run for the March to the Sea*: by Kevin Dougherty at *Mississippi History Now*, an online publication of the Mississippi Historical Society.

harassing foraging raid or other expedition in that direction.[195] Farragut's attack on Fort Powell was a part of Sherman's feint or delusion. But Farragut did not get the "feint" part of his attack order and was serious. If he had the opportunity to take and hold Fort Powell and to get his ships into Mobile Bay before the *Tennessee* crossed the Bar into the lower Bay he certainly would have done so.

From the Confederate perspective Farragut certainly appeared serious. General Maury at Mobile on February 14 wrote to General Samuel Cooper Adjutant General at Richmond that Farragut was in Pensacola a few days prior with eight mortar boats and four steamers to attack Grants Pass the next day. His fleet a few days later was reported to be off Mobile Bay.

Maury's effective strength had been increased to 10,050 of all arms. He said that he needed 6000 additional good infantry to successfully hold Mobile. He had plenty of breadstuffs and a fair supply of other subsistence. To hold off Sherman's expected attack he said he would need ordnance, experienced heavy artillerymen and some clever engineers – engineers experienced under fire.[196]

---

[195] Official Records Army, volume 34/2, page 266.
[196] Official Records Army, volume 32, page 736.

CHAPTER 6

The First Battle of Mobile Bay

The Union mortar boat flotilla took up position to shell Fort Powell on the evening of February 15, 1864 and opened fire at about 9 A.M. on the 16th. The fort's gunners replied infrequently to the enemy bombardment. Few of the projectiles from either side found their mark.

To assist the gunners of Fort Powell, the engineers took triangulations from Cedar Point and Fort Powell and each of the mortar boats. They had earlier measured the distances between the flagpole on Cedar Point and that of Fort Powell and Dauphin Island.[197] Calculating the distance from Fort Powell to an anchored mortar schooner in the sound was a matter of geometry. With the distance known from a point on Powell and a point on Cedar Point the angles would be taken from Powell to the target and from Cedar Point to the target and with that information the distance from Powell to the target could be calculated.

After the bombardment opened on the 16th, there was a weather delay. On February 19 Maury reported that the attack had not been renewed because the weather was too bad for action.[198] Mortar schooners needed relatively calm water to achieve any degree of accuracy. Ships at sea could fire their smoothbore guns from a rolling deck at point blank range by judging the roll or by bouncing their cannonballs off the water into opposing

---

[197] National Archives, record group 109, chapter 3, volume 12, Engineer Department Records.
[198] Official Records Army, volume 32/2, page 769, Maury to Polk February 19, 1864.

vessels. Accurate mortar fire required a stable platform.

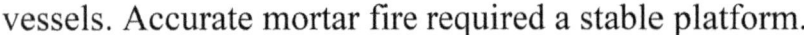

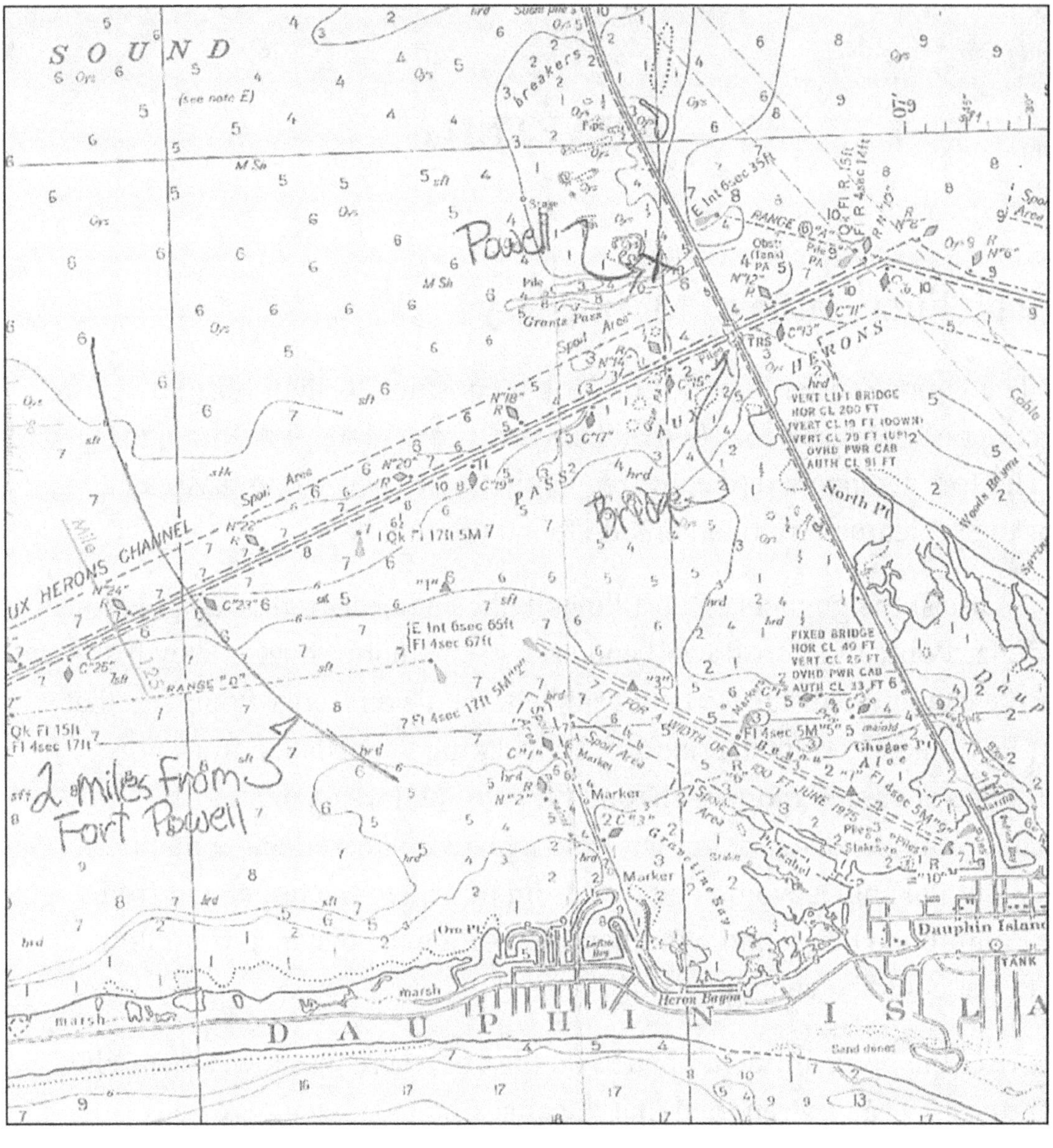

Navigation Chart of the area with 2 mile arc marked from Fort Powell

In February the wind in Mississippi sound is often from the north, northeast or northwest. In the summer the prevailing winds are from the southwest but often from the north or southeast in the mornings. A south wind would have allowed the mortar schooners to lie in the lee of Dauphin Island. In the winter they had to anchor up fully exposed and rolling in the prevailing north winds coming down Mobile Bay.[199]

---

[199] The author has a house on Dauphin Island looking directly over the area where Farragut's fleet concentrated for the bombardment and can attest first hand to the ferocity of the winter storms.

The wind would not necessarily be at an angle allowing mortar firing off one anchor. They could not fire directly ahead or directly astern because the mortar was located between the masts. Drawings from the period show the schooners firing at an angle of 10 to 15° off the bow. Stern anchors may have been required to secure those angles. Therefore, the wind would usually be from a side angle causing rolling in the 75 to 110 foot round bottomed sailing schooners.

Confederate headquarters in Mobile received daily reports unless there was heavy fog. During this period the defenders of Fort Powell used a light signal to communicate with Fort Morgan every night. Fort Morgan sent the nightly news on to Mobile by telegraph.[200]

Engineers

When Farragut moved his mortar schooners into position in Mississippi Sound some two miles west of Fort Powell, Major General Jeremy Gilmer, commander of the Military District of Georgia and South Carolina, headquartered at Savannah, was ordered to Mobile.[201] He was detailed for special duty during the siege of Fort Powell to inspect the defenses and to advise and assist.[202] He arrived in Mobile on the 22nd after travelling for 52 hours. In Mobile he stayed with General Maury and Colonel

General Jeremy Gilmer (Miller, *Photographic History of the Civil War*)

---

[200] *Williams*, letters page 128.

[201] Jeremy Francis Gilmer was born in North Carolina February 23, 1818. He graduated from the United States military Academy in 1839 whereupon he entered the U.S. Army. He constructed fortifications and conducted surveys until 1861 when he resigned. Gilmer then received a commission of Major of Engineers in the Confederate states Army and served as Chief Engineer on the staff of Gen. A. S. Johnson until his death at the battle of Shiloh April 6, 1862, where Gilmer was also severely wounded. In August 1862 he was assigned to the office of Chief of Engineer Bureau in Richmond, Virginia and promoted to Col. of Engineers. In August 1863 he was promoted to Major General and ordered to Charleston, South Carolina to direct the defense of that city. He returned to Richmond in June 1864 where he directed the Engineer Bureau until the end of the war. After the war, he was a director of the Georgia Central Railroad and President of the Savanna Gas-light Company. He died on December 1, 1883.

[202] Jeremy Gilmer Collection, University of North Carolina, he was ordered to Mobile by General Withers February 23, 1864, he resumed his position at Savannah March 17, 1864.

Von Sheliha after finding that room and board at the Battle House ran $15-$18 per day. While in Mobile he attended Von Sheliha's wedding. He considered the attack on Fort Powell to be most probably a feint to keep Maury from sending troops to reinforce Polk then on the Tombigbee opposite Sherman.[203] "If for this purpose alone, it has been a complete success."[204]

On February 27, Gilmer reported to Richmond that work on the Mobile defenses was being pressed with zeal. On the 29th he reported that the enemy had not fired on Powell for three days. "By earnest appeals in person and with General Maury I have induced Admiral Buchanan to send his smaller ironclads [the *Tuscaloosa* and *Huntsville*] to take position inside of Grants Pass.[205] Also the ram *Baltic*, clad with iron in front." Efforts to bring the *Tennessee* over Dog River bar were underway. She was expected to join the other ironclads within a few days.[206]

The Confederates, in the meantime, were keeping a watch on General Sherman's transports on the Mississippi River. If the transports from Vicksburg were going north, then Tennessee was their objective. If they were going south, that would have meant reinforcement for the troops assigned to assist Farragut in an attack on Mobile. General Gilmer stayed in Mobile until it was determined in early March that Sherman's transports were heading north.[207]

---

[203] General Polk was facing Sherman in central west Alabama.
[204] The Battle House is a hotel in Mobile.
[205] *Alabama Historical Quarterly*, The Civil War letters of Robert Tarleton, edited by William N. Still, Jr. states at page 56 that the Confederate fleet was lined up at anchor at the rear of Fort Powell.
[206] Jeremy Gilmer collection, Southern Historical Society papers, University of North Carolina, Chapel Hill, entries for February 22, 27 and 29, 1864.
[207] Jeremy Gilmer collection, Southern Historical Society papers, University of North Carolina, Chapel Hill.

The Bombs Fly

Bombardment of Fort Powell sketched February 23, 1864 (Harper's Weekly, April 24, 1864)

Even with calmer water the mortar and gunboat fire was not accurate. On February 24th, the Union fleet fired 373 shots at the fort. Three shells struck the bombproof and two struck the parapets. There was no damage, and no casualties. They resumed firing the following morning. [208]

Throughout the battle, Colonel Williams continued to send letters every few days to his wife. He wrote on February 27: "I wrote to you on the 25th, but believe I did not mention the lively time we had about 10 o'clock that morning – A gunboat came in on my left quite close, and endeavored to dismount my guns by an enfilade fire – I opened on the bold rascal with all my guns, and both sides had a warm time of it for half an hour – at the end

---

[208] Official Records Army, volume 32/1, page 401, Maury to Cooper.

of that time, he drew off having been hit more than once – The firing was furious…You may rest easy when you hear the big guns – the enemy won't take Fort Powell very soon that way – I am taking every precaution to punish them if they try to assault me in the night."[209]

A night assault would have meant an attack by sailors and Marines in large rowboats some capable of carrying 40 – 50 men. The western approach to the fort was shallow and bristling with chevaux-de-frise and log booms as obstacles. The forts Garrison had muskets that would fire buck and ball (giving a shotgun effect) as well as minie' balls, shotguns, pistols, hand grenades, bayonets and swords, and perhaps knives and pikes. They were ready to repel boarders on their tiny ship like island fort. The heavy guns would fire clusters of small balls known is grape shot and the forts field pieces would fire cans of small iron balls known as canister shot. The fort had boats for picket duty and with a fleet close, Williams may have placed boats in the sound on this duty. The only method available for lighting the approach to the fort was large iron baskets of light wood such as was placed on pilings on the west channel bank opposite Fort Morgan although there is no record of such being used at Powell. There would be no boat assault since Admiral Farragut did not consider such to be feasible.

More Batteries

By February 29th batteries were under construction on the Little Dauphin Island beach,[210] at Sughee Point as well as on Cedar Point to prevent the Union forces from establishing land batteries against Powell. The ironclads *Huntsville*, *Tuscaloosa,* and *Baltic* remained stationed at the east end of Grants Pass. They were positioned to be in sight of the enemy as a deterrent and to meet his fleet should the fort be silenced and an attempt be

---

[209] Williams, letters page 129.
[210] General Page Telegraph Book, Southern Historical Society Collection at University of North Carolina, entry for March 17, 1864, telegraph from Maury: "Try tonight to take the Parrot gun to Battery Tracy on Little Dauphin Island along the beach." Following the fall of the lower Bay line the name "Battery Tracy" was given to the former Appalache Battery at the head of that river north of battery Huger.

made to run past it into the Bay after removing obstructions.[211] A run through the pass would have been a most unlikely event.

Farragut was not optimistic. In a letter to the Commander of the Eastern Gulf Squadron on February 19, he said that he feared that he would lead a life of idleness for a month or two, as the Government appeared to plan the campaigns, and Mobile does not seem to be included just yet. He said that the troops from Vicksburg are on a handsome raid (referring to Sherman). He said that he should have to content himself going along the coast and pestering all the people he can "get at." "I am now trying to clear out Grants Pass. The enemy has established a very strong battery of about six or eight guns about the middle of it, and I wish to remove them if I can, but the difficulty is the shallowness of the water. I cannot get within 2 miles of them. I hope when the wind changes to the southward it will enable me to get within 3/4 mile nearer. We have had a very cold norther blowing for the last three days, but I hope it is at an end."[212] Northers meant rolling mortar schooners, lower tides and less water for Farragut's gunboats.

Mortar from Schooner Orvetta, now a memorial in Bristol, New Hampshire

Captain Drayton of the *Calhoun,* with of the bombardment squadron, wrote to Captain Jenkins of the *Richmond* then on blockade duty off Fort Morgan on February 24: " We are hammering away at the fort here, which minds us about as much as if we did not fire – that is, the fort – for the men skedaddle as soon as the fire is it all brisk, although they will keep up anything like a fair fight, as they did with me for two hours yesterday in the *Orvetta*, and until the others commenced action, when they retired. We cannot get inside of 2 miles at the nearest, and to do this every vessel is at least a foot in the mud, so that should the tide fall suddenly God knows when we would get off, although I

---

[211] Official Records Army, volume 52/2, page 631, Colonel J. C. Ives to President Davis February 29, 1864.
[212] Official Records Navy, volume 21, page 94-95, Farragut to acting rear Adm. Theodorus Bailey February 19, 1864.

suspect you people, who are rolling about outside, would be delighted to remain a week or so in such a quiet berth as this is."[213]

Torpedo Problems

The Confederates were surprised that Farragut's mortar schooners and gunboats were crossing and re-crossing the area where torpedoes had been previously placed without generating any explosions.

The torpedoes were of Mr. Singer's design. These used a complicated mechanism with a trigger releasing a spring loaded striker that struck an exploder cap. After Farragut broke off his attack the Confederate Engineers examined the torpedoes and found that teredo worms, oysters and barnacles had formed shell clusters on the top of the torpedo between the exploder caps and the spring-loaded trigger. The springs and the triggers worked, but the force of the strikers blow was deadened by the accumulated oyster and other shells, thus no explosions.[214] Even with the knowledge of the spring loaded trigger problem nothing was done to correct it and there were similar results with the torpedoes on August 5, except for the one newly placed that destroyed the *Tecumseh*.

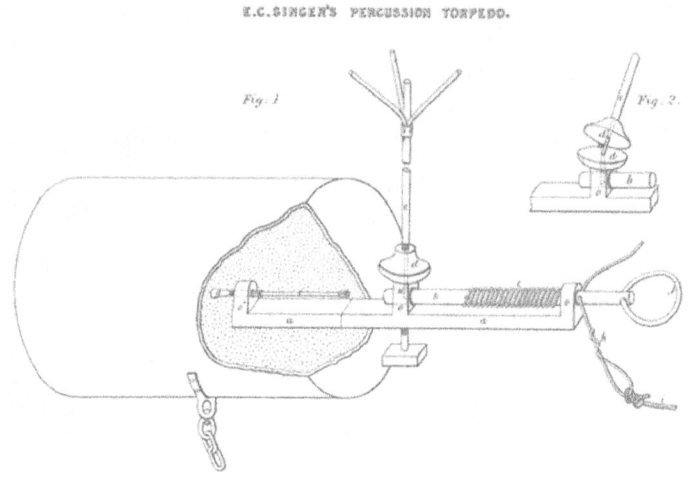

Singer torpedo (Von Sheliha, *Treatise on Coast Defense*)

---

[213] Official Records Navy, volume 21, page 95.
[214] *A Treatise on Coast-Defense*, Von Sheliha, page 229.

Standing Fast

Farragut's mortar schooners and gunboats renewed their attack on February 23 and continued the bombardment the next two days. On the 23rd they fired slightly more than 300 shells at the fort, but caused little damage and no casualties. During the attack on the following day, the fleet threw nearly 375 shells towards the fort. Again, few struck their target, and those had no serious effect. The fort's gunners initiated the action on February 25 by firing on the squadron. Despite 470 shells fired in reply by the Federals, the fort sustained less damage than it had the previous day, although the garrison lost one man killed and two wounded.[215] By the 28th, it was apparent to Farragut that he was not going to drive the defenders from Fort Powell.

Mortar Schooner (Images of War)

With the low winter tides and his steamers drawing 8 1/2 feet, he could not approach closer than 4000 yards or some 2 ¼ miles. He could not get within 800 yards of the fort in small boats so he could not assault it. But, he concluded that his continued action was assisting General Sherman by keeping up the idea of an attack upon Mobile, which attack was looked for hourly by the Confederates. "Would that were true; now is the propitious time."[216]

The *Tennessee* was attempting to work her way over the bars into the lower Bay. The draft of the Tennessee was too great to allow her to pass over Dog River bar immediately south of the City. To reduce her draft as much weight as possible, including her guns, was removed from the vessel. That was somewhat risky since there would be a period of time when she

---

[215] Bergeron, *Confederate Mobile*, page 134.
[216] Official Records Navy, volume 21, page 97.

would have been defenseless if Farragut had dashed in before her ordnance was replaced.

Removing the *Tennessee's* guns, stores and ammunition still did not reduce her draft sufficiently to cross the bar. The naval constructors then set about to build camels to lighten her draft. Camels are large wooden boxes shaped to fit snugly alongside the vessel's hull. These were sunk alongside, lashed to the vessel with chains then pumped out raising the vessel with them. Unfortunately, the first camels were either accidentally or by sabotage burned when they were nearly completed and a second set had to be built. The camels eventually were successful in reducing the draft of the *Tennessee* so that she cleared the bar into the lower Bay.

If the *Tennessee* got there before Farragut it would have been imprudent for him to go in without one or more Ironclads. "Because she could lie in shoal water where our ships could not get at her, and could knock our vessels to pieces, but if we go in before she gets over the bar, our gunboats will destroy her on the bar if she attempts to cross with camels."[217] The *Tennessee's* draft was 14 feet, which was not much less than the 17 foot draft of the *Hartford*. The *Huntsville* and *Tuscaloosa* with drafts of 7 feet or the *Baltic* at six and one half feet were shoal water boats.

Fort Powell did not escape damage from the bombardment. Sand[218] rather than brick was the most effective way to stop a large projectile. The shot and shell striking the fort would bury into the sand, explode, and then when the firing ceased, the garrison at the fort would fill in the holes with sand kept on hand for that purpose. Even though Fort Powell was unfinished and in need of constant repair, the engineers did not retain Negro laborers there since the Federals were liable to shell the place at any moment.[219]

---

[217] Official Records Navy, volume 21, page 96, Farragut to Gideon Welles, February 28, 1864.
[218] Some deserters reported in March 1864 that the bomb-proof of Powell was covered with 10 to 15 feet of oyster shells. Official Records Navy, volume 66, page 13. Sand was probably the principal component of the structure although the records show the use of oyster shells they were probably in the lower levels as a shell exploding in a pile of oyster shells would likely generate a shrapnel like affect. I have not seen any tests of the effect of artillery shells fired into a pile of oyster shells.
[219] Official Records Navy, Series One, volume 21, page 880, letter from Lieutenant Simms, Commander, *CSS Baltic* to Commander Catesby Ap R. Jones.

In early March, Fort McAllister on the Georgia coast was bombarded. The engineers there found that an 11-inch solid shot penetrated 9 feet 10 inches in the sand; an 8-inch rifle shell penetrated 3 feet 6 inches in sand.[220] The 13 inch mortars thrown at Powell penetrated the earth cover of the bombproof as deep as 3 1/2 feet, and upon exploding opened a crater of 7 feet in diameter.[221]

The fort's gun captains were improving their aim. Farragut reported on March 1 that they opened on his mortar boats with five heavy rifled guns and struck the mortar schooner *John Griffith* four times in succession.[222]

S-19

The Naval Ordnance Works in Selma shipped to Adm. Buchanan a 7-inch Brooke double banded rifle number S-19 in January.[223] The gun was loaned to the Navy and installed at Fort Powell. As was discussed earlier the gun was not proof tested.

A Union Parrott rifle with broken muzzle (*The Photographic History of the Civil War*)

During the bombardment S-19 had been fired 55 times at elevations of 21 1/2°, 15°, 10°, and 8° with powder charges of 12 pounds for shells of 95 pounds. Seven of the shells, also made at Selma, burst in the gun. On March 28 after firing 26 times within an hour and 50 minutes the gun became quite hot at the muzzle and exploded. The elevation that day was 10° with the last shot being at 8°. The shell bursting in the gun broke about 10 inches from the muzzle with the break being generally perpendicular to the axis of the bore.[224] First Lieutenant Frederick Ferguson of Company C, First

---

[220] Official Records Army, volume 14, page 222, report of John McCrady, Captain and Chief Engineer State of Georgia.
[221] *Treatise on Coast Defense,* by Victor von Sheliha, London, 1868.
[222] Official Records Navy, volume 21, page 98, March 1, 1864.
[223] Official Records Navy, volume 21, page 868.
[224] Official Records Navy, volume 21, page 882, report of Lieutenant Colonel James M. Williams, March 7, 1864. Page Telegraph Book, entry March 29.

Alabama Artillery Battalion, father of Hill Ferguson, commanded gun S-19 during the bombardment.

Bursting of guns was an occupational hazard of the men handling those large and dangerous weapons. Previously a rifled and banded 32-pounder had burst at Powell. Colonel C. S. Stewart was killed by a bursting gun at Fort Morgan. On February 16 while firing on Fort Powell the *J.P. Jackson* burst her rifled gun but no one was hurt.[225] On March 19 a 6.4-inch Brooke gun at Battery Simpkins on the Atlantic Coast burst with about 15 inches of the muzzle being blown off. But that gun had been fired between 1700 and 1800 times, notwithstanding the gun was considered to be serviceable and remained in use. Gun S-19 was also considered to be serviceable after the end of her barrel blew off. The gun crew did not necessarily agree.

Lieutenant Simms, of the *Baltic*, giving a naval perspective, said some beautiful line shots were made with S–19: "Am satisfied, at least one of the mortar schooners would have been sunk if sailors had been handling it, but unfortunately, those who were working it knew not how to sight a gun. Six of their shots went between her masts, too high, and yet they never thought of depressing the gun."[226]

Explosion of gun on U.S.S. *J.P. Jackson* February 16, 1864 while firing on Fort Powell (Frank Leslie's Illustrated Newspaper, April 2, 1864)

John M. Brooke, the designer of the gun, wrote to Buchanan from his Office of Ordnance and Hydrography in Richmond that Army columbiad powder was much stronger than the Navy powder of large grain. He said the charges of Army powder for 7-inch rifles of his design, such as S-19, should be from 8 to 10 pounds with shells and from 10 to 13 pounds with bolts. High charges should not be used unless required to produce effective results with wrought iron bolts on ironclads, otherwise, the guns

---

[225] Official Records Navy, volume 21, page 98.
[226] Official Records Navy, volume 21, page 880, Simms to Jones, March 5, 1864.

may be injured.[227] At the time the gun burst the Army crews were using 12 pounds of powder with shells, presumably Army columbiad powder.[228]

March-Friendly Ironclads in the Lower Bay

The large number of shells the Federal fleet continued to direct at Fort Powell resulted in some casualties and damage. At least five shells burst in the officer's quarters demolishing them. Lieutenant Cogburn and Sgt. Stanard were slightly wounded on the 16th. On March 1st the Union Navy fired 567 projectiles of which 20 struck the island and three the bombproof.

The accuracy of the mortar fire was no doubt a disappointment to Farragut. The Mortar Schooners and their 13-inch mortars had been with him at New Orleans and on the Mississippi and afterwards on patrol in Mississippi Sound. Their mortars and crews were worn out. Following their withdrawal from the Fort Powell bombardment they were sent home to New York. All the mortars were in need of replacing and the crews had suffered from yellow fever the previous summer.[229] The Captain of the *Sea Foam* reported that her mortar was: "much worn and scarcely to be depended upon for accuracy or endurance."[230] The others were in much the same condition.

Drawing of the vessel the Union Navy thought was the *Ram Tennessee* approaching Fort Powell. The *Tennessee* was still grounded on a bar in the upper Bay at the time. This must be the *Huntsville* or the *Tuscaloosa*. (Official Records Navy)

---

[227] Official Records Navy, volume 21, page 885, telegram John M. Brooke to Commander in Charge Mobile, Alabama, March 8, 1864.
[228] Shells exploding in Brooke guns were a continuing problem. The *Nashville* off Spanish Fort in March 1865 was firing on the Federal troops besieging the fort. She could not fire over friendly forces because of the shells exploding or breaking up in the barrels of her Brookes.
[229] Official Records Navy, Volume 21, page 243.
[230] Official Records Navy, Volume 21, page 240, May 3, 1864.

On March 1st Admiral Farragut reported to Gideon Welles Secretary of the Navy that to his great surprise, the Ram *Tennessee* appeared in full view in the Bay opposite Grants Pass where he had been at work all day shelling Fort Powell. "They (the fort) opened upon our mortar boats with five heavy rifled 100-pounder guns and struck the *John Griffith* four times in succession. We silenced the fort in one hour and a quarter, and they did not again open fire, but kept their flag flying until after sunset, when we ceased firing."[231]

Farragut Withdraws

On that same day, Farragut began withdrawing his flotilla from Mississippi Sound.[232] He explained to General Banks: "the *Tennessee* could be in shoal water alongside the beach inside of the peninsula, and then prevent the approach of your troops towards Fort Morgan, and that our ships, even after passing the forts will not be able to get at her, at least none of the larger vessels. Mobile will have to be left until the arrival of ironclads, when that will be God only knows."[233] In fact, the *Tennessee* did not arrive in the lower Bay until the 18th of May.[234] Farragut or his officers in the Sound mistakenly identified either the *Huntsville* or *Tuscaloosa* as the much anticipated *Tennessee*.[235]

C.S.S. *Tennessee* (U.S. Navy Art Collection, Washington D.C.)

---

[231] Official Records Navy, volume 21, page 97.
[232] Official Records Navy, volume 21, page 98, Farragut to Captain T. A. Jenkins, Senior Officer, Commanding Blockade off Mobile.
[233] Official Records Navy, volume 32/3, page 12.
[234] *Letters of Robert Tarleton* Edited by William Still. Tarleton was ecstatic in a letter from Fort Morgan May 18, 1864. "*we are expecting a grand sensation in a few days. The *Tennessee* is in sight about ten miles up the bay and they have only to take the camels from under her then she will be ready to go out and raise the blockade," page 59.

To the Confederates it was not yet clear that Farragut had abandoned his attempt on Fort Powell. On March 3, 1864 General Maury reported to Secretary of War Seddon that for 17 days the enemy's fleet had been attacking Fort Powell and in that time, nearly 2000 shot and shell have been thrown at the fort without doing any injury to it which could not be repaired each night by a few hours' work. The fort, he said, was stronger than on the first day. Continuing, Maury stated: Lieutenant Colonel Williams, commanding, a very gallant and energetic officer, was struck and bruised by a fragment of shell; four privates were slightly wounded, and one private had been killed with no other casualties.

Fort Powell held the Pass. Lieutenant Colonel Williams and his garrison had won the first Battle for the Bay. On March 4, the Mobile Daily Advertiser reported that "Fort Powell is absolutely intact..., stronger than on the first day's attack." The garrison, the report continued, is "in fine spirits and enjoying the boxes and barrels of roast turkeys, hams, pies, biscuits and cakes, which the ladies sent to them."

Immediately after Farragut withdrew, Williams was congratulated by Maury and given a period of leave to his home in Mobile. Major D. Truehart commanded the fort for a few weeks then Major W.C. Capers took over until Williams returned.[236] By May, Williams was restored to his "pet fort," and on May 12 happily wrote to his wife that "I am the keeper of the keys of Mobile again..." He also noted that improvements made during his absence: "Will be found to be rather inconvenient in service - though they look pretty enough."[237] He did not specify which improvements could be inconvenient.

The defenses of the Pass were being reinforced. Maury had previously ordered batteries placed on Little Dauphin Island and on Cedar Point.[238] That work was about to begin.

---

[235] *The Gulf and Inland Waters, the Navy in the Civil War* by Alfred T. Mahan page 223.
[236] Official Records Army, volume 21, page 883. Official Records Army, volume 21, page 894.
[237] Lieutenant Colonel James M. Williams and the Fort Powell Incident by John Kent Folmer, the *Alabama Review*, April 1964, page 120.
[238] Official Records Army, volume 57, page 402.

CHAPTER 7

Cedar Point and Chugee Point

o March 1864, the Red River campaign commenced which diverted Federal troops from Mobile.

On March 2, 1864 Von Sheliha ordered Captain Howard of the engineers to proceed with 100 Negroes and the necessary overseers to Cedar Point to construct a small work in lunette shape as ordered by Major General Gilmer. He was also to take charge of the construction of the works at Fort Powell with Mr. Biberon as assistant. Captain L. J. Freaux, engineer at Fort Gaines, was also ordered to push the work at the extreme point of Dauphin Island (Sughee Point) as vigorously as possible.

The Sughee Point works' right flank, according to instructions received from General Gilmer, was to be positioned so that a well and a recently dug grave would be nearly in front of the right-hand gun chamber. It's left flank was to extend far enough toward the house on the point to give the requisite space for four guns. He noted that the cedars would have to be left standing even if it was necessary to build the parapet around them. Timber was to be cleared only to give the guns a sufficient field of fire. He was to mount two 32-pounder rifled and banded guns

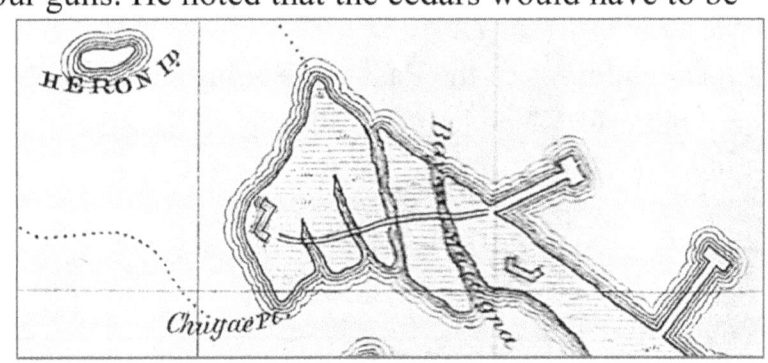

Batteries at Sughee Point and Little Dauphin Island (Parker, *Battle of Mobile Bay*)

at the two salients right and left, and two guns on siege carriages between them with traverses for their protection. Platforms were sent March 2, along with 3000 feet of 3-inch plank for the construction of temporary magazines.[239] Secrecy was still the order of the day.

The guns for the Sughee Point Battery had to be transported from Mobile Bay across Little Dauphin Island and several sloughs or bayous all bridged with a tread way. The engineers found they could not transport the banded 32-pounders weighing some 5 to 6000 pounds to the battery across the intervening bayous and instead determined to arm it with lighter Parrott guns on siege carriages.[240] Even the Parrot guns could not be moved into the battery until a bridge across a bayou was completed.[241] Eventually a strong bridge about 100 feet long was constructed crossing a bayou between the beach on Little Dauphin

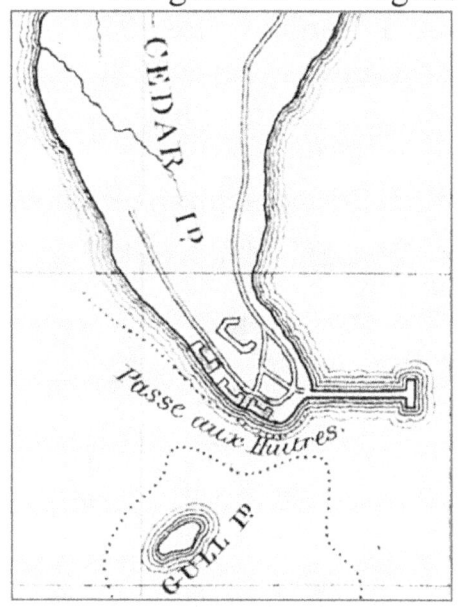

Lunette Battery at Cedar Point (Parker, Battle of Mobile Bay)

Island and Sughee Point.[242] A wharf leading to 6 feet of water off the Little Dauphin Island beach was constructed for the Sughee Point tread way as well as one for the small battery on the beach south of the Sughee Point wharf. On March 17 1864 Page was directed by Maury to maintain a "proper" guard at the point of Little Dauphin every night.[243]

The Battery at Cedar Point was of lunette shape for 4 guns.[244] The bombproof measured 12 feet by 50 feet and was originally intended for redoubt G in the

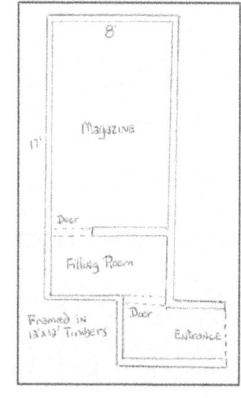

Typical magazine for small battery (sketched by Author from a drawing at Tulane U.)

---

[239] Official Records Army, volume 59, page 578.
[240] National Archives, Record Group 109, chapter 3, volume 12, Engineer Department Records, March 18, 1864.
[241] Page Telegraph Book, Page to Maury, entry of March 17, 1864.
[242] Official Records Army, volume 52, page 586, Union correspondence, Meyer to Granger 1865.
[243] Page Telegraph Book, March 17, 1864.
[244] National Archives, record group 109, chapter 3, volume 12, Engineer Department Records, March 19, 1864.

Mobile defenses.[245] Redoubt G was a much larger work for seven heavy guns. The Cedar Point battery would have been more similar to lunette D in Von Sheliha's defense line around Mobile.

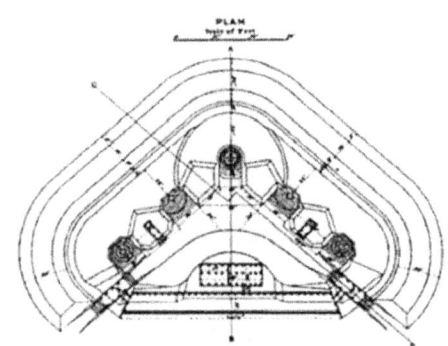

Lunette D Mobile defenses *designed by Von Sheliha (Official Military Atlas)*

Being isolated, the Cedar point lunette may have used a larger bombproof for storage and workshops as was done at Powell. Nevertheless, it appears to have been a big bombproof for the size of the battery.[246] The framing for bombproofs was prefabricated in the engineer shop in Mobile and then erected on site.[247]

On March 7, Daniel Geary, Ordnance Officer at Mobile issued to Captain C.C. Scott at Cedar Point projectiles for 6-pounder, 12-pounder howitzer and 24-pounder smoothbores, for the battery there at the time.[248] By the end of March the battery at Cedar Point was nearly completed.[249]

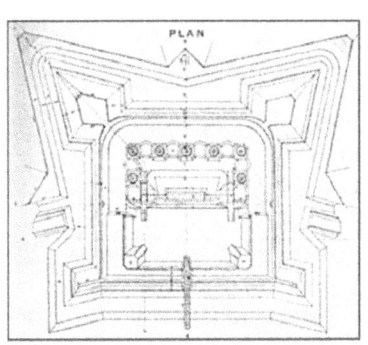

Redoubt G Mobile defenses *(Official Military Atlas)*

---

[245] Redoubt G was located between Monterey and Catherine Streets just north of Government Street in Mobile.

[246] See *The Official Atlas of the Civil War* plate CVIII.

[247] National Archives, record group 109, chapter 3, volume 12, Engineer Department Records, March 2, 1864

[248] Daniel Geary papers Mobile Public Library Mobile, Alabama. There is no reference in the Geary papers to ordnance sent to or received from Powell. Powder was distributed from the magazines at Fort Morgan. Apparently ordnance for Gaines and Powell was also.

[249] National Archives, record group 109, chapter 3, volume 12, Engineer Department Records, Report of operations for month of March.

A Naval Man Commands the Forts

General Richard Lucian Page replaced General Higgins as commander of the lower Bay line, which included Fort Powell, in March 1864. Page was a former naval officer, having served in the United States Navy from 1824 to 1861. He served on the U.S.S. *Constitution*, commanded the brig *Perry* on the African station, the *Independence* during the Mexican War and ended his naval career as commander of the sloop-of-war *Germantown*. He was on the *Germantown* at Hong Kong as late as December 1859.[250] When Virginia seceded he resigned and joined the staff of the Governor of Virginia. He later commanded some batteries near Norfolk, Virginia.[251]

General Richard L. Page (1807-1901)

Needed was a man who knew how to handle "great guns."[252] Page certainly fit that requirement. General Page was a Navy man through and through and had a very high regard for the Federal Navy. He tended to think of the Union ships as invincible. He thus had little confidence in his forts' ability to stop the Union Navy.[253]

24-pounder 1864

By the end of March 1864, the work at Cedar Point was garrisoned and armed with 24-pounders and fieldpieces but no long range rifled guns.

---

[250] Log of U.S.S. *Germantown*, Richard L. Page Collection, University of North Carolina. The guided missile frigate FFG5 was named for him in 1967.

[251] General Page survived the war and lived at Norfolk Virginia to the age of 94 years. He died at his summer home at Blue Ridge Summit, Virginia, August 9, 1901. *Mobile Press*, August 10, 1901.

[252] Bergeron, *Confederate Mobile,* page 81. In Pages log book entries he refers to heavy guns as "great guns". Admiral Buchanan used that terminology even referring to shore batteries. Heavy guns on ships were routinely referred to as "great guns."

[253] General Richard L. Page Telegraph Book, Southern Historical Society Collection, entry of March 17, 1864. William Llewellyn Powell for whom the fort was named was also a former navy man placed in command of forts for the same reason.

Fisheries

The Confederate Government was trying to reestablish the Mississippi Sound fisheries as a food source for Mobile, and the battery at Cedar Point was important to protect the fishermen from the Union blockaders.[254] The City's military commanders relaxed restrictions on fishing in the Sound. Fishermen and oystermen had been restricted to the Bay to keep their vessels out of Union hands. Those restrictions placed the oyster reefs west of Powell off limits. General Mackall issued an order allowing oystermen to go 3 miles west of Grants Pass in search of their catches. All fishermen who wished to take advantage of these relaxed restrictions had to register their boats with

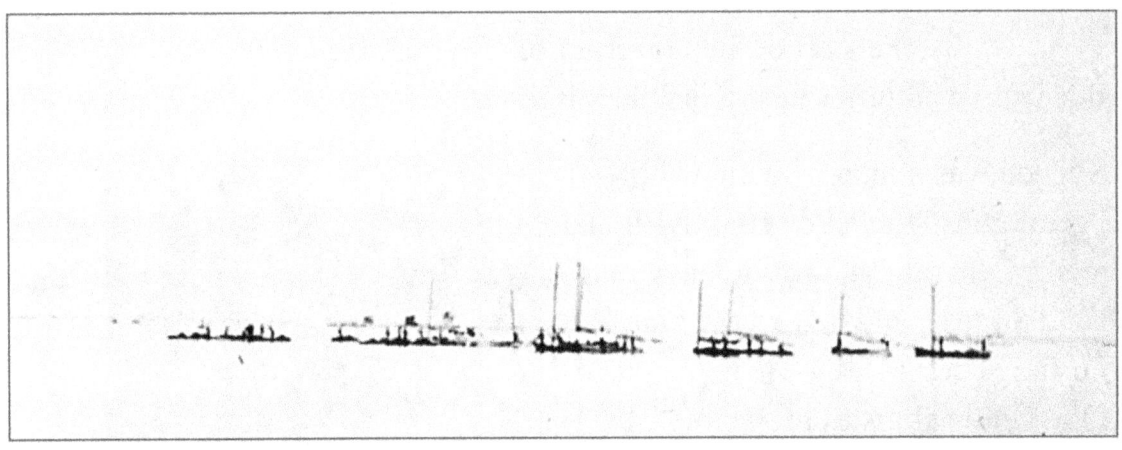

Oyster fishing fleet off Cedar Point about 1900 (Lewis Hine Collection, U. of Md. Baltimore County)

the Army and comply with any regulations established by the naval commander.[255]

The fishery was also important for the troops. The government had seines at Forts Morgan and Gaines for procuring fish for the men. The seine at Gaines was turned over by the 21st Alabama to the 1st Alabama Artillery Battalion when they were relieved at Cedar Point.[256] On April 28 Page

---

[254] Page Telegraph Book, entries of March 28 and 30, 1864.
[255] Bergeron, *Confederate Mobile,* page 100.
[256] Page Telegraph Book, entry for April 7, 1864.

asked for permission to purchase another seine for the 21st Alabama for $1200.[257] He received authorization for the purchase that same day.

There was no source other than cisterns, which were inadequate, for fresh water at Fort Powell. Drinking water was brought from springs on the Eastern shore, and stored in iron tanks and two cisterns as well as 15000 gallons in a floating tank barge in the rear of the fort. The fort drew rations every two months, which were kept in the bombproof.[258]

Going Home

Homesick Louisiana troops with access to boats and a short rowing distance to Union Navy ships in Mississippi Sound was a problem. For instance, on about March 21st eight men from the 12th Louisiana Battalion deserted from Fort Powell in the post boat.[259]

A Beautiful Little Work

The 21st Alabama then at Pollard was ordered to report to Page at Fort Morgan on April 17, 1864. Units of the 21st were assigned to Powell, Gaines and Cedar Point.[260] The 21st had been ordered to the field on April 4, 1864. It was brigaded with the 17th and 29th Alabama regiments and ordered to Rome, Georgia. It stopped at Pollard, Alabama on the Mobile and Montgomery Railway. There then occurred a dispute over jurisdiction or command and the regiment was sent back to Mobile. A May,1864 requisition by Lieutenant William J. Brainard indicated there was one

---

[257] Page Telegraph Book, entry for April 28, 1864.
[258] Official Records Navy, volume 21, page 372. Page Telegraph Book, entry for April 18, 1864.
[259] Page Telegraph Book, Entry for March 22, 1864.
[260] Page Telegraph Book, entry for April 17, 1864.

officer, two subalterns and 54 noncommissioned officers and privates in company K, 21st Alabama at Fort Powell.[261]

With the departure of Farragut's bombardment flotilla the Confederate engineers brought back the slave laborers and resumed construction work on the fort. Colonel and Assistant Inspector General George B. Hodge in a report to Inspector General Cooper dated April 13, 1864 said that Fort Powell was in the process of being greatly strengthened since the last attack of the enemy upon it: "It is, however, much to be regretted that the laboring force at the disposal of the chief engineer is greatly inadequate and daily diminishing. The impressed labor is being hourly returned to the planters, and no sufficient means as yet been provided to supply."

As to the design of the works protecting Mobile, Hodge stated: "They evidence a scientific proficiency in engineering unsurpassed, if equaled, by anything on this continent, and are themselves the most eloquent evidence of the educated skill of the engineer in charge, Lieutenant Colonel Von Sheliha."[262] Von Sheliha was obviously pleased with his design because at about the same time, he reported to Colonel A. L. Rives, Acting Chief Engineer, Richmond, that Fort Powell was not only a very strong work but also "very neat in appearance."[263] At about this time British traveler Fitzgerald Ross visited Fort Powell: "a beautiful little sand work in Grants Pass."[264] This was high praise indeed for Mobiles' Prussian Engineer.

Armament at Fort Powell as of April 23, 1864 consisted of two 8-inch columbiads, two 7-inch Brooke rifles, one 32-pounder rifled, one 32-pounder smoothbore, two 24-pounder siege howitzers and two 12-pounder iron howitzers. There were 136 armed men at the post. Their weapons were 135 Austrian rifles caliber .54, 25 double-barreled guns and 22

---

[261] *Mobile Confederates from Shiloh to Spanish Fort* by Arthur E. Green, page 54
[262] Official Records Army, volume 32/3, page 779.
[263] National Archives, record group 109, chapter 3, volume 16 Engineer Department Letters, Department of the Gulf Records April 1864.
[264] *Cities and Camps of the Confederate States,* by Fitzgerald Ross.

Whitworth Rifle

revolvers.[265] One of the fieldpieces was a long range British built Whitworth steel rifle that was ordered to be sent to Fort Morgan on March 24th.[266]

Sughee Point was considered by the engineers as a key position in the western part of the lower Bay line. Unfortunately, the lack of labor and transportation rendered it necessary to abandon that work in late April until the redoubt east of Fort Morgan was finished, after which work was to resume.[267]

Grants Pass was obstructed. But Von Sheliha could not obstruct the main ship channel. General Maury wanted, even at that late date, to keep a narrow channel in front of Fort Morgan open for blockade runners. In any event in April, Von Sheliha began trying to sink some timber obstructions in the main ship channel, but could not do so because of the currents.[268]

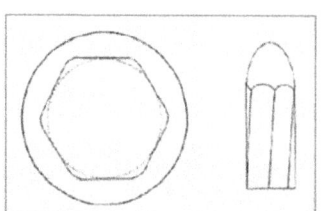
Whitworth rifling and projectile

Running the Blockade

Why was it important to keep the port of Mobile open to blockade runners, principally to and from Cuba, even if that meant leaving an unobstructed passage immediately in front of Fort Morgan as an invitation to Farragut's fleet? Why go to great effort and expense to defend Mobile? Let us look at those questions.

---

[265] Official Records Navy, volume 21, series 1, page 894.
[266] Official Records Navy, volume 21, page 891.
[267] Official Records Navy, volume 21, page 893 – 894. Ammunition report for Fort Powell for the week ending April 23, 1864. Von Sheliha to Captain Fremaux Engineer in Charge Lower Bay Line, April 22, 1864.
[268] National Archives, record group 109, chapter 3, volume 16, Von Sheliha report for the month of April 1864.

After the fall of New Orleans in April, 1862 Mobile was the principal Confederate seaport and city on the Gulf. The population grew during the war from approximately 30,000 to about 40,000, including many refugees from New Orleans and other threatened points. The primary importance of Mobile was as a seaport, since she had only modest manufacturing capabilities and was never a great armory or producer of war materials. Mobile was nevertheless considered important, but its significance was mostly psychological rather than strategic. In February 1865, General Richard Taylor, whose command included Alabama and Mississippi, stated: "Should we lose Mobile, we will lose everything west of the Chattahoochee. For these reasons I contemplate holding Mobile to the last."[269]

The *Denbigh* at Mobile (Thomas C. Healey, 1820-1889) Peery Collection, South Carolina Historical Society, Charleston, S. C.)

Mobile, up until the harbor was sealed by Admiral Farragut's fleet, remained a center for blockade running. After 1863 the blockade became more effective, greatly reducing the number of successful blockade runs. During the war some 225 blockade running ventures were attempted from Mobile, with approximately 180 being successful. By the summer of 1864 only a few specialized vessels continued in the blockade running occupation, but some of those ships, particularly the *Denbigh*, made the run to and from Havana on a regular schedule. Yet the blockade runners could not fill the most critical shortage at Mobile, for the true shortage in 1864 was men; men to shoulder the muskets, men to build the forts, and men for the barricades. The other great shortage was iron to armor the several vessels awaiting such and to cast the great guns and projectiles for the forts around the city. The shortage of iron was principally also one of manpower - manpower needed to mine the ore and coal and to process it into the iron plates and ordnance.

---

[269] Richard Taylor telegraph book, Tulane University, New Orleans.

The blockade runners could not bring the needed men but they did bring high-value cargoes. The insulated wire for electrically detonated torpedoes, rifles, some cannon, medicines and paper for the engineers to write their reports, came through the blockade. All of these commodities were useful and from a psychological point of view the idea of Mobile as a seaport could not be ignored.

Fort Powell (Frank Leslie's Illustrated Newspaper, April 2, 1864)

June 1864-Not Enough Hands

By the end of April 1864, the west face of Powell was completed and the parapet on the east face was being strengthened.[270] In June 1864, Lt. Gallimard was assigned as engineer at Fort Powell. Even though the engineers were paying three dollars per day for Negro laborers and $3.50 per

---

[270] National Archives, record group 109, chapter 3, volume 16, Engineer Department letters, Department of the Gulf, April – September 1864, Von Sheliha report for month of April 1864.

day for Negro mechanics, they could not find enough workers.[271] Engineering Department records show a daily whisky ration was issued to slaves working on the lower Bay line (including Fort Powell) in early May 1864 for medical and health purposes.[272]

Sketch by artist E.B.Hough from which the above April 2, 1864 *Frank Leslie's* illustration was prepared.

Captain L. J. Fremaux, Engineer in Charge of the Lower Bay line, reported on June 2, 1864 that the work on Little Dauphin Island (Sughee Point) was ready to receive guns on the west end, but the work had been stopped for want of labor. At Fort Powell, as usual, there were not enough hands, yet all the other work on the Lower Bay was cut back or stopped and every available man put to work at Powell. But the number of laborers was still insufficient.

Maintaining the labor force at Powell was difficult. They were confined on an island with access to small boats. There was usually a Union vessel in sight in Mississippi Sound. Desertions to the enemy by black and white laborers were frequent. In early June, for instance, four sod-layers were sent to Fort Powell, but only two arrived as the other two deserted. The engineers had to threaten the white workers with discharge from the Engineering Service before they would go to Powell. A discharge from the Engineering Service meant a transfer to the Army.

---

[271] National Archives, record group 109, chapter 3, volume 16, Engineer Department records.
[272] National Archives, record group 109, chapter 3, volume, 16 Engineer Department records report of May 9, 1864.

Transport was also a problem. Bricks, timber, etc. were sent to Powell by the *Baltic* or by flats towed by the *Dorrance*. The large steamboat *Baltic*, formally the ironclad ram of that name, was one of the engineers most useful boats but was worm-eaten, not seaworthy and the crew shorthanded. The *Baltic* was soon sent up to Mobile as unseaworthy.

Even with the shortage of transport the steamer *Dorrance* delivered to Fort Powell on June 11, 4000 feet of three-inch plank, 660 feet of 8 x 12 timbers, 420 running feet of 6 x 12 timber, 150 cartloads of brick bats, 150 cart loads of sods,[273] 50 cords steamboat wood, one new skiff and two oars. No additional guns were available at Mobile for the fort at that time.[274]

During this time Fort Powell was being expanded to the south and west beyond its rock breakwater. A base of brickbats was laid to the west and sand filled behind a new wooden bulkhead. The fort was evolving into the neat polygonal work envisioned by Von Sheliha.

The work of finishing the Cedar Point battery had come to a halt. All but two of the workmen on the wharf deserted to the enemy. Since April not one slave could be obtained to finish the sodding and covering of the bombproof.

Engineer Fremaux said he required 282 workers on Fort Powell, but had available only 182. For Cedar Point he needed 104 and for Little Dauphin Island he needed 304, for which he had none. There was also a shortage of workers at Fort Morgan, which required 200 workers, but only had 68 and Fort Gaines required 300 workers, but only had 46. His total force of workers was 296, while his requirement was 886, a shortage of 590 hands.[275]

---

[273] Sods or turfs were used instead of wood for interior slopes. The sods were cut with short bladed grass and thickly matted roots and were 12 inches square (stretchers) and 4 1/2 inches thick and others (headers) 18 inches long, 12 inches wide and 4 1/2 inches thick. The sods were partially dried and laid with the grass down and watered as needed until the grass covered the exposed areas. The top layer was placed with the grass upward. *A Treatise on Field Fortification* by D. H. Mahan, 1852, pages 36 – 37.

[274] National Archives, record group 109, chapter 3, volume 16, Engineer Department letters, telegrams Von Sheliha to Gallimard, June 9, 10 and 11, 1864.

[275] Official Records Navy, volume 21, page 900 – 902. Official Records Navy, volume 21, page 903, letter Page to Jones June 26, 1864 as to the *Baltic* being sent up to Mobile.

The Cedar Point Battery was still manned and armed. But the two 24-pounders were replaced in mid-June with fieldpieces.[276] On July 21th the two 3-inch rifles and the two-12 pounder siege guns on Little Dauphin Island were also ordered sent up to Mobile.[277]

Inspection

The ordnance Department in Richmond periodically sent an inspector to Mobile to report on the condition of the ordnance stores in the defensive works. On July 26, 1864, Colonel S. Crutchfield reported as to the shot and shell at the Bay forts and batteries (including Fort Powell): "Great carelessness and ignorance are displayed by the ordnance sergeants in their neglect of these [referring to shot and shell]. The most common faults I noticed were allowing them to become rusty and dirty and then endeavoring to remedy it by excessive lacquering. In the Bay forts and batteries the light dry sand is constantly drifting about whenever there is any wind, and of course readily adheres to freshly lacquered shot and shell, making their outsides rough and irregular and consequently considerably increasing their dimensions in some directions.

"Very little attention is paid to the proper piling of them, in such cases they are scattered carelessly through the damp bombproofs, where they suffer much from rust. Strapped shells are piled up three and four tiers deep by which means the sabots are split, the straps broken or slipped and the interior of the shell exposed to moisture. The same may be noticed of the shot. Unstrapped shells are not piled with the fuse holes down and great neglect exhibited in keeping dry loaded shells."

Powell was also cited for having a "good deal" of ammunition for large guns that had to be corrected and reduced in weight and the battery had no scale for that purpose.[278]

---

[276] Page Telegraph Book, entry of June 17, 1864.
[277] Page Telegraph Book, entries of July 21, 1864.
[278] Daniel Geary Papers, Mobile Public Library.

Colonel Crutchfield also said that in nearly all of the batteries there were shells of various patterns and weight collected early in the war rather as experiments and makeshifts than otherwise. Those makeshifts would prevent all uniformity and accuracy in firing while "many of them are dangerous to the safety of the guns." He probably included the Skates pattern projectiles in these experimental and makeshift patterns.

For instance, on September 3, 1861, Leadbetter asked Skates and company to experiment with leather disks two inches thick bolted to the flat base of shells, the discs were to expand into the rifling. Experiments in Britain concluded that sawdust between a cartridge and shell could replace the metal cup. Metal was always in short supply in the South. The navy tried but General Raines thought it would not work.[279] On September 12 Leadbetter sent to Skates plans for making a shell designed by Mr. Read, where there was fitted to the rear of the shell a wrought iron cup that expanded into the grooves in firing which he said was believed to be excellent. The Read projectile was used in almost all of the rifled 32 and 42-pounder guns in the Mobile area. On September 5, 1861 Skates had agreed to furnish shells for rifled 32-pounders that were turned down to fit the bore. This description seems to fit the projectiles which I refer to as Skate's projectiles but others call Read-Parrots that have been found in the Mobile area.[280]

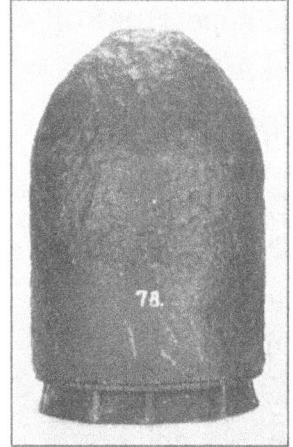

32 pounder Read/Parrott

The Mobile Advertiser and Register on August 28, 1862 reported that Colonel George A. Smith tested shells of his own design by firing them at targets. The paper did not give a description of the shells or how they differed in design from others.

There have been a number of Skates/Read-Parrot projectiles found in the Mobile area. I have seen none with a sabot. Several of these came from Fort Powell. One that I examined was ready to fire. There was a piece of tarred twine carefully placed under the fuse to seal it. There was no evidence

---

[279] National Archives, Mobile Squadron Papers, September 25, 1864.
[280] National Archives, record group 109, chapter 3, volume 1, Engineer Department letters.

of a sabot. There have been some such projectiles found with a pre-engraved lead sabot.[281] Perhaps some later projectiles had lead sabots while earlier ones had some experimental sabot. When the encrustation from the Powell finds was chipped away, any remaining evidence of a tarred rope sabot or a leather disk disappeared.

The bombproofs of all the various batteries in the Mobile area were framed up with heavy timbers laid side-by-side forming the roof which was then covered with sand or dirt. Without some waterproofing they could not be expected to be dry. For at least some of the bomb proofs the engineers found a quantity of bitumen from some unknown source with which they attempted to waterproof the magazines. This substance has the appearance of asphalt used to pave our streets. I've seen no comments in the records as to the effectiveness of these waterproofing efforts. I delivered a sample of this type waterproofing from Fort Jeb Stuart in Von Sheliha's line of works around Mobile to the History Museum of Mobile several years ago.

The Union Navy was constantly picking up deserters and "contrabands"[282] in Mississippi Sound. They interrogated all of these men and often acquired useful information. One of the strangest of these reports came from Lieutenant Commander DeKrafft of the Mississippi Sound Squadron on June 30, 1864. He reported that the rebels had two or three armed launches from Mobile in the vicinity of Grants Pass waiting for the opportunity to get out to Pascagoula where two companies of Cavalry were stationed: "One of these launches is armed with a revolving boat gun."[283] Nothing further was heard of this proposed expedition or the gun.[284]

---

[281] *Heavy Artillery Projectiles of the Civil War* by Kerksis and Dickey, pages 183-84. *Civil War Heavy Explosive Ordinance* by Jack Bell page 389.
[282] A period term used by Union authorities to denote Slaves that that made their way to Union lines or ships and freedom.
[283] Official Records Navy, volume 21, page 253.
[284] From bits and pieces of information the Union thought the Confederates were organizing an expedition to Ship Island to recapture lightly guarded prisoners being held there. A worthy objective but no actual attempt was made.

During the month of June Farragut was increasing his forces off the mouth of the bay. On June 14 admiral Buchanan wrote to Catesby Jones in Selma; "17 of Farragut's vessels off today. We expect an attack soon."[285]

---

[285] Official Records Navy, volume 21, series 1, page 902.

CHAPTER 8

July-The East Face

Down Time

There was precious little leisure time for the garrison of Fort Powell. Although no daily log exists of the garrisons activities, they were necessarily highly regimented. Even though the troops would not normally have been required to work in the construction of the Fort, there was much to do. Drilling at the guns and maintaining them were important. The small island was in many ways like a ship at sea. Every iron object, including big guns and projectiles, was exposed to the salt air and spray, and became rusted. The troops used sandpaper to clean the guns, tallow to grease the wheels and oil on elevating screws.

In the ordnance warehouse at Mobile there were kegs stored for distribution to the batteries of white lead paint, venetian red paint, chrome yellow paint, lamp black, linseed oil, varnish, turpentine, and the necessary sandpaper, brushes etc. Projectiles had to be cleaned and painted, with each type receiving its own special identifying colors. Some batteries painted their gun carriages. The wooden carriages were painted white at Battery Gladden. We do not know if such was the case at Powell.

A general order issued in January, 1863 in Mobile required heavy artillery officers to follow the drill in the book *Instructions for Heavy Artillery* by the old US Army published by West and Johnson, Richmond, Virginia, 1862. No change or alteration in the drill was allowed.[286]

---

[286] Daniel Geary papers, Mobile Public Library.

For the garrison stuck on a small island their entertainment came whenever and from wherever they could find it. They fished, gathered oysters, swam, gambled, used their seine and invented distractions for their off duty time.

In one of Williams' letters he described one way the troops found to amuse themselves: "I was interrupted by the shouts of the men, and going out to see what was the cause of the excitement, I discovered three or four of them sailing toy boats, like so many schoolboys – two of these tiny sloops were racing and the excitement was great, and many bets were taken in pieces of tobacco – I was boy enough myself to watch them for half an hour, an interested spectator not so much of the boating as of the boatman – poor fellows. They have a dreary enough time of it, and I like to see them able and willing to make the best of everything and amuse themselves – the men I have are cheerful and obedient – I could not be more pleasantly situated."[287] Later at Spanish Fort Williams wrote that while half his soldiers were digging trenches, the rest, "like so many school boys," were shooting marbles outside his tent.[288]

Williams had a small sailboat with which he sailed about the lower Bay. His quarters were in the house alongside the wharf. The summer heat led him to also pitch a tent on the bombproof where he would take shelter when it rained, but otherwise he preferred the open air and sand for a bed.

Williams wrote on July 31, 1864: "The sea is rippling gently under the house, and continuously invites me to plunge in for a bath – an invitation that is accepted two or three times a day. Crab lines hang out of the windows and from the 'back gallery' and are occasionally drawn in for the benefit of our dinner table – a foot-tub is full of the ugly things, who are tumbling about, pinching and clawing each other viciously – and reaching up to grab each unfortunate that is added to their number."

Williams continued: "speaking of crabs reminds me of an amusing trick that was played off upon some of the officer's the other night – we keep

---

[287] *Williams*, letters page 132.
[288] *Williams*, letters page 158.

our smoking tobacco in a 100-pound Brooke shell box: a crab was put in the box, of course, when anyone went in the dark to fill his pipe the crab would try to grab his hand – one after another fell into the trap but would say nothing about it and watch for someone else to go there."[289]

For the engineers there was no respite. Engineer Captain J.V. Gallimard was ordered on July 10, 1864 to take charge of the works on the lower Bay line, consisting of Forts Morgan, Gaines, Powell, the works on Little Dauphin Island and Cedar Point, as well as the channel obstructions. He was given instructions as to what work to do on each of the above.

As to Fort Powell, he was, in the order indicated: (1) to mount the guns on the east face, (2) build the parapet and traverses of the east face and (3) complete the work on the proposed plan. He was told that want of laborers would prevent him from completing at that time, the important defenses on Little Dauphin Island and Cedar Point. He was to finish at once the telegraph line from Mobile to Cedar Point to Fort Gaines.[290] The telegraph line was soon completed.[291]

The shortage of workers continued to be a problem. Impressment officers were sent across the State to secure the slaves for the work. Until those workers were available steps were taken[292] to obtain a working force of about 2000 for all of the defenses around Mobile from the slaves engaged in the salt works upriver in Clark County and at Bon Secour.[293]

On July 11th Von Sheliha again instructed Gallimard to give immediate attention to the east face. The armament of the east face was to consist of one 7-inch Brooke gun in the south east salient, one 10-inch

---

[289] *Williams,* letters, page 134.
[290] Official Records Army, volume 78, page 707.
[291] On the Eastern shore a telegraph line ran from Fort Morgan to a cavalry picket post near Gulf Shores and then up the east side of the Bay to connect with the Mobile to Montgomery line near Blakely.
[292] On July 10, 1864, Von Sheliha passed on to General Maury information from Colonel Blount, caretaker at the forts at Oven and Choctaw Bluffs that about 3000 Negroes were engaged at the salt works in the Oven Bluffs area, and another 1200 at Bon Secour that might be obtained for the needed labor force. National Archives, chapter 3, volume 16, engineer Department letters, Department of the Gulf April – September 1864.
[293] Official Records Army, volume 39, page 705, Letter from Von Sheliha to acting Chief of Engineer Bureau, Richmond, July 11, 1864.

columbiad in the center, one 32-pounder on the north east. The 10-inch was to range southeast and towards Cedar Point.

Time was running out.

Final Preparations

The engineer's July report on Powell was as follows: "the guns on the east face – one ten-inch columbiad, one 7-inch Brooke gun, and one 32-pounder rifled, which will be exchanged for one ten-inch columbiad – have been mounted and protected by temporary parapets. The gallery on the south side has been framed and raised. The area of the work has been extended towards the west by making a foundation of brick-bats, on which the parapet will be built. The whole work is surrounded by booms; the east and north faces are protected by wooden chevaux-de-frise, but the first being liable to become water-logged, and the latter to destruction by barnacles, and additional row of chevaux-de-frise, made of short pieces of railroad iron, of which there was a large quantity taken from Battery Gladden (late Pinto), has been constructed."[294]

Some of the above planned work was done. Railroad iron obstructions were in place around the fort. The second ten-inch gun was never placed on the east side. But the work was being pressed towards completion as fast as the available manpower allowed.

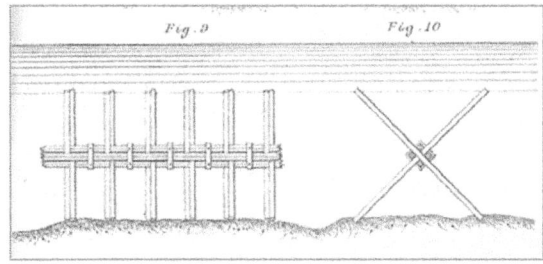
Chevaux- de fries made from railroad irons removed from Pinto Battery that were previously removed from Bragg's Pensacola to the eastern shore railroad (Von Sheliha)

On July 29, 1864 Union troops were boarding their transports in Algiers, Louisiana for the Mississippi Sound and a landing on the west end of Dauphin Island. These troops were to invest Fort Gaines.

---

[294] Official Records Army, volume 39, page 730.

In early July General Maury had begun receiving reports that naval reinforcements were on their way to Farragut in the Gulf. Mobile was the logical place for Farragut to use those reinforcements. On July 4, 1864, General Samuel Jones at Charleston had written to Maury: "A Yankee surgeon, captured near here yesterday, says a fleet of monitors had started to Mobile, from which much is expected. I give you the information for what it is worth." And on the seventh: "Thirteen steamers passed here yesterday going south, probably you will see them." [295] Two monitors, after a coaling stop at Key West, steamed to Pensacola and two come from the Mississippi River and then all moved into position off Mobile Bay. The forts' garrisons worked, exercised their guns, fished and otherwise entertained themselves while the storm approached.

August-Coming Ready or Not

By early August, Farragut had massed his fleet, including his four long coveted ironclads, for a run up the ship channel, past Fort Morgan and into Mobile Bay.[296] The timeline for that battle is as follows:

- o August 3 – Union forces land on Dauphin island and begin investment of Fort Gaines
- o August 5 – Passage of Fort Morgan by the Union fleet, and engagement in Mobile Bay.
- o August 5 – Union monitor Tecumseh sunk by torpedo off Fort Morgan.
- o August 5 – Fort Powell evacuated.
- o August 8 – Surrender of Fort Gaines.
- o August 9 – 22 – Siege of Fort Morgan.
- o August 23 – Surrender of Fort Morgan.

---

[295] Official Records Army, volume 35, pages 556 and 557.
[296] On August 1 there were 23 Union vessels off Fort Morgan. The first monitor arrived July 21 and by August 1 three were inside Sand Island with steam up. Attack was considered to be imminent and women and children were sent away on July 21. The fourth and final monitor arrived August 4. Farragut was ready for his charge into the Bay on the 5th of August. Page Telegraph Book, entries July 20, 1864 through August 4, 1864.

A conjectural rendering of Fort Powell immediately prior to the Battle (by the Author)

U.S.S. *Conemaugh* (US Naval Historical Center)

Assistant Engineer Lt. G. W. Mader[297] was in charge of construction at Fort Powell in early August. On August 2, Von Sheliha asked him if the guns on the east face were ready to fight. Apparently Mader responded in the affirmative, because on August 4, Von Sheliha reported to Gilmer that Powell was in good defensible condition.

The Garrison commanded by Lieutenant Colonel Williams for the coming fight consisted of two companies of the 21st Alabama, and a portion of Captain James M. Culpepper's South Carolina Battery, a total force of about 140 men.[298]

Union Admiral J. C. P. DeKrafft on his flagship *Conemaugh* along with the *J.P.Jackson* and *Narcissus* moved into range in Mississippi Sound on the morning of August 5, 1864 and opened fire on Fort Powell. At about the same time Admiral Farragut, with his 14 wooden vessels lashed together two by two with his monitors leading, moved up the ship channel toward Mobile Bay. The Battle of Mobile Bay was underway.

The Run past Fort Morgan

A lack of iron and shortage of labor, meant Admiral Buchanan had only one rather than four ironclads capable of operating in the Lower Bay. However that one vessel was the *Tennessee,* generally considered to be the most formidable of the domestically built Confederate vessels. It was supported by three wooden, partially-armored gunboats - the *Selma, Morgan* and *Gaines*. The Confederate fleet

---

[297] Deserters with knowledge of the Mobile defenses useful to the Union were not limited to laborers, seamen and troopers. Engineer Mader crossed the lines in March 1865, carrying with him a detailed description of the Mobile defenses. Mader was from Louisiana, commanded a mortar battery at Pensacola in 1861 and served as engineer at Fort Morgan, Fort Powell, and on the upper Bay defenses. Alabama Department of Archives and History folder W – 27. Official Records Army, volume 49, page 864. Official Records Army, volume 49, page 876.

Another Confederate engineer by the name of Ross went over to the Union January 15, 1865 with detailed knowledge of the Mobile defenses. Ross considered the line of fortifications around Mobile almost impregnable to an assault. His information may have contributed to the Union Army's decision to attack at Spanish Fort and Blakely rather than attack directly from Pascagoula against the Mobile fortifications. Official Records Army, volume 49, page 636.

[298] *Confederate Mobile,* page 139.

was no match for the fleet of four Union monitors and 14 powerful wooden vessels assembled off the mouth of Mobile Bay on August 5, 1864.

Torpedoes, forts and obstructions were the first line of defense of the Bay with the fleet in a support role. This was the great mistake of the Generals and Admirals involved in the defensive planning for Mobile. As a practical matter the lower Bay forts were useful only to support the fleet and blockade runners. Much of the very heavy expenses incurred in strengthening the forts could have been used for the production of ironclad gunboats. The Confederate Engineers first priority should have been the establishment of rolling mills and steam engine manufacturers in support of the fleet. A dozen Confederate ironclads could have defended the entrance to Mobile Bay even with minimal onshore defenses but one ironclad could not defend it even with the assistance of mighty Fort Morgan. But that decision was not for the local engineers and despite their best efforts, with the resources allocated to them, the lower Bay forts were only partially ready to receive the Union fleet.

Running in *(Harper's Encylopedia of U.S. History, vol6, 1912)*

The west side of Fort Powell facing Mississippi Sound was complete as was the piling and torpedo obstructions in the channel giving it the ability to resist any naval assault from the west. The east face was not ready. Farragut would have to take Powell. He had to bring his troops, supplies and siege train thru Grants Pass in order to subdue Fort Morgan. He would have to take it from inside the Bay. Fort Morgan and the Confederate fleet did not stop Admiral Farragut. If he had not succeeded in forcing an entry on August 5, he likely would have later. But the union victory in the battle of August 5, 1864, the Battle of Mobile Bay, was not a foregone conclusion, not because of the fighting spirit of Admiral Buchanan or the strength of his vessels or the guns of Fort Morgan, but because of the torpedoes, a threat to any vessel that should strike them.

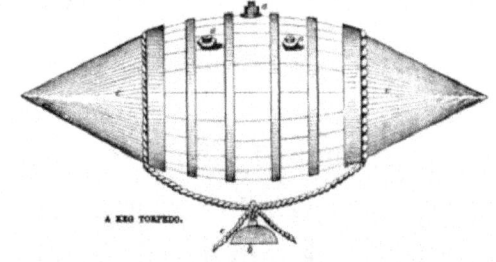

Raines torpedo

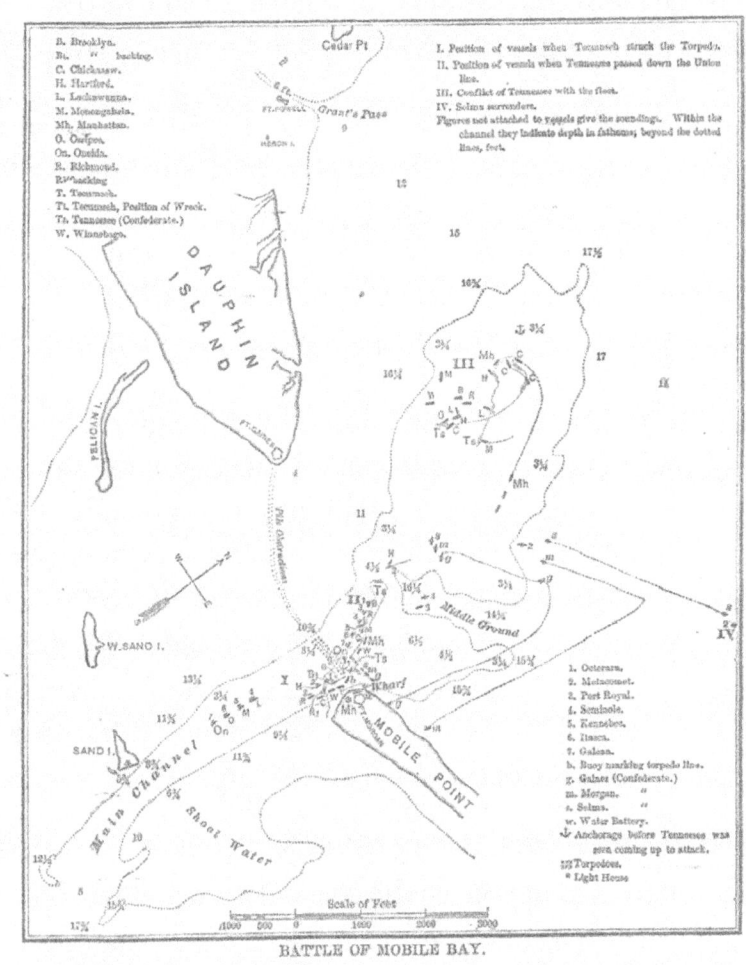

Map from Alfred T. Mahans book *The Gulf and Inland Waters,* 1883

The mouth of Mobile Bay, between Forts Morgan and Gaines, is three miles wide - the west two miles are shallow and were obstructed by green heart pine piling, sunk well into the sand. The east mile of the entrance in front of Fort Morgan was obstructed by 134 Singer torpedoes and 46 Raines torpedoes in three rows in echelon secured by chains to anchors. The distance from the water battery at Fort Morgan to the first of the torpedoes was 226 yards. That 226 yard gap had been left for the passage of blockade runners and the occasional sortie of a gunboat to assist such runners.

The reliance on torpedoes by the engineers for the eastern mile was not by choice. They would have preferred to have pilings or rafts or sawyers or all of those in combination with torpedoes, as were used in the upper line of obstructions. But the Bay would not allow it. The channel was too deep, the bottom too loose, and the currents too strong. The only obstructions available for the deep water channel were torpedoes and if they failed, there was nothing to block the entrance but Fort Morgan and Buchanan's squadron, which vessels did not mount spar torpedoes. The Confederate Army and Navy, including the inflexible Admiral Buchanan, had complete disdain for the torpedo – the public had no confidence in anything but the torpedo.

Early on the morning of August 5, 1864, the Union Fleet moved up the ship channel toward Fort Morgan. Admiral Farragut's battle plan for that morning was simple in concept, but the same tidal currents that frustrated the Confederate engineers made it unworkable. The four lead monitors, impervious to shot and shell, but slow and unwieldy, were to move into the gap between the fort and the torpedoes and hold their position, shielding the wooden vessels from the fort and the *Tennessee*, while the wooden vessels, lashed two by two, with the *Brooklyn* and her consort in the lead and Farragut in the *Hartford* following, were to dash through the gap between the Monitors and the torpedoes and take possession of the Bay.

Because of a flooding tide and west wind, the unwieldy Monitors were unable to hold their position in front of the fort, and they moved slowly to the west to maintain steerage, blocking the entrance to the gap. Captain Craven on the leading Monitor *Tecumseh*, moved farthest to the west and when the *Tennessee* also moved to the west behind the torpedoes, Captain Craven ordered his ship to follow in an effort to shield the wooden vessels from the fire of the *Tennessee*. In so doing, the *Tecumseh*, in her ponderous waltz with the *Tennessee*, moved into the waiting torpedo field. One torpedo of Mr. Singer's design functioned perfectly and the *Tecumseh* sank immediately. Of her crew of 114, only 21 escaped. Captain Craven went down with his ship.

As the *Tecumseh* sank, the leading wooden ship, the *Brooklyn*, stopped in the channel, with the remaining three Monitors blocking the gap. With the effectiveness of the torpedoes apparently proven by the *Tecumseh's* fate and with the *Brooklyn* unable to proceed through the gap the rest of the fleet piled up behind her. The Confederate gunners had easy targets and did not fail to find their mark, causing a rising number of casualties in the Union fleet.

The heretofore invincible Admiral Farragut's plan for battle was in shambles and only he could give the orders that could win or lose the battle. A lesser man might have hesitated, but not Farragut, and with a "Damn the torpedoes, full speed ahead," or some such statement,[299] he moved the *Hartford* around the *Brooklyn* into the line of waiting torpedoes.

But Farragut had an unseen ally in the battle. He was assisted by barnacles, oysters and toredo worms that affixed their shells to the spring loaded striker pins of Mr. Singer's torpedoes deadening the force of the trigger spring and preventing the explosion of most of the torpedoes.

The run into Mobile Bay, August 5, 1864 (Naval Historical Center)

If the torpedoes had functioned, the *Hartford* and her consort, the *Metacomet*, would likely have shared the fate of the *Tecumseh*. If the *Hartford* had been lost, and with the gap still blocked by the Monitors, would the rest of the fleet have attempted to force their way through the line of torpedoes? The risk to vessels and careers was so great that the other captains would have been unlikely to make the attempt and the fleet may have on that day been repulsed.

---

[299] For a detailed discussion of Farragut's statement and of the battle see *West Wind, Flood Tide, The Battle of Mobile Bay* by Jack Friend.

At that critical time Admiral Farragut asserted himself, risked a great gamble and won. His gamble that the torpedoes would not explode and sink his vessel was hedged to some extent by intelligence estimates that only one in ten of the torpedoes were operable because of the length of time in the water. Farragut's intelligence reports could not have been very comforting to him when he passed into the mine field past the turbulent waters covering the *Tecumseh*. The greater the risk, the greater the glory, and so it was.

That Farragut's calculated risk worked is history. The *Hartford* steamed through the torpedo field and the rest of his fleet followed in its wake, scattering the Confederate gunboats as they went. Buchanan in the *Tennessee*, like the Light Brigade at Balaclava, charged into the cannons of the 17 Union vessels, which battered that great ship into submission. For the naval participants on both sides there was shared glory in the greatest naval battle of the war.

For those in charge of the forts, only General Richard L. Page of Fort Morgan was considered to have fought his fort well. General Page, the old naval captain and a contemporary of Farragut and Buchanan was determined to match their exploits. Notwithstanding, once the Union siege guns and mortars were in position on August 21, the fort was able to survive their pounding for only one full day before surrendering its 600 men and 46 artillery pieces on August 23, 1864.

All of the officers responsible for the defenses of Mobile Bay knew and acknowledged that once the Union fleet controlled the bay, Fort Morgan would fall. All knew that Fort Gaines was weak and indefensible and that Fort Powell was not completed on her bay side. In the heat of battle, all the assessments of the vulnerability of the Lower Bay line were forgotten.

Colonel Anderson, with a reinforced garrison of 864 men, surrendered Fort Gaines on August 6th. Fort Gaines was untenable with a hostile fleet in the bay. On August 6, General Page first said that Fort Gaines was a weak fort and could not resist attack by water or by land. Shortly thereafter, he said the surrender of Fort Gaines was: "A deed of dishonor and disgrace to its Commander and garrison."

The press and the public roundly condemned Anderson for the manner in which he surrendered his fort. At the time of the surrender of Fort Gaines, there were 1500 Union troops in position to bombard the Fort from behind protective sand dunes and a Union fleet in the Bay. The supporting earthworks recommended by the engineers to the west had not been constructed. The reinforcement of Fort Gaines by 276 local defense troops and marines from the city on August 4 was a mistake. 150 men could have protected the Pelican Pass Ship Channel, while 864 was too small a number to resist with a fleet in the bay and a Union army on the island. Notwithstanding that Gaines had only a limited capability of defense, the local military authorities and the public, given the example of Buchanan and Page, expected the Fort commanders to resist and were extremely disappointed when they did not do so.

Admiral Buchanan had recognized that his reputation rested not on whether he won or lost, but how he fought. He fought and lost and Farragut and his fleet was in control of the lower Bay.

Adm. Franklin Buchanan C.S.N. (Naval Historical Center)

CHAPTER 9

The Storm from the East – The *Chickasaw*

The real damage to Fort Powell came not from the Union Mississippi Sound bombardment flotilla, but from the guns of the double turreted Monitor *Chickasaw*.

U.S.S. *Chickasaw* (Naval Historical Center)

Farragut was in the Bay but he still had to take Grants Pass. He could not supply his fleet in the Bay or bring in transports with troops and siege guns to take Fort Morgan without access to the Pass. He had to drive Williams from Fort Powell and do so quickly, solely as a naval operation. Powell's defenses of heavy guns with canister and grape, several fieldpieces and muskets together with booms and chevaux-de-frise effectively prevented any possibility of assault by troops in boats.

On the afternoon of August 5th Farragut ordered the light draft monitor *Chickasaw* to bombard Fort Powell. The *Chickasaw* approached Powell from the southeast or east. That side of the fort was unfinished.

Mounted on the east side was a 7-inch Brooke rifle, a 10-inch columbiad and perhaps a 32-pounder or a rifled and banded 32-pounder. The last inventory of guns included a 32-pounder but indicated that it was to be replaced by a larger gun. Williams does not mention the gun in his report nor is it in the Union inventory.

Maury reported the fort had 8 heavy guns, which must have included the 32-pounder. Either the gun was too far to the north so that it could not bear on the action, it had been removed but its replacement not delivered and mounted, or Williams simply did not consider it part of his heavy ordnance and treated it like one of his uncounted field pieces. The south side also had a 7-inch Brooke rifle (S-19) that was not fully protected.

Chickasaw attacking Fort Powell August 5, 1864, Federal fleet in background *(Battles and Leaders of the Civil War, 1884-1887)*

The final engineers report shows a temporary east side parapet. A "temporary parapet" of sand could have been some 6 to 8 feet thick, more or less, rather than the designed 25 feet. Williams indicated in his after action reports that the parapet facing Gaines and little Dauphin Island was nearly complete but the rear had "only been commenced." Even if he had thrown up a temporary parapet of sandbags it is unlikely that it would have stopped an 11-inch shot and a few 11-inch shells could have blasted large holes through it opening up the backside of the magazine.

The *Chickasaw* was a double turret *Milwaukee* Class river monitor built in Carondelet, Missouri and commissioned in May 1864.[300] During the Bay Battle she harried the *Tennessee* from short range astern, jamming her rudder chains with 11-inch smoothbore Dahlgren projectiles weighing about 166 pounds. She fired at the *Tennessee* 48 solid shot and four steel shot.

The *Chickasaw* was 220 feet long and 56 feet wide with two Ericsson turrets. On her overhanging hull sponsons she had 3 inches of iron over 15 inches of pine. Her deck had only three-quarter inch iron plates over 8 to 12 inches of pine, but her turrets had 8 inch thick iron armor.[301]

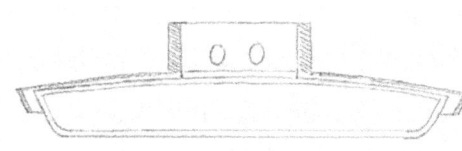

Cross section of *Chickasaw* (sketch by Author)

At about 2:30 p. m. the *Chickasaw* was ordered to attack Ft. Powell. She drew only 6 feet and was able to steam up to the pier at the fort.

The *Chickasaw* was the only fully operational ironclad then available to Farragut. Of the four ironclads that went into the battle, the *Tecumseh* was sunk at the outset by a torpedo; the *Manhattan* lost the use of one of her two guns by the dropping of an iron fragment into the vent. She was only able to fire six of her 15-inch shot during the entire action. One of those six, however, breached the plate of the *Tennessee*. The turrets of the other shallow draft monitor, the *Winnebago,* were inoperable and could not revolve; forcing her to aim by turning the vessel and making her rate of fire extremely slow. The *Chickasaw* had the requisite shallow draft and was still in good condition with both turrets and her four 11-inch guns operational.[302]

---

[300] Donald L. Canny, *The Old Steam Navy*, volume 2, Naval Institute Press. After the War she was converted to a ferry and not scrapped until 1944.
[301] *The Old Steam Navy*, volume 2, page 117
[302] *Letters of Captain George H. Perkins*, published 1886, page 126.

Captain Perkins was ready for the fight. While executing his orders to bombard the fort, Captain Perkins removed several barges from alongside or near the Powell wharf. In his after action report Perkins wrote: "in the afternoon of the same day (the 5th), I again got underway, and brought a large barge – the *Ingomar* – out from under the guns of Fort Powell, exchanging several shots and being struck three times. On the morning of the 6th, I proceeded again to Fort Powell, which I found deserted and blown up. I towed out another barge. In the afternoon I advanced and shelled Fort Gaines." [303]

George H. Perkins from his book *Letters of Captain George H. Perkins*, published 1886

A New Orleans newspaper, discussing Perkins taking the *Chickasaw* under the guns of Fort Powell reported as follows: "Lieutenant Cmdr. Perkins, of the monitor *Chickasaw*, steamed off in the direction of Fort Powell, and then discovered, a short distance from the fort, and within easy range, a barge at anchor filled with stones. It was the intention to sink it in the channel at Grants Pass, for the purpose of obstructing it. The *Chickasaw* passed between the fort and the barge, securing the latter with cables, and towed the barge off, the fort firing in the meantime." [304]

Colonel Williams, commander of Fort Powell reported that at about 2:30 P.M., one of the enemy's monitors came up within 700 yards of the fort firing rapidly with shell and grape. Farragut in his report of August 8 wrote: "we took some covered barges also from Fort Powell and Cedar Point which will do us good service as a workshop." [305]

Another report stated that the *Chickasaw* came within 350 yards of the fort and fired 25 11-inch shells. These shells so displaced the sand on the rear of the work that Williams feared for the magazine if again attacked.

Williams decided to abandon the fort. The log of the *Chickasaw* recorded firing only 35 shells total. Colonel Williams on Powell reported

---

[303] *Perkins* letters, page 134.
[304] Perkins letters, page 141.
[305] Perkins letters, page 142.

that the *Chickasaw* fired both shell and grape. An 11-inch solid shot recovered from the fort is in the History Museum of Mobile. The *Chickasaw* appears to be the only vessel that fired 11-inch projectiles into Powell.

Prizes

Prize money[306] may have encouraged Captain Perkins to bring his vessel so close to Fort Powell. Perkins could have accomplished his mission by shelling the fort from a longer range without approaching the end of the pier. The close approach was necessary only to capture the barges. On August 2, three days before the battle, he wrote to his mother: "you must look out for my prize-money. I shall try and leave a few lines for you just before the action, and if anything happens to me they will be sent you."[307] Prize money was clearly on Perkins mind.

Inside a Monitor's turret (*Harper's Weekly*, Feb. 3, 1866

The award of prize money was only available in strictly naval operations. When Mobile surrendered, no prize money was awarded for the numerous vessels captured there because it was a joint Army-Navy operation. Even though Union infantry was ashore on Dauphin Island, the Mobile Bay battle was considered to be strictly a naval operation.

Captured prizes were surveyed and appraised and those documents along with statements detailing the action and which vessels were within hailing distance were sent to the clerk of the U.S. District Court in Boston, Key West, or to the District Court in New Orleans for adjudication. The vessels in Mississippi Sound, although within signal distance were separated

---

[306] Prize money as a reward for risking oneself to take enemy vessels during wartime was a part of U.S. law up until World War One. The last prize case to be adjudicated was from the Spanish-American war.

[307] *Perkins,* letters page 129

from the action by Fort Powell and a narrow obstructed channel, and therefore did not participate in the Mobile Bay prize moneys.[308]

The *Ingomar* was appraised at $3000. The hull, anchor and chain was worth $1500 and the steam machinery $1500. The value was reduced because the surveyors found the hull was greatly injured from teredo worms. There was deducted from the monies, court costs, in the case of the *Ingomar* $75.92. The *Tennessee's Hospital* was appraised at $7500. The coal barge at $6000 and the water tank at $2000. The *Tennessee* sold for $96,000 and the *Selma* for $154,550.35.[309] The amount of prize money was considerable for vessels not necessarily needed in a war that was nearly over.

Battle of Mobile Bay prize money was paid to the admiral, captains, officers and crews for the taking of the *Tennessee*, the *Selma*, the four lighters including the *Ingomar*, and even the guns and machinery removed from of the sunken *Gaines* and the blockade runner *Ivanhoe*.[310] Apparently the hulk loaded with rocks anchored off Fort Powell that was intended to be sunk in the channel had no value. The prize court records, if such exist, for the ordnance from the *Gaines*[311] have not been located even though there is a report indicating that the guns were to be sent to Pensacola for appraisal, which was then to be sent to Boston for adjudication.[312]

The only guns on Fort Powell that would bear on the *Chickasaw* were the east face 10-inch columbiad, and two 7-inch Brooke rifles including the razeed Brooke gun.[313] Gun S-19 was on the southeast corner facing toward

---

[308] Official Records Navy, volume 21, page 670.

[309] Archives Branch, Federal Archives and Records Center, Waltham, Massachusetts, record group 21, Records of the U.S. District Court for the District of Massachusetts, December term 1865.

[310] Suit was filed at Boston on January 19, 1865 on the *Selma, Ingomar* and Three Lighters and on October 6, 1865 in the Eastern District of Louisiana on the *Tennessee*.

[311] Official Records Navy, volume 21, page 696, Farragut to Wells stating that all guns from the *Gaines* had been salvaged.

[312] Official Records Navy, volume 21, page 696.

[313] Gun number S-19 was a naval gun loaned to the army. In sailing Navy terminology, a razee was a cut down warship. You take a three decker and remove the upper deck or a two decker and remove the second deck you have a razee. In the Revolutionary war, the British cut down two deck 74's to make a razee (not a frigate) and sent them to search for the *Constitution*. The U.S.S. *Independence* was a razeed 74 gunner. The Civil War Union *Cumberland* was a razee. Official Records Navy, volume 14, page 284. Secretary of the U.S. Navy from March 1857 to March 1861 Mr. Isaac Touncey recommended in December 1860 that several steam frigates then out of repair should be razeed and converted into efficient sloops of war. Congress did not make the necessary appropriations. Official Records Navy,

Fort Gaines but could traverse to the east over the unfinished temporary parapet. The 10-inch columbiad and the 7-inch rifle on the east face were not manned. The elevating mechanism on the rear of the 10-inch was broken by a shell fragment early in the action, effectively disabling the unmanned gun. The east face Brooke was considered by Williams to be too exposed and was also not manned.

The *Chickasaw* approached from the rear unfinished side of the fort. The guns on that face were sheltered by the temporary parapet only. Williams in reference to S – 19: "The gun was loaded with great difficulty, there being no platform in the rear…and the delay occasioned by a sponge head pulling off in the gun I succeeded in firing but three shots from it while the ironclad was within range."

Only the Brooke gun in the southern angle fired on the *Chickasaw*. One of the shots from the Brooke penetrated the *Chickasaw's* lightly armored deck and on rebounding out caused friction that set fire to the hammocks stowed below.

Blown Up

Generals Page's order was to; "Hold as long as you can." Williams decided he had done so and evacuated that night. Williams made the correct decision.

As soon as it was sufficiently dark to hide his movements, Williams evacuated the garrison. Lieutenant Tom Savage of the Mobile Battle Guards, and Private Desport, of the Mobile Cadets number 2, were left in charge of a detail with orders to spike the guns and prepare a train and match to explode the magazine as soon as they discovered that the garrison had reached the

---

volume 4, page 303. Apparently to the naval officer, anything that was cut down or shortened or shot away was razeed.
    Naval officers and Williams in referring to S-19 after the explosion reduced the length of its barrel referred to it as the "razeed gun." The term is an interesting description, hence the reference.

mainland. The tide being low, every man reached Cedar Point in safety and marched thence to Mobile. The fort was blown up at 10:30 P.M. [314] Williams, in his after action report states that Lieutenant Jeffers, acting ordnance officer, was to spike the guns. A Union vessel reported 12 men on the Fort after the garrison left and prior to the explosion. [315]

Fort Powell's magazine exploding (*Frank Leslie's Illustrated Magazine*, September 24, 1864)

---

[314] *The Mobile Cadets 1845-1945,* author unknown, edited by William S. Coker page 126.
[315] A requisition by Captain Melville C. Butt for company C, 21st Alabama, indicated that the men of that company lost their clothing in the evacuation of Fort Powell. *Mobile Confederates* by Arthur E. Green, page 54.

Williams described the event in a report to General Maury dated August 7: "When the enemy's fleet passed into the Bay the garrison consisted of two companies of 21st Alabama Regiment and a part of Culpepper's battery, in all of about 140 men. Water for 30 days was protected from the enemy's fire in the bombproof and other stores for two months. The front face of the work was nearly completed and in a defensible condition, mounting one 8-inch columbiad, one 6.4-inch rifle, and two 7-inch Brooke guns. The face looking toward Gaines and Little Dauphin Island was half finished. The parapet was nearly completed, but traverses and galleries had only been framed. The rear had only been commenced. Two guns were mounted, one 10-inch columbiad and one 7-inch Brooke rifle. They were without parapets and exposed from the platform up. This part of the fort was strewed with large quantity of lumber, which was being used in the construction of galleries, magazines, etc.

"During the morning the fort was shelled from five gunboats in the sound at long range. The fort was hit five times, but no particular damage was done. I replied with the four guns bearing on that side, with what effect is not known. About 2:30 p.m. one of the enemy's monitors came up within 700 yards of the fort, firing rapidly with shell and grape. I replied from the 7-inch Brooke gun [razeed] on the south angle. It was protected by an unfinished traverse, which, however, would not permit it to be depressed sufficiently for ricochet firing. The gun was loaded with great difficulty, there being no platform for the gunners in the rear, owing to which the delay occasioned by a sponge head pulling off in the gun I succeeded in firing but three shots from it while the ironclad was in range. One shot struck on the bow with no apparent effect. The ironclad's fire made it impossible to man the two guns in the rear, and I made no attempt to do so. The elevating machine of the 10-inch columbiad was broken by a fragment of shell. A shell entered one of the sally ports, which are not traversed in the rear, passed entirely through the bombproof, and buried itself in the opposite wall. Fortunately it did not explode. The shells exploding in the face of the work displaced the sand so rapidly that I was convinced unless the ironclad was driven off it would explode my magazine and make the bombproof chambers untenable in two days at the furthest. To drive it from its position I believed impossible with my imperfect work, and so telegraphed to Colonel Anderson, commanding Fort Gaines, that unless I could evacuate I would be compelled to surrender within 48 hours. His reply was: 'Save your garrison when your fort is no longer tenable.' At the time his dispatch was received it was becoming dark. The fleet had not moved up to intercept my communication with Cedar Point. I could not expect to have another opportunity to escape, and I decided promptly that it would be better to save my command and destroy the fort than to allow both to fall into the hands of the enemy, as they certainly would have done in two days. The tide being low, I marched my command to Cedar Point without interruption or discovery. In one narrow channel I found the water overhead, and in crossing it I damaged my ammunition and lost a few muskets (a special report of which will be made). Lieutenant Savage was left in the fort with orders to prepare a train and match to explode the magazine is soon as he discovered that I had gained the mainland. Lieutenant Jeffers, acting ordnance officer, was directed to spike the guns at the same time. The fort was blown up at 10:30 p.m. Every man was brought off safely to Cedar Point, thence to the city." [316] The pathway marked out through the shallows early in the war to Cedar Point was used.

U.S.S. *Estrella* off Pensacola Naval Yard 1866-1867

The U.S.S. *Estrella* observed from Mississippi sound, at about 9:45 PM, troops evacuating the fort by way of the "reef" leading from the fort to the mainland. They judged that there were about 100 to 150 evacuees who

---

[316] Official Records Navy, volume 21, series 1, page 560, also Official Records Army, volume 39, series 1, page 444.

seemed to be in great haste, "as they took nothing with them." The captain of the *Estrella* stating that at 11:45 P.M. a signal was made to him to engage the enemy and they steamed up to an easy range of 2000 yards and commenced firing. Their Schenkle shells tumbled badly and they had to use solid shot. The fort did not reply and they could see only some 10 or 12 men remaining on it.

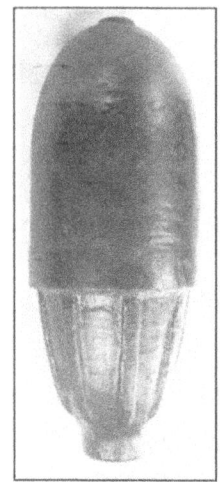
Schenkle shell without the paper sleeve sabot

No one from the fort reported the late night naval activity.[317] Obviously, Williams and the *Estrella* were not operating with synchronized watches.

Maury wrote on Williams' report that "Colonel Williams should have fought his guns. Fort Powell should not have been surrendered." Williams was relieved from command pending investigation.[318]

On August 12 Maury wrote of Williams to Secretary of War James A. Seddon at Richmond: "Lieutenant Colonel Williams, of Fort Powell, abandoned and blew up his work without having a man injured, nor had any injury been inflicted on any part of his fort. He reports, one of his gun carriages disabled, and one gun temporarily out of use by careless loading. He had under his bombproof fully thirty days water and two months provisions. He had hand grenades, revolvers, muskets, and howitzers to defend his fort against launches, and eight heavy guns to use against the ships. The fort had just been connected by telegraph with Fort Gaines and with Mobile.

"On the morning of the fifth there were seventy Negroes with trenching tools in the fort. The guns on the east face of the work were mounted and in fighting order, but were not yet covered by the parapet, and

---

[317] Official Records Navy, volume 21, page 504.

[318] In fairness, in a letter condemning Williams for evacuating he stated that this was the "same Commander who in a spirited manner sustained the attack of Farragut some months ago." Official Records Army, volume 39, page 426.

[318] Official Records Army, volume 39, page 428.

[318] *Sketches of Mobile,* by Bernard A. Reynolds published in Mobile 1868. Reynolds was a captain with the 21st Alabama Regiment, and was captured with Colonel Anderson at Fort Gaines.

the men servicing them would have been exposed as are sailors on an ordinary man–of–war. It is altogether probable that a faithful service of their battery for half an hour would have driven off or sunk the only boat attacking its eastern face, and that it might have been held long enough to compel the fleet put to sea, or at least enable Mobile to prepare for a land attack."[319] Obviously Maury had never been toe to toe with a Union monitor with 11-inch guns.

Although there was recrimination at the time the general postwar conclusion was that tactically once Farragut's fleet was operating inside Mobile Bay, the fate of the forts was sealed as they could not be provisioned and would have fallen to the Union Army and Navy siege guns any way. That is what actually happened. Admiral Farragut in a letter to General Canby considered Page's criticism of the other fort commanders unjustified.[320]

Williams was subsequently vindicated at his court martial which found he had "acted with sound discretions in obedience to the letter and spirit of his orders." On September 1, Special Order Number 245 officially announced his acquittal and stated that he was "Released from arrest and will resume his sword." General Maury and Taylor disagreed but the judgment of the court was final.[321] In September 1864 Williams commanded Redoubts 4, 5, 6 and Battery K in the Mobile defenses. The Cadets and Battle Guards of the 21st were at Battery Huger, and then were joined at Blakely by the six companies of their regiment paroled after their surrender at Fort Morgan. The other two companies, captured at Fort Gaines, never rejoined as they were retained on Ship Island to the close of the war. Ship Island Prison was not a pleasant place. Grave records there from October 17, 1864 to January 3, 1865 show the deaths of 54 men from the 21st Alabama and 8 from the 1st Alabama Artillery Battalion.

---

[320] *Sketches of Mobile,* by Bernard A. Reynolds, published in Mobile 1868.
[321] LT. Colonel Williams and the Fort Powell Incident, by John Kent Folmer, *The Alabama Review*, April 1964, page 132.

Roster
Mobile Cadets Co. "K"
21st Alabama Regiment C. S. V. Paroled at Cuba, Miss.
May 5, 1865

1. 1st Lieutenant   W. J. Brainard
2. 2nd "   A. F. Hurtel
3. Sergeant-Major   Green, J. S.
4. Sergeant   Bullock, J. S.
5. "   Partridge, Thad.
6. "   Stanard, C. LeB.
7. Corporal   Brothers, T. S.
8. "   Bruce, W. J.
9. Private   Candlish, W. G.
10. "   Crawford, T. E.
11. "   Couch, J. E.
12. "   Couch, O. W.
13. "   Covington, G. B.
14. "   Coyle, Jas.
15. "   Davidson, J. A.
16. "   Dorman, T. T.
17. "   Gale, E. B.
18. "   George, R. B.
19. "   Harrall, E. W.
20. "   Hopper, H. H.
21. "   Kieman, F. J.
22. "   Langdon, C. C. Jr.
23. "   LeBaron, Alex.
24. "   Minzie, F. J.
25. "   O'Conner, R. E.
26. "   Owen, F. A.
27. "   Penny, F. T.
28. "   Richards, C. R.
29. "   Richards, W. W.
30. "   Russell, G. A.
31. "   Stanard, W.
32. "   Stanton, F. N.
33. "   Sayre, M. A.
34. "   Sheffield, W. H.
35. "   Shivey, F. M.
36. "   Vail, L. C.
37. "   Walker, R. H.
38. "   Waring, M. M.
39. "   Wilmarth, A. M.
40. "   White, R. R.
41. "   Wolfe, W. T.

Company that surrendered with Williams (Coker, *The Mobile Cadets 1845-1945*)

In March 1865 Williams had again been placed in command of the reorganized 21st Regiment then engaged in the defense of Spanish Fort. After the evacuation of Mobile the Regiment was surrendered at Cuba Station, in Sumpter County, near York, Alabama, on May 6, 1865.[322]

---

[322] See Timeline of the 21st and Lt. Colonel Williams attached as an Appendix 1.

Years later, on May 1, 1890, Williams wrote in the margin of his personal copy of Foxall Parkers' *Battle of Mobile Bay*: "The facts which [sic] does not appear in the record is that a scapegoat had to be provided to bear the load of sins, which left our position and [sic] easy prey for Farragut."

Continuing his margin notes Williams wrote: "The bay side of Fort Powell had been left unprotected while our engineers were engaged in many absurd works, and some which deserve a worse name – such as the construction of batteries near Fort Morgan for no other purpose than the protection of blockade runners in this swash channel. That the staff of the general commanding was interested in this money-making business was an open secret.[323] While I commanded at Fort Morgan I repeatedly called attention to the fact that we could not successfully oppose an attempt to pass the fort, unless the channel was effectively closed with torpedoes – no attention was paid to this as to do so would stop the blockade runners – Such torpedoes, as were placed were carefully buoyed.

"My opinions on this subject, afterwards so signally and fatally confirmed, were shared by every intelligent officer who was familiar with the position. Sgt. William Demony, who made the copies of my monthly reports as to the condition of the fort, once asked me, if I did not fear to give offense at headquarters, by repeating each month, in the same language, my suggestions as to the necessity of torpedoes."

"I am very well satisfied that I did give offense, and but for the independent integrity of the court-martial in the case of Fort Powell, I would've been ruined and disgraced by the speculative gentleman [sic] who were unfortunately, my military superiors." Williams appeared to be still bitter thirty years after the fact.[324]

---

[323] General Maury was himself, as late as May 1864, ordering items for his personal account through the blockade. See *The Denbigh's Civilian Imports* by J. Barto Arnold III, pages 204, 205 and 206.

[324] Lt. Colonel Williams and the Fort Powell incident, by John Kent Folmer, *Alabama Review* April 1964 pages 134-135.

The garrisons of Fort Powell and Gaines were mostly local. The public strongly agreed with Williams and with Colonel Anderson who surrendered Fort Gaines that the evacuation of the one and the surrender of the other were proper. Generals Maury and Taylor did not want the paroled Garrison of Gaines to return to Mobile and asked that they and Williams be transferred out of Mobile as their presence; "may injure the *morale* of the other troops."[325]

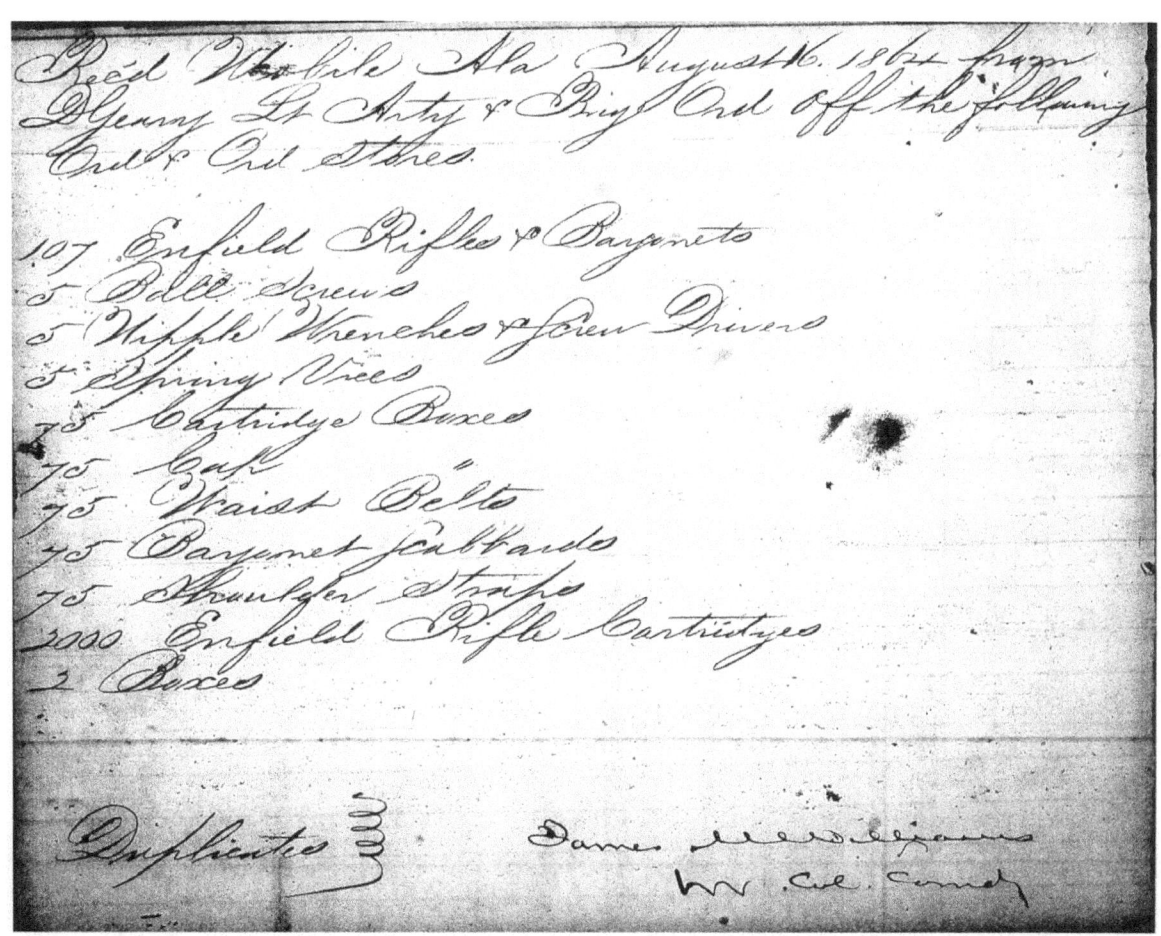

Voucher for rifles and equipment issued from the ordinance warehouse in Mobile to William's troops while he was stationed in the Mobile defenses (Daniel Geary Papers, Mobile Public Library)

---

[325] Official Records Army, Dyer's Compendium, part 2, page 741, Maury to Bragg September 14, 1864.

Chapter 10

Final Days of the War

Fort Powell after the explosion (*Frank Leslie's Illustrated Magazine*, September 24, 1864)

The Confederate service of Fort Powell was over. On August 6 at 5:00 P.M. one officer and ten U.S. Marines with their haversacks and 2 days rations were detailed to the now Union vessel *Selma* for Fort Powell.[326]

The following day Acting Master, Timothy Pomeroy of the U.S.S. *Estrella* (one of the Mississippi Sound squadron vessels) landed at Fort Powell at 7:00 a.m. to hoist the flag and to do a survey. He reported: "I found it had been blown up, turning the center directly out over the parapet. It is nothing but a heap of rubbish in ruins, with a deep tunnel – shaped hole in the center, which was filled with water. There are some remaining

---

[326] Official Records Navy, volume 21, page 51.

portions of the magazines for shell and some shells in them in good order. It had the appearance of being evacuated in great haste, as some of the clothing of men and officers are still remaining in their quarters. There is a long wharf leading out on the northeast side of the fort, at the end of which is 5 1/2 or 6 feet of water; lying alongside is a barge, capable of carrying from 100 to 150 tons of coal, in good order. On the wharf are the quarters of the soldiers, in which are some few muskets, canteens and privates' clothing, which is of little value. I found in the fort the following guns and ammunition:

"On the northeast corner, 2 ammunition chests with spherical case. One 10-inch columbiad, perfect, with carriage; 1 iron fieldpiece, 3 6/8, with carriage; 1 fieldpiece, 4 5/8, with carriage, right wheel broken; one fieldpiece perfect.

"The following on the east side: One pivot gun, dismounted and partly buried; one chest of hand grenades, perfect.

"In the bombproof that is partially demolished is the following shell: Forty-seven shell for 7-inch gun, in good order, in boxes.

"Southeast corner: One 7-inch rifle pivot gun, in good order, on carriage; one fieldpiece, 4 1/2 inch, in good order, on field carriage.

"South side: One 7.6 gun, smoothbore.

"Southwest corner: One 7-inch rifle gun, partly buried up; has about 1 foot of muzzle broken off.

"West side, in bombproof, partly buried up, a quantity of projectile shells for rifled guns.

"West side: One 8-inch gun, smoothbore, on carriage, partly covered up in rubbish.

"On the southwest corner: One 5 and 6/8 fieldpiece, on carriage, in good order.

"This comprises all the armament I could see. Still I think there is another rifle gun buried upon the west side. These guns are all of rebel manufacture.

"There are large quantities of square fine lumber in good order, which may be useful to fleet in repairing the damages; also some three and four inch planks."[327]

The power of the explosion was such that it blew out the bottom of the magazine to a point below the waterline.

By the morning of August 9th whatever efforts were required to open the obstructions in Grants Pass had been completed and the Union Army moved its transports containing about 2000 troops and their siege material and train to Pilot Town (Navy Cove) east of Fort Morgan. The transports passed without interruption within 2 miles of the fort, and commenced landing at a wharf left in good condition at about 11 a.m. The siege of Fort Morgan was about to begin. [328]

The Union Army apparently maintained a Garrison garrison on Powell even though the fort had been turned inside out by its magazine explosion.[329] A lithograph published in New Orleans by Capt. William S. Trask appears to show mounted guns and numerous soldiers cabins on the Fort post explosion. Trash was with the six Michigan heavy artillery that was the garrison at Fort gains from August 23, 1864 to July 9, 1865.

---

[327] Official Records Navy, volume 21, page 505.
[328] Official Records Army, volume 39, page 412.
[329] The rarely reached goal of the ordnance officers was to have on hand in each battery 200 rounds per gun. General Maury's report of August 8 (Official Records Army, volume 34, page 428) states that the outer line of defenses for Mobile being Forts Gaines, Morgan and Powell were supplied with 300 rounds per gun while those near the City had no more than 200 rounds per gun. Each of the 8 heavy guns would have some 25 projectiles in service magazines that should not have been involved in the explosion. At 8 pounds of powder per round plus rounds for the field pieces there could have been in excess of 15,000 pounds of powder in the magazine when the fuse was lit.

Union occupation of Fort Powell (lithograph by Manouvrier & Simon, New Orleans. Artist Capt. William S. Trask of the 6th Michigan Heavy Artillery then the garrison of Fort Gaines. View from NE to SW)

Cedar Point Occupied

After the evacuation of Fort Powell and during the siege of Fort Morgan, Union General Granger had additional troops sent to him to either use in the prosecution of his siege or to occupy Cedar Point.[330] On August 14, 1864 Granger decided that as soon as he received the two additional regiments, he would make a lodgment and a redoubt at Cedar Point. He deemed it important to hold a position on the mainland to facilitate the deserters,[331] contrabands and refugees that were arriving at his lines on a

---

[330] Official Records Navy, volume 21, page 528, Canby to Farragut.

[331] Desertions were taken seriously by Confederate authorities. As late as March 11, 1865, Private Frank Hoover, Company B 22nd Louisiana was sentenced to be shot and sent to Spanish Fort for execution in the presence of the troops. National Archives, Record Group, 109, chapter 2, volume 100. On March 18 Williams wrote that on the day before, the brigade had witnessed a military execution of which he was in charge; and on March 31, Privates Thomas Elam and Elijah Winn, both local men who had deserted from

daily basis.[332] Six regiments and a battery (about 4000 troops) occupied Cedar Point on August 25. They found there one 12-pounder howitzer abandoned by the Confederates.[333] That large force did not remain long.

The Confederates could not contest the Union occupation of the Point. General Gardner at Mobile was aware that Grangers forces were there, but they appeared to him to be merely making a temporary incursion. He had limited troops, and could not move outside of the breastworks of the Mobile defenses with the militia[334] he had available.

Fieldpiece

Gardner was correct and the Union generals soon pulled their troops off Cedar Point. Farragut had his ships in the Bay, and had taken the forts at the entrance of the bay, but there were not enough Union troops to move against the City of Mobile itself. Farragut wrote on August 27, 1864, to Secretary of the Navy Gideon Welles that he was now a little embarrassed by his position. He had taken the forts at the entrance of the Bay, which was all he had ever contemplated doing to begin with. He considered an army of 20 to 30,000 men necessary to take the city of Mobile and almost as many to hold it. The double ender gunboats and the Mississippi River Monitors were the only vessels that could reach the city's defenses. His larger vessels could not approach within 12 or 15 miles of the upper obstructions.

It was evident to Farragut that the army had no men to spare, beyond those "sufficient to keep up an alarm, and thereby make a diversion in favor of General Sherman." He told Welles that he disliked the idea of making a show of attack, unless he could do something more than making a menace, but he was willing to do so if that's what the department wanted. He had been in the Gulf and the Caribbean for nearly five years out of six, was tired

---

the 21st Alabama in September 1863, were shot by a firing squad. *Mobile 1865* by Sean Michael O'Brien page 117. Mobile Register and Advertiser, April 2, 1865.

[332] Official Records Army, volume 39, page 252.

[333] Official Records Army, volume 39, page 422.

[334] Often during the Civil War there were no regular Confederate troops stationed in the City. All guard duty was done by militia units. History Museum of Mobile, Diary of Lieutenant Mumford, entry July, 1864.

and wanted to go home. Shortly thereafter, he turned over his command and headed north.[335]

Union Major General Edward R. S. Canby agreed with Farragut but did not have the forces to do more. On August 22, 1864 Canby wrote from New Orleans to General Granger commanding U.S. forces at Mobile Point: "the occupation of Mobile and a demonstration up the Alabama would favor Sherman's operations greatly, and if I can get the force it will be done. I advised the Admiral when I was over that I could not materially increase your force, and he concurred with me in the opinion that it would be unwise to make any direct attempt upon Mobile until this could be done. We can still make such demonstrations from the Bay and from the Mississippi as will materially aid Sherman."[336]

Gen. Edward R. S. Canby
(Harper's Weekly, April 15, 1865)

Both sides thought that they did not have enough troops to either take or hold Mobile. At the time both sides overestimated the land forces of the other. General Maury stated: "The enemy has in this vicinity a reported land force of about 12,000 men at Pensacola, on Ship Island, on Dauphin Island, and Mobile Point. The fleet is very large. The shameful surrender of Fort Powell and Gaines has opened the way for the enemy, and he can tonight land his troops within 5 miles of the city and invest it. There is in this whole district about 6000 troops of every description, about 1000 of them have been under fire, the rest are state reserves and militia and the old men and boys of the town, all recently organized and armed. The works are strong. The supply of ammunition is short. The people are in good heart and seem resolved to have their city defended at all hazards. The noncombatants will not go away. The subsistence supplies are abundant for a proper garrison for six months. Fort Morgan still holds out against the heaviest attacks ever made on any of our forts."[337]

---

[335] Official Records Navy, volume 21, page 612, Farragut to Gideon Welles, August 27, 1864.
[336] Official Records Army, series 1, volume 78, page 288 – 289.
[337] Official Records Navy, volume 78, pages 795-96, Maury to Taylor, August 23, 1864.

The fundamental error of the Confederate authorities was the assumption that the occupation of the city of Mobile was Farragut's objective rather than the occupation of Mobile Bay. The heavy spending on forts for the defense of the Bay and City meant fewer funds and resources were available for the construction of ironclad gunboats and that deficiency doomed Mobile Bay.

- September 2, 1864 Atlanta falls, which with the victory at Mobile Bay, gave the North a sense the war was winnable, resulting in the reelection of Lincoln

The Confederates maintained a cavalry picket at Cedar Point. From a lookout point there, a tower or a tall tree, they watched the Union activity in the Lower Bay and reported by telegraph. On October 7, 1864, the *Tritona* with the Admiral Thatcher on board saw a fire on the land near the Point. The "tinclad no. 48" (the *Rodolph*) stood in and fired a few rounds to which there was a reply from a battery on shore.[338] At least a few fieldpieces were at Cedar Point.[339]

In the spring of 1865, the Union army began its push up the Eastern Shore to invest the newly built Confederate works at Spanish Fort and Blakely.

On March 16, 1865 Union Major General Edward S. Canby asked Admiral Thatcher to assist in the movement of troops to the eastern side of

---

[338] Official Records Navy, volume 21, page 808, October 7, 1864.

[339] On October 6, 1864 Confederate Captain Frank Moore, commanding special scouts was provided with 25 men and initially a section of artillery with two rifled pieces. He was to be on the lookout for a particular steamboat that was thought to be trading with the Union and to burn all cotton and naval stores liable to fall into their hands. By way of postscript the order was changed so that only one piece of artillery was to be sent and that he was not to interfere with the steamboat. It was thought that if he did the Union forces would certainly establish a picket at Alabama Port (just north Of Cedar Point) and deprive them of their watching post. Official Records Navy, volume 21, page 914, Gardner to Captain Frank Moore October 6, 1864.

the Bay.[340] A column of 9000 men was to start the next day from near Fort Morgan up the coast, crossing or turning at Bon Secour Creek, crossing the east branch of Fish River as low-down as practical, and striking the north branch near Dannelly's Mill, where the crossing would be made. Another column of 10,000 men would move by water, with the Admiral's help through Bon Secour and Fish River bays, debarking at a point about 1 mile below Dannelly's Mill.

Canby decided to make a demonstration on the west side of the Bay by landing a brigade of about 2000 men on Cedar Point. That landing would be limited to a feint for the purpose of distracting the Confederates from the movement on the east side of the Bay. He asked for the Navy's cooperation in transporting the troops.[341]

Skirmish at Fowl River Narrows

A brigade of the third division of the sixteenth corps under Colonel J.B. Moore consisting of the 44th Missouri, the 33rd Wisconsin, the 72nd Illinois ("Chicago Board of Trade Regiment") and the 95th Illinois together with a two-gun section of artillery was designated to occupy Cedar Point and advance as far as Fowl River. They landed on March 18 after repairing the pier to land the units' horses. They completed the debarkation of the brigade on the 19th. They then moved forward in the direction of Fowl River where they skirmished with the Confederate cavalry until dark.[342]

The troops were traveling light, without land transportation, except for six ambulances. The men carried five days cooked rations in their haversacks. The commander was instructed to make as much display of force as he could without neglecting any security precautions and by the

---

[340] Farragut had turned over the fleet to Thatcher shortly after the battle of Mobile Bay and returned to New York.
[341] Official Record, Navy volume 22, page 65.
[342] Official Records Army, volume 49, page 133.

construction of roads, bridges, etc. convey the impression that his command was the advance guard of a much larger force.[343]

The incursion of Colonel Moore's brigade is referred to in *Dyer's Compendium*, Part 3 (Regimental Histories for the Union units involved) as: "Expedition from Dauphin Island to the Fowl River narrows March 18 – 22." The skirmish of the 19th is referred to in compilations of battles and skirmishes as "the skirmish at Fowl River Narrows." *The Official Military Atlas of the Civil War* plate XL.

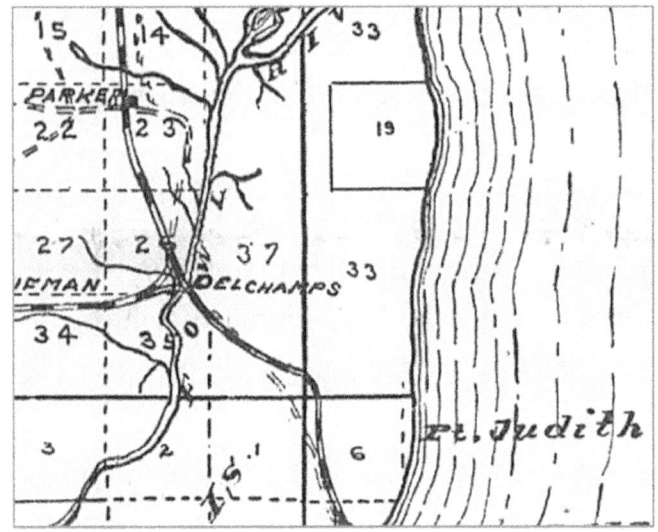

Fowl Rivers narrows (map by Widell, Theodore, Alabama Department of Archives and History,1907)

Earlier, in justifying the removal of guns from Powell, General Withers stated that there was a good road from Cedar Point to the interior. If so there must have been a bridge over Heron Bay cutoff not shown on contemporary maps. The map does show the road from Alabama Port to Fowl River, which maps of the 1890s show as the "Delchamps" community. There was apparently a ferry across the River at the narrows. The road west of the River went toward Bayou La Batre with a fork north to Mobile.

In October Captain Frank Moore and his Special Scouts were the Confederate force in the area. I have not located any Confederate reports of the skirmish. The Confederate skirmishers could have been Moore's group or the City Troop, Partisan Rangers or the Alabama and Florida cavalry (Lieutenant Colonel S. J. Murphy). All these were small, no more than company size units involved in scouting in the area.

The special scouts were apparently an experienced group used for intelligence gathering and covert operations.[344] Whoever they were they did

---

[343] Official Records Army, volume 49, page 16.

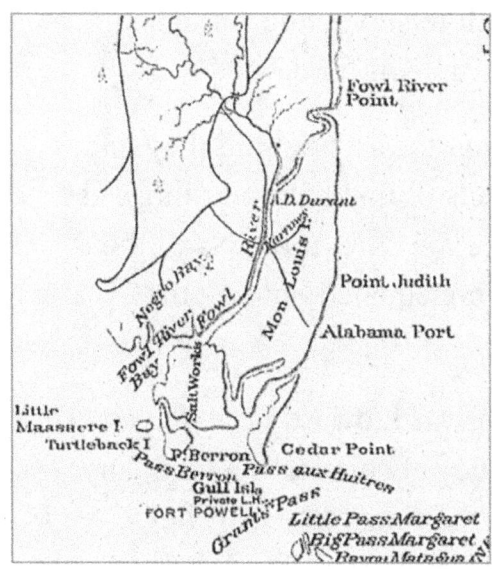

Cedar Point to Fowl River (*Official Atlas of the Civil War*)

not run in the face of overwhelming force but retreated skirmishing toward the river, and when the Union troops withdrew back toward Alabama Port they advanced and continued to harass them.

Details of the incursion exist from the point of view of the 95th Illinois. The 95th landed without opposition. As they approached on their transports they saw a company of Confederate Cavalry, who had been watching the movements of the Federal Army, move away toward Fowl River.[345]

The troops of the 95th reported: "Important batteries had been erected here in a former day by the rebels, intended to command Grants Pass but they had been evacuated since the great victory of Admiral Farragut in Mobile Bay in the summer of 1864. There was no dirt soil in this locality, and these rebel forts were constructed entirely with oyster shells, which abounded here in superfluous quantities. The oyster shell fortifications displayed something of Yankee ingenuity, and to us who were accustomed to a different material, presented a novel and interesting appearance."

When they came ashore they found and disarmed several large torpedoes concealed along the broken wharf.

"The 95th camped that night on the point near the rebel look-out, and was ordered to be ready for a forward movement on the following day. The regiments were instructed to beat tattoo several times each, which would give the impression that a large Federal force had landed. The troops were now camped by the celebrated Cedar Point oyster-beds, and soon after landing the surf was alive with wading soldiers, skirmishing not with rebels,

---

[344] Official Records Army, volume 49, page 1214.
[345] The details of the 95th Regiment's March to the narrows is told in the *History of the 95th Regiment Illinois Volunteers,* by Wales W. Wood, Esquire, Chicago, 1865.

but after oysters, of which they brought skiffs-full to shore, and furnished the camps with large supplies of this luxurious article of food."

They enjoyed the oysters, but not the mosquitoes. They said they had never experienced such large-size ravenous insects of that nature as those at Cedar Point. "Oysters and mosquitoes seem to be the chief products of the locality, and the abundance and luxury of one were equaled only by the multitude and inflictions of the other."

On March 19, 1865, the brigade moved forward toward Fowl River and Mobile. After proceeding a short distance, they encountered a company of Confederate cavalry, who had been watching their movements. They immediately deployed skirmishers and the cavalry retreated. They then marched until dusk with the regiments in line of battle in the thick pine woods, several miles north of Cedar Point. Orders were here issued for the regimental bands to beat three tattoos each that evening, as well as a corresponding number of reveilles on the following morning, varying tunes each time, to accomplish the deception intended.

Unfortunately, the 44th Missouri had but recently formed a regimental drum corps and they did not know a variety of tunes. Whenever they attempted the various changes of reveille or tattoo "the inevitable result was a monotonous, discordant production, little worthy of the name of music. If you listen to them once, you could afterward easily detect them among 1000 well-trained bands. For this reason, the drum corps of the 44th was not the best possible instrument with which to deceive the enemy in the manner proposed."[346]

The next day the brigade moved forward a few miles to a small creek where more torpedoes were found. After shelling the opposite shore the troops counter marched and returned to camp 2 miles from Cedar Point where they remained until the afternoon of the 22nd, when they embarked for Fish River. There they rejoined the Army marching on Spanish Fort and Blakely.

---

[346] The *Mobile Register and Advertiser* published a letter dated April 12, 1865 from William J. Fulton age 15 to his sister describing the Federal regiments marching into Mobile after the surrender. He said the bands consisted of 10 fifers and 10 drummers and were the "poorest bands in Yankeedom."

In April 1865, Spanish Fort and Blakely fell opening the way to Mobile. The Confederate forces at Mobile evacuated to Meridian and Demopolis. On April 12 the Mayor of Mobile surrendered the city to Union General Canby. The defense of Mobile was over. General Lee had surrendered at Appomattox on April 9, General Taylor at Citronelle on May 4 and General Kirby Smith the Trans-Mississippi forces on May 26.

The War was over.

Chapter 11

Post War

The New Channel[347]

Fort Powell today is under some 3 to 5 feet of water. At low tide a few of the perimeter rocks are visible. When the tides are ebbing and flowing there is a substantial current from the Bay into Mississippi Sound and vice versa. Fishermen who are unaware or do not see eddies over the rocks risk damage to their boats and motors and most avoid the area. Oystermen who work the reef are aware of the hazard.

Following the war the fort was simply abandoned and the sand transported from the Fort Morgan peninsula washed away with each hurricane and storm. In the winter, storms from the north blow down Mobile Bay, generating substantial waves. In the summer afternoon storms frequently blow through from the northwest generating equally substantial waves from Mississippi sound.

By the 1880s Corps of Engineers maps showed sand still piled on the site of Fort Powell. In 1906 John Grant's toll collector/lighthouse keeper's house was still standing on piles on Grants Island/Fort Powell. The expense accounts for the McGill estate which purchased the pass from the heirs of Grant in 1887 showed revenues of $1498.25 and expenses of $1119.80 from the operation of the pass from May 18, 1888 to December 24, 1889. Those expenses included payments to keeper Mr. John Reed, oil apparently for the light, lumber, shingles, nails, caulking etc. for maintaining the house. The

---

[347] Unless otherwise noted Illustrations for the following chapters are from the collections of Bill Armistead, David Smithweck and the Author.

keepers did not collect tolls but recorded passages; this information was sent to Mobile where a representative collected the tolls from the owners of the vessels.

The hurricane of 1906 washed the sand out from under the keeper's house leaving it on piles sitting over water. The storm also blew out some windows and did other damage. The 1906 storm was powerful and blew away the houses of the bar pilots at Navy Cove and destroyed the railroad from Fort Morgan east along the peninsula.

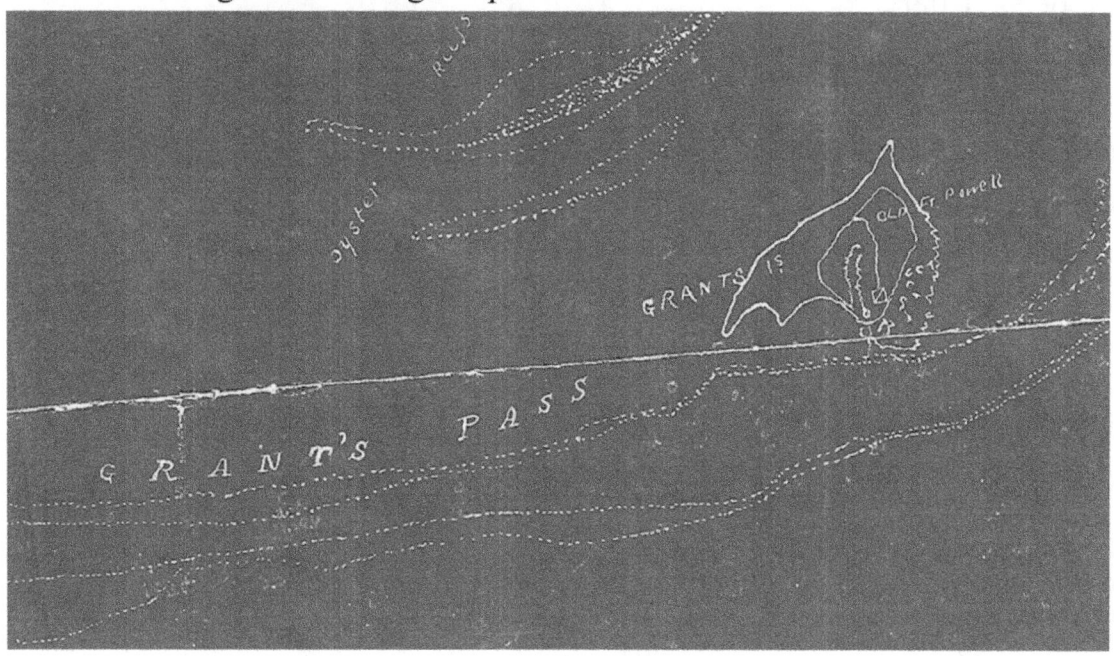

Corps of Engineers survey 1884

Today only oyster shells and the perimeter rocks mark the location of Fort Powell. No evidence remains of the battery built on the beach at little Dauphin Island or at Sughee Point. The Cedar Point battery was built to some extent of oyster shells. There remain several small mounds of shells that could be remnants of those works. A railroad and highway was built in a north-south direction across Cedar Point. The shell mounds/earthworks would have provided a convenient construction material for the base of either. Every storm from the southwest cuts farther into the shore and reduces the size of the remaining oyster mounds.

There were a number of surveys of the area made from the 1880s through the 1920s. The Corps of Engineers was interested in completing the intra-coastal waterway which was the greatest project of that organization during the era between the great wars. The Corps has a long history in the area. Because of the danger posed by Gulf storms, the necessity of deepening the Pass aux Heron channel between Mobile Bay and Mississippi sound was recognized at an early date. Congress authorized the project in 1828 but after several years of fruitless effort the work was abandoned.

Captain John Grant, as described earlier, developed a better dredging system, and in 1839 was given a 25 year monopoly under which he improved the channel and charged a toll for its use.

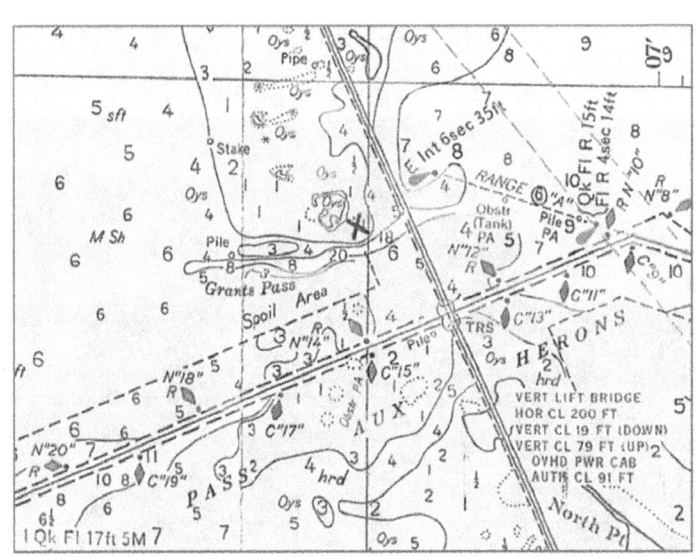

Modern navigation chart, X marks the location of Fort Powell

The obstructions placed in Grants Pass during the Civil War partially filled the ends of the channel. Some additional dredging was done shortly after the war but none after 1869. Although Grant and his successors continued to charge tolls, the larger vessels that had used the pass were forced to take the outside route.[348] In 1913 Congress authorized the Corps of Engineers to dredge a channel 10 feet deep by 100 feet wide through the oyster reef. This work, a part of the intra-coastal waterway was completed in 1914. The channel was increased to 300 feet width in 1930. During World War II the channel was enlarged to 12 feet deep and 150 feet wide.[349]

The Corps of Engineers did not deepen Grants Pass but dredged their channel through Pass aux Heron about 1800 feet south of Grants channel.

---

[348] By the 1880s the Grants Pass channel had become irregular in width along its course and was only about 65 to 70 feet wide in its narrowest part. It could still accommodate vessels of over 7 feet. During the year closing September 30, 1882, 486 vessels, ranging from 25 tons and upwards, with the draft from 5 to 9 feet made use of the channel paying fees of $4,500 to Grant who died in 1884. Chief Engineer's Report, 1895 page 1718. Date of death from Findagrave.com.

[349] *A History of the Mobile District U.S. Army Corps of Engineers 1815 to 1971,* page 62.

John Grant had died in 1884. In 1887 his heirs conveyed the franchise from the State to Felix and Arthur McGill. In 1908 the property was deeded from the heirs of the McGills to the Catholic Bishop of Mobile. The Bishop of Mobile in 1955 deeded the property to the Mobile Area Chamber of Commerce. In 1974 the Chamber of Commerce deeded Grant's interest in the Pass franchise to the University of South Alabama. By that time Grants Island/Fort Powell had long since been eroded away. In 1982 the Pass and 7644 acres were patented to the University of South Alabama by the State of Alabama.[350]

The southern route was taken to avoid conflict with whatever title the Bishop may have claimed and/or the necessity of negotiating for whatever rights the Bishop claimed at the time.

As a consequence of the Corps decision to use the Pass Aux Heron route the new, wider 1914 channel did not impact the site of Fort Powell.

A Railroad?

Several maps from 1880 through 1910 show a railroad running across a bridge from Cedar Point to Dauphin Island just east of Fort Powell at about the location of the present highway bridge.[351] The Dauphin Island Railroad and Dock Company or the Mobile and Dauphin Island Railroad ran from Cedar point to Alabama Port across the Fowl River narrows to Halls Mill to Mertz and thence to the Mobile docks. Part of the right-of-way was later used by the Bay Shore Line (Mobile & Bay Shore Line).

---

[350] For a time-line history of possession and ownership of Fort Powell see Addendum Number 2.
[351] Corps of Engineers Library map collection drawer number 1, maps 2-6, Grants Pass Railroad bridge location 1893. 1889 map by Paul C. Boudousquie, Alabama Department Archives and History map collection among others.

One of the first railroads proposed from Mobile was for a line to Dauphin Island. In the American Railroad Journal and Mechanics Magazine volume 2 – New Series volume 8 published in 1839 we find: "the harbor of Mobile Bay at the town being too shallow for large ships, and gradually becoming worse, it has been found necessary to construct a Railroad 28 miles in length to Cedar Point on the Gulf, where the largest vessels lie in safety."

During the 1880s the Dauphin Island Railroad and Dock Company was organized with plans to build a railroad from Mobile to Dauphin Island where docks would be built along the east side of Little Dauphin Island to accommodate deep draft vessels.

On February 5, 1906, an Act of Congress authorized the company to construct and maintain a bridge or viaduct across the water between the end of Cedar Point and Dauphin Island. The company was also authorized to build wharfs and docks out from the west end of Little Dauphin Island into the waters of Mobile Bay and to dredge a channel to the terminal.

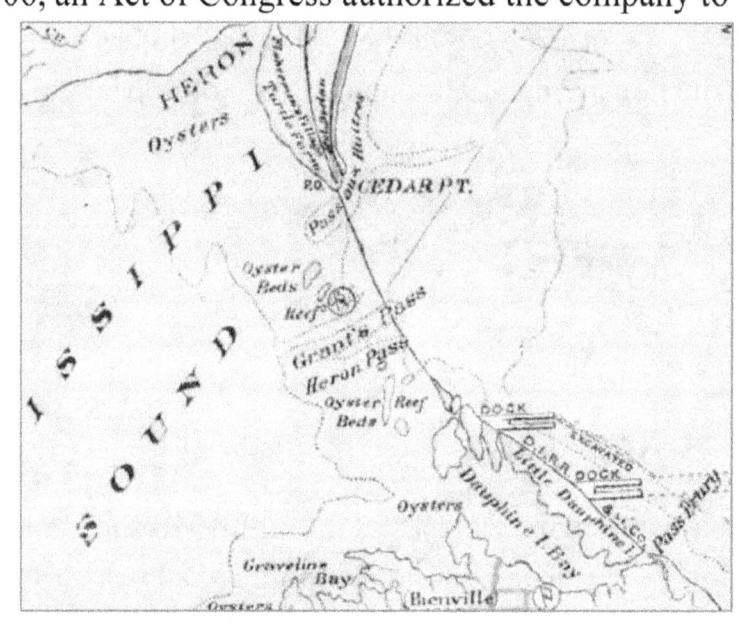

Map of proposed railroad to Little Dauphin Island (Boudousquie, Paul C., Ala. Dept. Archives and History)

All construction was subject to the requirement that such bridge not obstruct navigation between Mississippi Sound and the Bay. The promoters of the venture planned to construct, in addition to cargo wharves, a large coaling terminal to accommodate steamships transiting the Panama Canal then under construction.

There was a report in the *Mobile Press* on February 17, 1911 that the Corps of Engineers was holding a hearing on March 2 in the matter of the proposed construction of a bridge by the Dauphin Island Railway and Harbor Company which would connect Dauphin Island with the mainland.

End of the line at Cedar Point (Bob Boykin Collection, Jim Hall, Dauphin Island Archive of Historical Data)

Some work was done on the Island for in January 1912 some 50,000 feet of lumber was shipped to the Island for construction of temporary wharves.[352]

The proposed railroad to Dauphin Island and a deep water port there was not the only one in the area. The Birmingham, Mobile and Navy Cove Harbor Railroad secured by an act of Congress on 20 July 1888, the privilege of using a 50 foot strip along the northern high water line across the Fort Morgan Military Reservation. The company purchased property on the Fort Morgan peninsular from Little Point Clear to Fort Morgan where a deep water terminal was to be built. Construction was underway east from Navy Cove when it was destroyed by the hurricane of 1906.

The railroad right-of-way from Fort Morgan ran eastwardly along the peninsula turning north to Bon Secour and Fairhope, thence north to the Bay at about the present location of Interstate 10. A trestle across the Bay along where Interstate 10 runs today was to connect the road to the Mobile docks.[353] A breakwater of ballast stones was started in the lower Bay by another company to build a sheltered anchorage but never completed.

None of the Railroads proposed were completed because of the hurricane of 1906 and the fact that during World War I the Corps of Engineers dredged a 17 foot channel into the port of Mobile which eliminated the necessity of any outlying ports.[354] In any event there was no

---

[352] *Mobile Press*, January 12, 1912.
[353] Map by Paul C. Boudousquie dated 1889.
[354] In the course of my law practice I represented Mobil Oil Company and rendered title opinions for them that covered the east end of Dauphin island, Little Dauphin Island, the shifting sand islands south of Dauphin island, the area between Little Dauphin island and Cedar Point and the western portions of the Fort Morgan Peninsula. I also represented the successors in title to the Birmingham Mobile and Navy Cove Harbor Railroad in a lawsuit in Baldwin County to clear the title to a large tract of property on the Fort Morgan Peninsula. On the other side of that lawsuit were several hundred descendants of the Mobile Bar

railroad constructed to Dauphin Island and thus no impact on the site of Fort Powell although it probably impacted the site of the battery at Cedar Point.

The Bridge

Lift span bridge to Dauphin Island (Dauphin Island Archive of Historical Data)

The present Dauphin Island Bridge was built after hurricane Frederick damaged the original one in 1979. The first bridge, with a lift span, was built in 1954 and opened to traffic July 2, 1955. Dredges were used along the west side of the bridge to enable the placing of power poles and to create a channel for the pile drivers and construction barges. The oyster shells and spoil removed by the dredges were piped off to the east. The dredging and construction work for the bridges were to the east of the site of Fort Powell and did not impact the remains of the Fort, but likely removed any evidence that may have remained of the pier and quarters.

There was dredging in the area of Cedar Point in about 1950 and again in 1954 and 55. Participants in those dredging operations reported that in 1950 they were looking for oyster shells and struck several cannonballs with the dredge cutter head under several feet of mud off

On Fort Powell 1968, Bridge in background

Pilots who formerly had a community at Navy Cove. The lawsuit was filed about 1968 and finally concluded about 2002. In the course of that protracted litigation title searches provided the details of the activities of the railroad companies which were to some extent covered in the book A *History of the Mobile District U.S. Army Corps of engineers 1816 to 1971*.

what was then Frank Collier's pier. The 1954 and 1955 dredging was in connection with the construction of the bridge. It is not known whether the bridge or road construction impacted the site of the Cedar Point battery.[355]

---

[355] Conversation with James McPhillips and Joe Helmsing of Southern Industries and with William P. (Skookie) Clark dredge operator with Radcliff Materials December 30, 1976.

CHAPTER 12

Centennial

One cannot say that Fort Powell was lost. The records were there. There were numerous books on the Battle of Mobile Bay that referenced Fort Powell. There were maps published as a part of the Official Records of the War of Rebellion and several books contained maps showing the location of the fort. Navigation charts showed Grants Pass.

Map with Grants Island south of Grants Pass (Wedell, Theodore, 1907, Ala. Dept. Archives and History)

The problem was that many of those maps placed the fort on the south side of Grants Pass on Tower Island, whereas it was actually located on the north side.[356] As a practical matter it was lost unless one was prepared to invest a large amount of time in research or happened upon an unmistakably Fort Powell artifact.

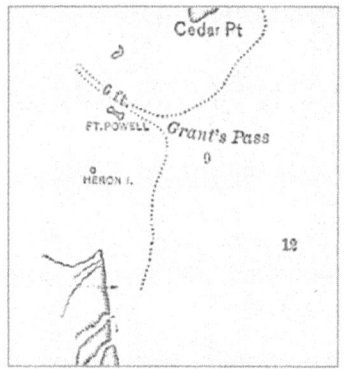

Another Map showing Fort Powell on the south side of Grants Pass (Mahan, Alfred T. *The Gulf and Inland Waters*, 1883)

But no one was that interested; that is not until the Centennial of the Civil War. During the Centennial years of the 1960s there was great renewal of interest in everything Civil War. Reenactment groups were formed all around the country. Each battle was marked with reenactments. In the Mobile area there were a number of reenactment groups including the still active 21st Alabama and the now inactive Lumsden's Battery.

---

[356] Jeffrey N. Lash, an archivist at the National Archives in Washington, D.C., in his article, *A Yankee in Grey: Danville Leadbetter and the Defense of Mobile Bay, 1861 – 1863*, fixes the location of Fort Powell as being on Tower Island. *A History of the Mobile District U.S. Army Corps of Engineers*, published by the Mobile District in 1975 indicates the same.

Spanish Fort, Fort Morgan, Fort Gaines and Blakely all had their battle reenactments. Blue and gray clad troops skirmished and lines of cannon fired during the restaged battles. There was great smoke and pageantry enjoyed by thousands of spectators. No such pageantry marked Fort Powell.

Lumsden Battery reenactment group

Small hand held metal detectors were becoming available to the general public during the 1960s. Forts and battlefields across the country were scoured by enthusiasts searching for minie' balls, artillery projectiles or for anything Civil War. All of the forts, batteries, and battlefields in the Mobile area received the attention of history buffs and relic hunters.

Not until the 1980s did the State of Alabama through the Alabama Historical Commission set up permitting processes for underwater exploration of battlefield sites or shipwrecks. During the 1990s the commission proposed and the legislature adopted regulations governing such activities. I served for a number of years on the Maritime Advisory Committee to the Alabama Historical Commission and was chairman of the group for a time. The Committee was tasked with reviewing all permits for underwater historical searches, reviewing proposed legislation and making recommendations as to such to the commission. Not that any such regulations mattered as far as Fort Powell was concerned. By that time the State had, on what appeared to be primarily political rather than purely factual and legal considerations, patented the title to the site of the fort to the University of South Alabama. Absent some agreement between the University and the State that the author is unaware of, it is not apparent that any State Agency not concerned with navigation or fisheries, has any jurisdiction over the water bottoms at the site of the fort.[357]Notwithstanding

---

[357] See summary timeline for the possession and title history of Fort Powell and Grants Pass attached as appendix 2. Code of Alabama sec. 41-3-5 may give to the State the exclusive right of explore

the area has been designated as a protected site by the Alabama Historic Commission and one would be prudent to consider it as such.

Several people in the 1960s begin searching for sunken cannons and sunken boats. An old fisherman told of a mortar in the Delta. A 13 inch Union mortar was raised and placed in front of the Department of Education building in Bay Minette. A Marine policeman told Civil War history buff Abner C. (A.C.) Jones about what locals called "The Old Oyster Cannon" under about 18 inches of water on the oyster reef near Grants Pass. Jones then contacted his brother-in-law Bill Armistead. Armistead and Jones went to the site and in a few hands on minutes concluded that the object was indeed a cannon and a large one.

William R. (Bill) Armistead

Bill Armistead is by profession a pharmacist (now retired) with an interest in history and a genius in organizing expeditions, land expeditions to search for a suspected Civil War site or camp or a march route or diving expeditions to look for boats or artifacts or simply to spend the day with like-minded friends in a crystal-clear Florida spring. I have fond memories of many such expeditions.

William R. (Bill) Armistead

---

an underwater fort although other statues limit those rights to items imbedded in State owned water bottoms.

Bill earned his pharmacy Degree at Auburn University where he was a fraternity brother of Milo Howard, who for many years was the director of the Alabama Department of Archives and History in Montgomery. Bill would from time to time send reports to Milo regarding new or suspected finds.[358] During the 1960s Bill, and a group of Civil War hobbyist begin collecting artifacts from the several sites in the Mobile area. Reenactments of the area battles required uniforms, muskets, pistols and all such accoutrements including full-size cannons. Bill would sell or trade for any of those and he was a dealer for a then state of the art brand of metal detectors. I still have the used Metro-Tech he sold to me.

Display case at Olde Fort Alabama

---

[358] One such formal report that Bill and I sent to Milo Howard contained the history of and drawings of the last Civil War fort built which was at Moscow, Alabama, south of Demopolis, along with my survey of the river adjacent to the site.

Armistead at his Museum

Bill founded the Southern Skirmish Association which organized mock battles and cannon, rifle and pistol shoots all over the southeast. As his collections and his friends collections grew Bill brought them all together at his Olde Fort Alabama Museum at Alabama Port about 3 1/2 miles north of the Dauphin Island bridge. The Museum was a tourist attraction through the late 60s and early 70s that was open weekends and some week days and staffed by Bill, his wife, his brother-in-law as curator and a mostly volunteer staff. The Museum was the headquartes for Lumsens Battery, a reenactor artillery battery armed with Bill's 3-inch ordinance rifle.

Area newspapers followed closely the activities at Olde Fort Alabama. Many of the pictures here are from newspaper clippings kept in a scrapbook at the Museum. The clippings are from newspapers and magazines across the southeast but principally the *Mobile Press Register*, *The Mobile County News*, *On the Go Magazine*, *Gulf States Guide*, *Foley Onlooker*, *Mobile City News*, *Mobile This Week*, *Shelby County Reporter*, *Alabama Journal* and *Pensacola News*.

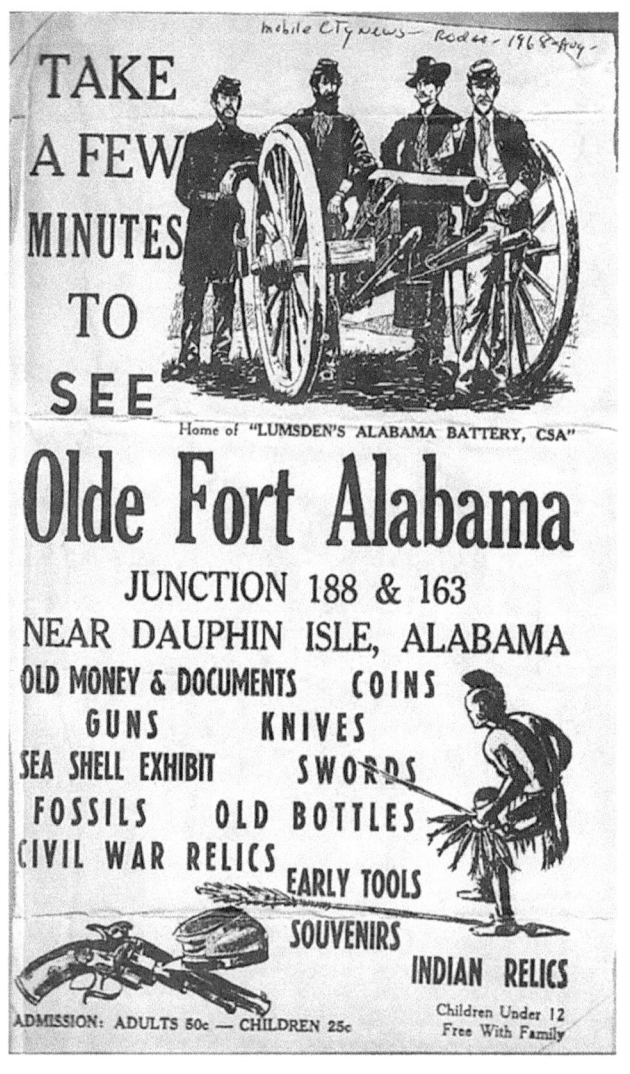

Advertisement 1968

Gun after being winched out of the bottom, Note the high-tech bilge pump on the barge

When Bill and brother in law A. C. Jones confirmed that the oyster reef cannon was indeed such Bill predictably organized his like-minded buddies to retrieve and preserve it. By then the site was identified as being the site of Fort Powell then under several feet of water. In April 1967 the group gathered equipment including timbers, come-a-longs and a small wooden barge.

"We spent weeks digging oyster shells from around it", Bill stated. "Sometimes there would be 20, 25 people in on the plan – anyone with a strong back or just interested in Civil War artifacts."[359] Moving the gun required more than just strong backs. As the gun is 10 1/4 feet long and weighed 14,850 pounds some heavy equipment was required.

On cross ties preparing to lift, Abner C. Jones on top of gun (J.C. Smallwood photo)

The best description of the effort that went into raising and preserving the cannon was found in *The Onlooker* published at Foley, Alabama, April 20, 1967. In the article bill recites a brief history of Fort Powell and states that the cannon was: "blown up and toppled over on its on its carriage, which was underneath the barrel which was found in the muck with the muzzle pointed up at an angle of about 30 degrees."

"Local oystermen told us there was a cannon out there around old Fort Powell that could be seen at low tide, so on a recent low tide Olde Fort Alabama's assistant director Clark Jones and I

---

[359] *The Mobile Press*, Suburban section, June 2, 2005, article by Deanna Burkett.

went out and searched and discovered the barrel almost totally covered with barnacles and oyster shells. This was in early April.

Volunteers preparing to lift gun,
Photograph provided by R. Stowe,
Archaelogical Services, Inc.

"So we probed it, ran a long steel rod down the muzzle which was at the 30 to 45 degree angle, and touched bottom at about 8 feet. Then we knew it really was a cannon.

"We probed around the outside of the barrel and hit a trunnion with the second probe. We pitched in and dug out the accumulated oyster shells and muck from around it and felt the trunnion under the water.

"Another thing which led us to believe there was one of the old Fort Powell guns down there, was one of the wheels of the carriage was uncovered in the oyster shells underneath the barrel.

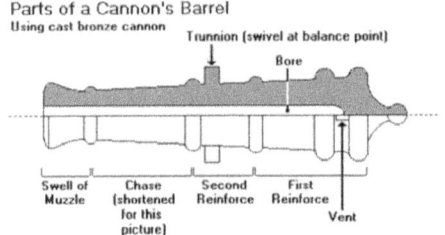

"So I contacted my friend John H. Nettles, Sr. a retired master steel rigger and salvage contractor, who offered his equipment, experience and time to help raise the cannon.

"I called on all my friends and associates who are all interested in Civil War relic collecting, and we began the longest five days hard work I've experienced in many a year.' Armistead said.

"Among those who helped were J. C. Smallwood, Dan Purvis, Frances Barrington, Dr. Sidney Phillips and sons Tex and ,Charlie , O. C. Miller, Jerry Price, Donald Pipkins, Jerry Davis, Woodrow Saranthus, Donald Whitney, Jim Bizjack and Andrew Baker. Jay Banks, his wife and sons Jimmy, Kirk and Bud came over from Metairie, Louisiana to help on the project. J. C. Smallwood took a number of photographs of the operation. Brother-in-law Jones was a regular.

"We spent five days working from 5 a.m. till dark almost every day, and it was work, digging, loading and unloading the barges which carried our tools and equipment, and fighting the tidal current as the tide changed from low to high.

"I consider it one of the greatest Confederate Civil War finds in the 14 odd years I've been collecting in South Alabama, Florida, Mississippi and Louisiana.

Into Stainless steel vat for preservation

"Now work is just beginning, as we must immerse the cannon into a bath of ten percent of sodium hydroxide for three to four weeks. The bath has to be changed then the whole gun covered with mossy zinc granules and submerged for another three to four week period, and then cleaned and lacquered.

On display at Alabama Point

"This process takes out all of the chlorides and all of the oxygen that has permeated the material during the last 103 years. At 14,850 pounds the tremendous weight involved made it impossible to load the barrel without extremely heavy lifting equipment.

"I talked to another waterfront friend, A. L. Morgan of Morgan Dredging Co., on Dog River, who has a large tug and barges, and he put me in touch with H. B. Erb, of

Displayed at the History Museum of Mobile

Erb's Wrecker Service. Erb drove a heavy duty wrecker truck aboard the barge, Capt. Morgan piloted us at high tide to the cannon site, and a few hours later Erb backed his wrecker truck off the barge at Dauphin Island and delivered the cannon to old Fort Alabama, where it was placed on display."

Armistead related that materials used to recover the cannon had to be brought to the site and assembled daily. The equipment ranged from shovels to railroad cross ties and even a jeep. They put Papa John's jeep on a 20 x 30 foot barge and ran it down the bay, pumping water to keep it from sinking. The jeep was offloaded onto a shell island that had built up behind Fort Powell and used its 5-ton winch to pull the cannon out of its bed. The wrecker was then barged to the site to pull the gun from the water. It took more than a month of effort to remove the cannon from the water then another eight months to preserve it. Armistead said "this pickling process" involved 800 gallons of water and 800 pounds of lye.

Slings were placed around the gun and crib work was gradually built up raising the gun to a level where it could be placed on a larger barge with Erb's wrecker, transported to Alabama Port and placed in a large stainless steel tank behind the "Olde Fort Alabama" Museum that Bill was then operating where the gun was preserved.[360]

Armistead with Gun at present location on Government Street

---

[360] The gun was preserved by placing it in a 10% lye solution (sodium hydroxide) for a few months, then thoroughly washed with freshwater, again covered in a 10% sodium hydroxide solution and packed with zinc for another few months after which it was washed, dried and painted. The process converts any absorbed chlorides into a stable zinc oxide. The stainless steel tank used for the preservation

In another article published in the Bayou la Batre weekly newspaper Bill stated that the gun was mounted on an iron center pintle barbette carriage of which one half was recovered. Bill surmised in a *Press Register* article, August 6, 1967 that following the magazine explosion had the gun not landed on its carriage crosswise at about a 30-degree angle it might have landed in the mud in such a way it would not been discovered. A solid brass caplock firing mechanism was still attached to the cannon. There was a projectile in the barrel.

Raising a flywheel from the Fort site

Bill's knowledge of the construction of the Fort was still sketchy at that time. He related to *The Onlooker*: "we do know that the installation was built largely on a wharf and the 'Fort' proper was made up of sandbags atop the wharf and scaffolding." Much research on that subject remained to be done.

The Flywheel on display at the History Museum of Mobile (Photo courtesy History Museum of Mobile)

The Fort Powell cannon was initially displayed at Armistead's Museum at Alabama Port. It was then donated to the History Museum of Mobile and was on display for many years at their Government Street location. The gun is now mounted near the Raphael Semmes monument in the median of Government Street

---

was later donated to the University of South Alabama Archaeology Lab. I last saw it in the 1980's at their Brookley Campus facility.

in downtown Mobile. The gun is commonly known as a 10-inch "Confederate Rodman" rifled to 6.4-Inch. It was cast by J. R. Anderson & Company (Tredegar Foundry) in Richmond, Virginia in 1861 and weighs 14,850 pounds.[361]

The gun is likely one ordered by then Major Danville Leadbetter, Acting Chief of the Engineer Bureau in Richmond. On September 2, 1861 he wrote to Captain Samuel H. Lockett at Fort Gaines that five columbiads and rifled guns had been ordered for arming Fort Gaines and thirteen for Fort Morgan. Two of those for Fort Gaines and some of those for Fort Morgan had already been forwarded. The order for armament of Fort Morgan consisted of five guns of the size and form of the 8-inch columbiad, bored as 24-pounders and rifled. The shot was about the weight of an 8-inch shot, with greater range, accuracy and power. Also ordered was a 10-inch gun, bored to a 32-pounder caliber and rifled and the remainder smoothbore 10-inch guns.[362] The 10-inch gun rifled to 32-pounder caliber describes the Fort Powell gun. [363]

---

[361] *Artillery and Ammunition of the Civil War,* by Warren Ripley.
[362] Official Records Army, series 1, volume 16, page 726.
[363] There may be another Fort Powell cannon among the several 32-pounders displayed at Fort Morgan. At page 108 the presence of such a gun on the northeast corner of the fort was noted. At page 119 it was noted that no such gun was listed in after action reports or inventories but was probably there. The *Mobile Press Register,* July 30, 1937, reported that among the cannon on exhibit at Fort Morgan was a 32-pounder, "the only known surviving relic of Fort Powell". The exact gun in the collection is not identified.

CHAPTER 13

Researching Powell

I grew up in Washington County, Alabama leaving there to take a degree from the Engineering School at Auburn University. The only history course that I took in high school or college was a U. S. Naval History course at the University of Alabama in about 1957. At the time had I not developed an interest in Civil War history. I was interested in the War of 1812, naval history and ships. I had read the Horatio Hornblower series in junior high school and that started my study of sailing navy history. I also started surface collecting for Indian artifacts at an early age and have from that time read everything I could find on the local Indians. Until I met Bill Armistead I had never done any Civil War research other than reading general histories.

I was in Mobile from 1961 through 1965 and then came back to Mobile in 1968 after completing law school at the University of Alabama. In the early 1970s one of my clients had a lease on the Fort Morgan State Park, except for the fort proper and the Coast Guard Station. Thus I had access to maps and surveys of the area which piqued my interest as to what Civil War artifacts might remain. I secured permission from the lessees to go search for such, subject to approval by the Fort Morgan Historical Commission[364] which operated Fort Morgan. Not knowing that such was not possible I proceeded to Fort Morgan and negotiated an agreement with my cousin Roger Lee Kirkland who was executive secretary/director of the Fort for the Fort Morgan Historical Commission at the time.[365] Roger Lee assured me that the Army had cleared the area of projectiles with their mine detectors in the 1950s and that I would certainly be wasting my time. That was almost a certainty, as my contract provided that if I found any projectiles, the first of any class of such recovered was to be properly preserved at my expense and

---

[364] The Alabama Historic Commission was created in 1966.
[365] Fort Morgan was transferred to the Alabama Historical Commission on January 12, 1977.

returned to the Museum at the fort. In the unlikely event that I should find any duplicates, I could keep them. No matter, as my primary interest was in the finding not the keeping.

That private permit granting permission to explore a historic site was one of the first in Alabama. I also received several more permits for other projects as will be related later. I did not own a metal detector and had never used one so I asked Read Stowe of the Archaeology Department at the University of South Alabama if he knew anything about metal detectors. He referred me to Bill Armistead.[366]

Bill was behind the counter at Dan's Drugstore in the southern part of the City when I introduced myself. I told him I had a contract that allowed me to search Fort Morgan, for which I needed a metal detector. I asked if he would be interested in participating to show me how to use such. He loaned me a detector shared his research and agreed to meet me at the site.

Author with Fort Morgan cannonballs

On the day appointed my wife Roxie, daughter Pamela and I showed up at Fort Morgan as did Bill and about six of his friends with metal detectors and shovels. We had studied the historical maps and overlaid them on recent surveys and determined the location of a mortar battery in the final Union siege lines. That was the target. We laid out a grid with stakes and lines and assigned a person with a detector to each search box. Roxie and I were assigned one of the squares.

---

[366] I had met Stowe earlier when I had called and inquired if he was interested in doing an archaeological survey for a client on a large industrial site in north Mobile County. He was interested and I think that was the first outside industrial contract job for the then fairly new Archaeology Department. Over the next 20 years so I was able to refer to him another half-dozen such contracts.

Daughter Pamela on Armistead's boat at Fort Powell

Within an hour Roxie had a huge signal about 10 feet from the airstrip. I called Bill over to check it out and his reaction was that it was much too big to be a cannonball and was no doubt a piece of track from the railroad that serviced the Spanish American War batteries. Notwithstanding I decided to see what it was and started digging. At a foot I hit a cannonball, then another and another and another. We had located 17 assorted cannonballs on a pallet.

GIs being GIs and it being August and hot and several miles back to the ammo dump, the projectiles had just been abandoned. There was a 7-inch solid shot, two 32-pounders, a 10-inch and a number of 8-inch mortar and columbiad shells. In all we found about 20 projectiles. I preserved all of them using lye and zink in 5 gallon buckets and delivered most back to Roger Lee at the museum.

I can identify my projectiles in the museum cases because everyone else painted their preserved artifacts with black rustoleum type paint. Mine were done with several brushed coats of artist acrylic final finish which is what I had available at the time and I liked the natural look.

Why did I tell that story? Not just because I find it interesting, I told it because it tells how and why I met Bill Armistead who introduced me to Fort Powell, loaned me his research notes gleaned from the Official Records and set me on a 40 year path of researching local history, searching for sunken ships and lost earthworks. I also spent some time in the water on Fort Powell and set about to determine how the fort was built and what

Author in diving gear at Fort Powell about 1978

it looked like in August 1864.

Fort Powell was Bill Armistead's project and it is not polite to interject oneself into someone else's project. So I set about to find some projects of my own. I had been certified as a scuba diver and bought a boat which I placed in dry storage at Dauphin Island Marina. It turns out that almost all of the underwater sites in the area are Civil War related. This led me to my researching all of the previously undocumented forts, batteries, ships and submarines in the area.

One of my first underwater projects was to research and locate the wreck of the Confederate vessel *Gaines* off Fort Morgan in the mid-1970s. With my research material I drew plans for and built a model of the vessel.

The major part of my law practice was Admiralty Law. I represented large ships, and most of my clients were in New York or Europe. Consequently I traveled to New York on a regular basis and when my business was concluded I would on occasion schedule a shuttle flight to Washington and spend a day or two in the Archives. A good law school student must know how to do research. A good all-around lawyer also must be comfortable with books and libraries and researching. I like to think that I was both for I always loved books and libraries and I believe I have a talent for research. Anyway I do love it.

I had annual Southeastern Admiralty Law Institute meetings in Atlanta and following which I and Roxie and daughter Pamela would drive over to Chapel Hill, North Carolina where I was working my way through the Southern Historical Society Collection. I visited libraries in New York, the New York historical Society, University libraries including Tulane University and started building a local history and particularly a local Civil War history library. I have many general Army and Navy Civil War books, but no specific Robert E. Lee or Stonewall Jackson books in my library. I do have Civil War books whose authors or subjects were affiliated with the Mobile area or relate to the local Indians or military history including ships, forts, railroads, maps etc.

I found it a mistake to study any one of the Mobile area forts in the abstract. Most of these works were designed by the same engineers. Structural details from one often translate to another. The original gun pits at Fort Powell were designed at about the same time as those of the Appalache battery (battery Tracy), and first generation battery's McIntosh and Gladden. The early gun platforms were mounted on pilings. The early three or four gun Fort Powell may have been constructed in the same manner, or not as the base was oyster shells rather than mud. Unlike Tracy, Gladden or McIntosh the few remaining scattered pilings give no guidance as to early gun placement and are as likely to be remnants of the keepers house as a gun emplacement.

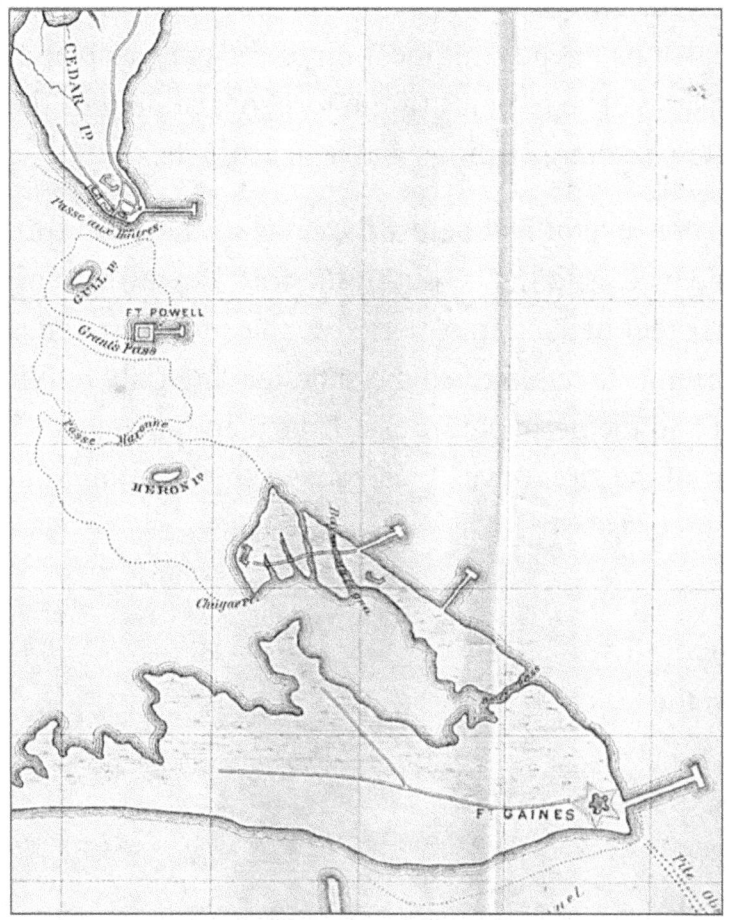

Contemporary Confederate Map (Foxhall Parker, *Battle of Mobile Bay*)

Armistead with his boat at the collapsed Dauphin Island Marina 1979

Von Sheliha learned from his experience at Island Number 10 where the gun platforms were also mounted on pilings. After a few fires over half of them dismounted. At his Mobile works (including Powell) and at Choctaw and Oven Bluffs, his guns were mounted on floating platforms. When the sand of the fort washed away all evidence of the placement of guns and magazines disappeared. The descriptions of Colonel Williams and the engineer's reports give us the general location of the guns as being on the west, east or south sides. The remains of the fort consist only of the perimeter rocks, a few scattered pilings and iron artifacts.

The artifacts are several feet below the level of the 1864 fort and also give little or no guidance as to the layout of the fort. Powell was principally built up on an oyster reef of sand transported to the site. Hurricanes, storms, waves and tidal currents have removed the sand leaving only a living, shifting oyster reef and the perimeter rocks. An exception appears to be the cannon removed from the site. It was located near the location indicated for it by the historical records.

None of the contemporary maps accurately depicted the plan of Fort Powell. The best of those maps, drawn by the Confederate Engineer in charge and signed off by General Page appears to depict the outline of the work at

Professional divers Chuck Hand and Pete Sughart (in hardhat) preparing to dive on C.S.S. *Huntsville* 1985

Cedar Point and the battery at Sughee Point. Fort Powell is represented by a simple square with an attached wharf.

My personal investigation of the site of Fort Powell consisted of 20 or more trips to the site from about 1974 until Hurricane Frederick destroyed the Dauphin Island Bridge and the dry boat storage facility at the Dauphin Island Marina in 1979. My boat was on the bottom of three tiers of boats inside the dry storage building all of which collapsed. Bill Armistead's boat was stored outside on the east side of the building which collapsed towards the west. He was able to move his boat out of the debris within a few weeks but I had to await the cutting away of the metal frames of the boat racks and building before my damaged boat could be moved. It was several years before the bridge and marina was rebuilt and I returned the boat to the Island. I did no on site exploration of Fort Powell after Hurricane Frederick. Other projects had my attentions and I had reached the conclusion that there was not much more to be learned about the design and construction of the fort from further exploration.

Raft up of boats alongside Sughart's boat on a *Huntsville/Tuscaloosa* dive. Bob Holcombe of the Confederate Navy Museum, Columbus, Georgia is in Authors boat facing aft toward motors. Jack Friend is in his boat on the far left corner.

I continued my research in books, archives and libraries. Before the Internet these searches required a great deal of travel and time. As I worked my way through archive materials, for instance, the Richard Taylor letter book at Tulane University, I made notes not only as to Fort Powell but as to all the forts, batteries, ships, submarines, operations etc. in the Mobile area.[367] Powell was usually far down my priorities list.

In about 1973 I negotiated a contract with Department of Archives and History and the Attorney General's office granting to me the exclusive right to search for and move enough mud to identify the Confederate ironclads *Huntsville* and *Tuscaloosa* in the Mobile River or the head of Spanish River and to search the Tombigbee River at Oven Bluff and the Alabama River at Choctaw Bluff. By 1980 I had a permit with the Alabama Historical Commission to search for and identify the Civil War submarine *Pioneer II*. Several years later I secured a second *Pioneer II* search permit jointly with the Baldwin County Historical Society and secured a grant from the Alabama Department of Conservation and Natural Resources. A university underwater archaeology group was brought in with no positive results.

The records available locally in the early 1960s all stated that the *Huntsville* and *Tuscaloosa* had been sunk in the Spanish River opposite Mobile. If you search the records indexed for those vessels only that will be the obvious conclusion. During the early 1960s a group of locals spent several summers in the Spanish River looking for the vessels. Not finding them and finding records where several heavily built vessels had been blown

University of South Alabama yacht during magnetometer survey of the *Huntsville/Tuscaloosa*

up in the 1870s as a part of the obstruction clearing program, they reasonably concluded that those heavily built vessels that had been exploded were the *Huntsville* and *Tuscaloosa*. In the early 1970s I read the same official Records but for all the Mobile squadron vessels. I found a reference related to the *Nashville* where she had picked up the crews of the soon to be

---

[367] I mention the Richard Taylor Letter Book because he is one of my favorite Civil War Generals. His book *Destruction and Reconstruction* is an excellent study of the war in the west and the final days in Alabama.

scuttled vessels at the *head* of the Spanish River. That is where I concentrated my search. In about 1974 Henry Baker came down from Selma to assist and a magnetic target was found there. I spent the next 10 years researching to try to determine if those vessels had been disturbed after they were scuttled and concluded that except for one small iron grabbing expedition they had not. My research also pinpointed the location of the vessels as the Mobile River at the head of the Spanish River.

In 1992 I published in *The Alabama Review*[368] an article titled: Submarines and other Secret Weapons Built and Tested at Mobile during the Civil War. The same article was later republished in the *SubCommittee Report*[369] magazine. Because of the great interest in Civil War submarines that resulted from the finding and recovery of the *Hunley* from Charleston Harbor my *Alabama Review* article was cited many times in other articles and in books. I have been told, but have not verified, that it is likely the article has been cited more than any other published in the *Review*. My sketch of the submarine *Pioneer* from that article is on the website of the Cabildo Museum of New Orleans to illustrate their artifact as it was tested during the Civil War. I have a sub bottom profiler target off Fort Morgan that I believe to be the *Pioneer II,* but I have not been able to confirm such.

During that same period I secured a permit from the Alabama Historic Commission and Corps of Engineers to move mud to identify the ironclads *Huntsville* and *Tuscaloosa* in the Mobile River, but only after I delivered a full magnetic survey of the site. I engaged Carl Helwig from New Orleans who made his living with a boat equipped with a magnetometer finding pipelines, anchors and such for the offshore oil industry. He brought his boat over and we did a magnetometer survey that showed that there were indeed two large iron objects in the search area. A detailed magnetic map was prepared of the site showing two very large anomalies that satisfied the Corps of Engineers and resulted in the granting of the permit.

With the assistance of a City of Mobile grant through a local Jaycee committee headed by Don Brannam, who was of great assistance as a

---

[368] Volume 45 no. 3, July 1992
[369] Issue 17, Summer 1994

volunteer diver on the project, I hired marine archaeologist Alan Saltus out of Louisiana and local professional divers Pete Shugart and Chuck Hand. After many dives and moving much mud with the professionals and numerous volunteers, many who were associates of Armistead, we were able to verify that the two large iron objects in the Mobile River were indeed Confederate ironclads. Following such I co-authored with Saltus a report to the Corps of Engineers identifying the vessels that up till then were thought to have been destroyed as a part of the Civil War obstruction clearing of the 1870s. All of this was obviously very time and resource consuming. Congressman Sonny Callahan, during this period, referred to me in a letter to the Alabama Historical Commission as a "historical activist." Whatever that is I suppose I was such.

Another major research effort during that period was the forts at Oven and Choctaw Bluffs in Clark County. I did on site surveys, including adjacent river bottom searches with groups of divers, prepared maps of the works, and wrote the then unknown history of those two powerful forts, together with the history of the Confederate Naval Yards at Oven Bluff and McIntosh Bluff and the three vessels built just upriver from Oven Bluff. The history was published in three volumes of the *Clark County Historical Society Quarterly* in 1995 and 1996.

In the early 1980s, I was appointed to the Board of the History Museum of Mobile where I enjoyed working with Director Caldwell Delaney and his successors. David Alsobrook, the current director of the Museum, spent many hours on an edit of this book. I served five terms as Chairman of that Board and as I write this I am still happily serving on that board. For a number of years I had shared research with and consulted with the Archeology Department of the University of South Alabama. In 1985 I was appointed Adjunct Research Associate in the Department of Sociology/Anthropology of the University of South Alabama by University President Dr. Whiddon.

In all my research I found only one detail plan of Fort Powell and one detailed description of the design and construction of the work. This description is found in the book *A Treatise on Coast Defense* by Victor Von

Sheliha published in London in 1868 and reprinted by the Greenwood Press in 1971.[370]

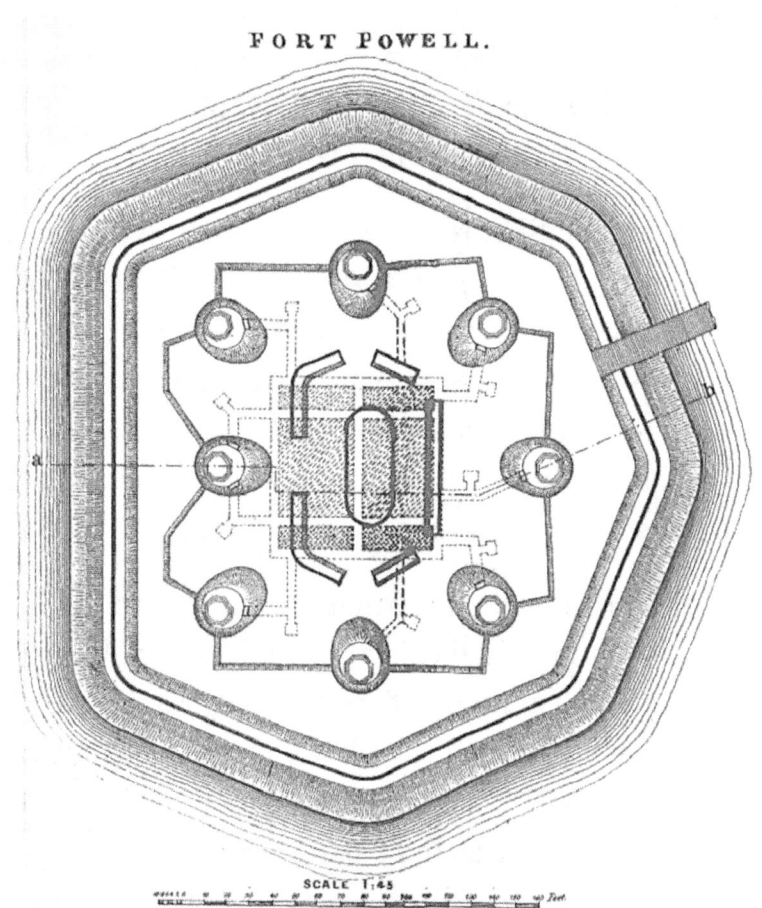

Fort Powell by Victor Von Sheliha

---

[370] My first awareness of this book was when I found an original edition in the Birmingham Public Library in the 1970s at which time I copied pertinent portions. I later found another original copy in the New York Public Library and then I found and ordered the Greenwood Press reprint edition. Today locating the book would be a simple Google search. What a wonderful resource the internet and the Google search engine are for running down such things.

Von Sheliha's drawing shows a perfectly symmetrical polygonal work. For years I was satisfied that as chief engineer and designer of the Fort his plan was correct. But was it? Von Sheliha wrote his *Treatise on Coast Defense* to demonstrate to European powers his experience in that field gained during the American Civil War and to assist him in the promotion of his patented torpedo boat. His book also included the latest European postwar innovations in coastal defense both actual and theoretical. Since Fort Powell was to illustrate the very latest technology in that class of coastal batteries then one would expect that his illustration of Powell to be neat and symmetrical.

The problem is that Von Sheliha stated that the fort was surrounded by perimeter rocks as breakwaters. The plans do not match the surveys or photographs of the perimeter rocks. Since the perimeter rocks were still in relatively straight lines I have assumed they have not been much shifted about by hurricanes or storms. The rock groins southeast of Fort Gaines have survived intact and in line through several hurricanes even though the sand that was attached to them has shifted several hundred feet.

A few years ago I organized all my materials on Fort Powell in preparation for a talk to a group of ladies on Dauphin Island. In preparation for the talk I did a painting and a model of the fort. Later, on reviewing such and particularly after studying surveys and photographs of the perimeter rocks I concluded that Von Sheliha's drawing no doubt was what he intended but not necessarily what was built as the rocks do not support his plan.

At the time I concluded that it was unlikely that the Fort would have been built outside of the perimeter rock breakwater. In January 2011 I gave another talk on the same subject and after another quick review changed my opinion and after reviewing several period drawings concluded that the fort was extended beyond the rock breakwater/perimeter. I decided at that time to put my thoughts on the subject on paper and to prepare conjectural as built plans of the fort.

The Rocks

Chapter 14

Description of the Fort

I have attempted to prepare a plan of the fort as it existed in August 1864. The starting point for a drawing is naturally Von Sheliha's drawings and description.

In his book at pages 38 – 42, in a chapter captioned "Guns mounted in barbette, even when protected by properly built traverses, may be silenced by concentrated fire from ships," Von Sheliha gives a detailed description of Fort Powell and the battery on Choctaw Bluff, on the Alabama River, 110 miles above Mobile. He considered those works to be good examples of state of the art earthwork forts. Nonetheless he concluded that the fleet would always get through unless the forts gunners were protected by ironclad walls and ship channels obstructed and mined.

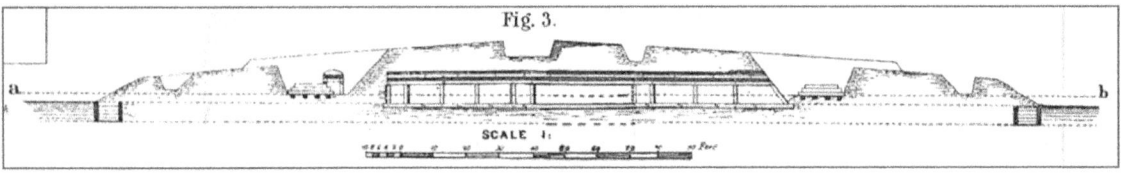

Cross section view of Fort Powell by Von Sheliha

Here is his detailed description of the fort:

"Fort Powell was built on a shell-bank, at high tide partially submerged. The terre-plein had to be raised 3 feet above high tide; and for this reason first a row of cribs (5 feet wide, 10 feet long, and 6 feet high, made of 12 each pine logs) was placed along the outside line of the basis of the work. For the filling of the space inside this line of cribs, oyster-shells were used till a level with low water outside had been reached. The cribs themselves were filled with sand, and protected by rocks on the outside. An attack from the west (Mississippi Sound) being to be expected first, the western face, first of all, was placed in a state of defense. The parapet was 8 feet high, 25 feet thick, had an interior slope of one third of its height, fell on the superior crest 2 feet, and had an exterior slope of 1 to 1. On each face of the work three guns were mounted, each standing in its own circular chamber, 18 feet in diameter at the bottom, and 24 at the top. These chambers were formed by heavy traverses, which being elevated 3 feet over the gun chamber, and reaching 9 – 12 feet over the superior crest of the parapet, extended to the bomb-proof, forming part of the parapet of the cavalier. The guns were mounted at a distance of 60 feet from center to center of their platform. In order to enable the parapet securely to withstand the effect of a heavy bombardment, it received not only the heavy profile of 25 feet, with an exterior slope of 1 to 1, but also a broad berm. On this berm another parapet, 4 feet 6 inches high, giving protection only against musketry, was built for the double purpose of gaining the greatest possible effective line of infantry-fire against boat attacks, and of giving the work at abundant supply of sand out of which to fill the sandbags necessary for the repairing the damages sustained by a heavy bombardment. A further judicious use of the large sand-masses required for the construction of this work was made by establishing traverse rifle-pits, and a line of infantry defense on the cavalier, which latter also served as position for two Whitworth guns. The bomb-proof contained the main powder-magazine, a shell and filling-room, a laboratory, a blacksmith-shop, water-tank, surgeon's-room, besides quarters for the men. A covered passage established safe communication between the gun-pits, and each gun had been provided with its own service-magazine. The traverses formed a kind of embrasures for the guns, allowing them a field of about 110° – 170°, which could be increased by cutting part of the traverses, or decreased by closing the embrasures with sand-bags. The importance of the steadiness of platforms, and the thorough securing of the pin of the chassis of the barbette-carriages having impressed itself on the mind of the chief engineer of department by his experience (dearly bought at Island No. 10, where of fifty-one guns, thirty-eight had dismounted themselves after the first fire, in consequence of badly-constructed platforms having settled in the new ground, extraordinary

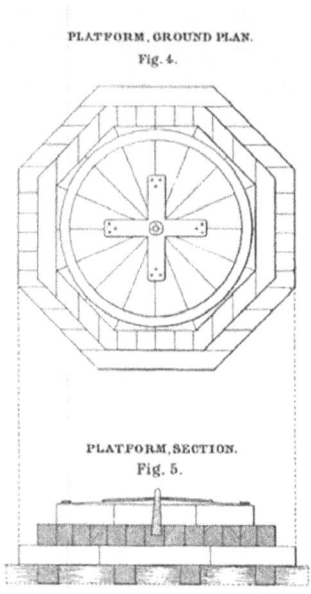

PLATFORM, GROUND PLAN.
Fig. 4.

PLATFORM, SECTION.
Fig. 5.

Plan for gun platforms at Fort Powell by Von Sheliha

care was bestowed on the laying of a firm foundation for the platforms And on making them as strong and level as possible. As a foundation served four sills, 12 x 12 inches, and 12 feet long, which were laid parallel to each other, at a distance of 3 feet from center to center; on these four other sills of equal size were laid cross-wise, with the same distance between them, the upper sills being let into the lower ones, so that the whole formed a level surface, which was 8 feet below the superior crest of the parapet. After the earth had been firmly packed in and around the sill-frame, the first platform, forming an octagon, and consisting of 14 pieces of sawn timber, 12 x 12 inches, was laid, and secured by bolts to be sill. On this another octagonal platform, consisting of 12 pieces of timber, of the same size (12 x 12 inches), and on this again a third platform, consisting of ten timbers, was securely fastened, the three platforms forming three steps, making it easy for the gun detachments, especially nos. 1 and 2, to step from their exposed position on the platform to a place giving them the advantage of being protected by the full height of the parapet. The pin rested on a disk of iron, half an inch thick, and was let through the whole of the upper and part of the middle platform; besides, it was secured by the pintle-cross, which consisted of two pieces of timber, 5 feet long, 10 inches wide, and 5 inches thick, securely fastened to the platform by iron bolts. The greatest care was bestowed on laying the traverse-circle level in all its parts. To prevent the accumulation of rain-water on the platform, planks tapering from the pintle-cross to the traverse-circle, and having a slope of one-half of an inch towards the periphery, were laid in addition. Auger-holes bored through these planks and the upper platform timbers, passing under the traverse-circle, formed small drains for water falling on the platform. The whole was saturated with rosin-oil, protecting the timbers against the influence of the weather.

"On coastal permanent fortifications foundations of granite or beton [concrete], and iron pintle-crosses, will naturally be preferred for platforms;

in provisional fortifications, however, when the engineer very often lacks time and material for carrying out more complete plans, the platform here described will be found to answer all purposes.

"The channel west of Fort Powell had been obstructed by torpedoes and a row of *chevaux-de-frise* made of railroad iron."

The above description is detailed and no doubt recites his instructions to his subordinate engineers and contractors. His plan that accompanied the description conforms generally to the above quoted description but the perimeter rocks on the site today do not. For instance, he says the guns are on 60 foot centers but the plan shows some centers to be 65 feet. Such discrepancy may seem minor but it opens the door to the possibility of more significant differences.

Which is controlling when it comes to attempting to recreate the as built plans, the plans or the perimeter rocks?

The Rocks

According to Von Sheliha's description, the rocks were placed on the outside perimeter to protect the cribs. The timber cribs and the sand filling the cribs did not survive the years of erosion. The perimeter rocks did.No records have been located that tell exactly when the rock breakwater was placed around the perimeter of the work. Etchings of the fort indicate they were in place mid-1863 and probably after the wharf was built since there appears to be a gap in the rocks where the wharf would have been located. We also do not know the source of the rocks. They were not local, but the engineers had a source up the Alabama River since we know that large rocks were brought down the Alabama River to Choctaw Bluff for use there as anchors for obstruction rafts.

Several aerial photographs exist of the site. None are entirely satisfactory as it is difficult to find the necessary combination of tide, wind, water clarity and sun angle for a clear image of the rock perimeter. The best aerial views perhaps are from Google Earth from 2006 and 2011. That site changes its aerial views every few years. We also have aerial photographs of the rocks from the 1970s.

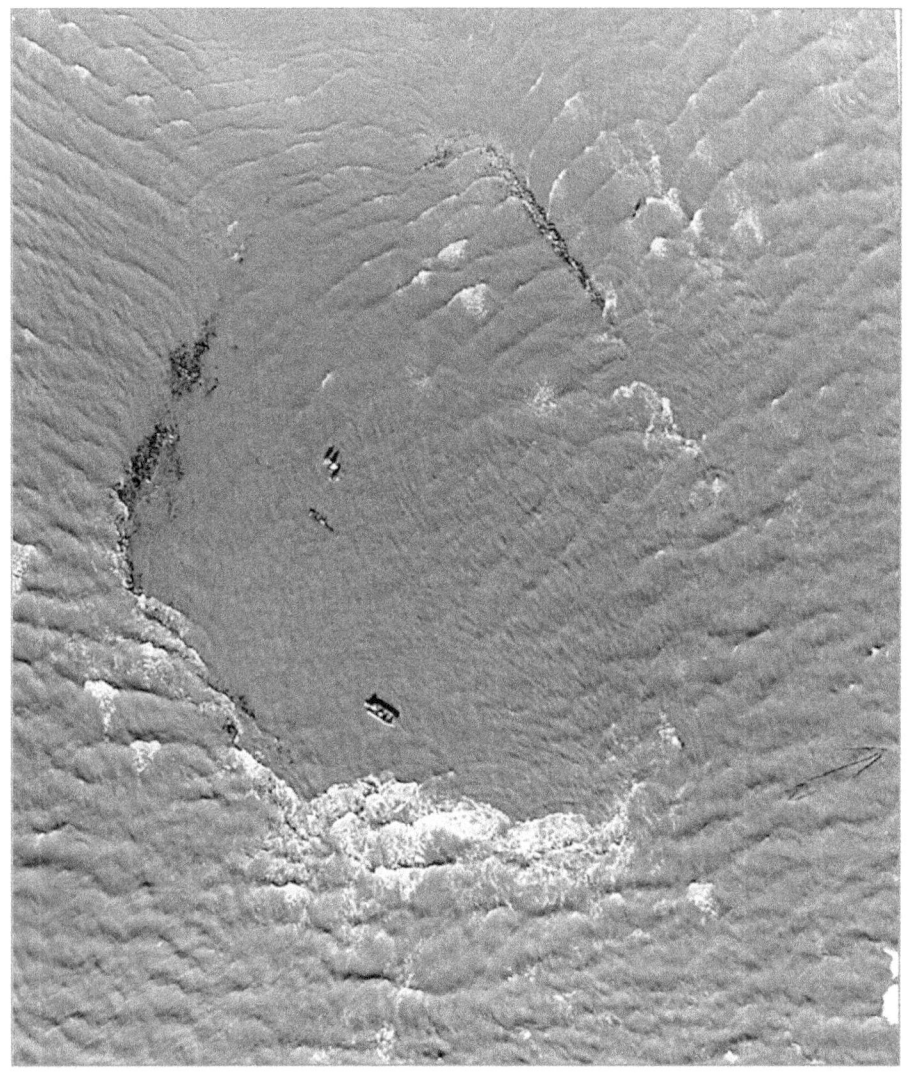

The rocks

Surveys were done in the 1960s and 70s initially by Armistead, by Odeus C. Miller and a third by Armistead and Smithweck. None of these conform exactly to the photographs attesting to the difficulty of locating the corners in the water. The photographs more closely conform to a smaller Von Sheliha's plan than do any of the surveys.

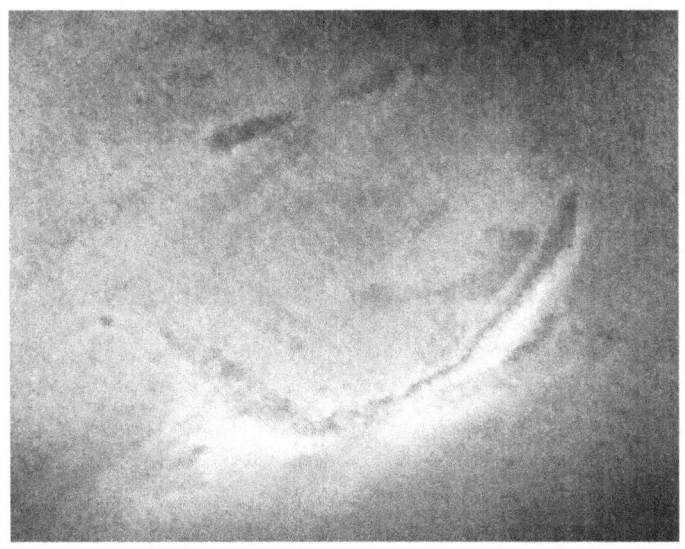
Google Earth view of the perimeter rocks

During the war there were several drawings of the fort published. These etchings were based upon drawings made by experienced and respected artists who would have been trying to deliver a realistic portrayal of the subject. The artists worked from Union gunboats some 2 miles or so from the Fort, but with a good spyglass they could pick out the details that could be seen from their viewing angle.

The drawing of the fort as it appeared in 1863 shows it to be within the rock perimeter. During early 1864 the fort was expanded to the west on a foundation of brickbats The later etchings, including the August 1864 drawing, show a wooden bulkhead/breakwater around portions of the fort.

When I initially studied and compared the various surveys, descriptions and drawings with Von Sheliha's plan, I concluded it was a plan of what he would have preferred, not necessarily what was actually under construction. However, upon further reflection, it is clear that Von Sheliha did design and actually build elaborate structures, indicated

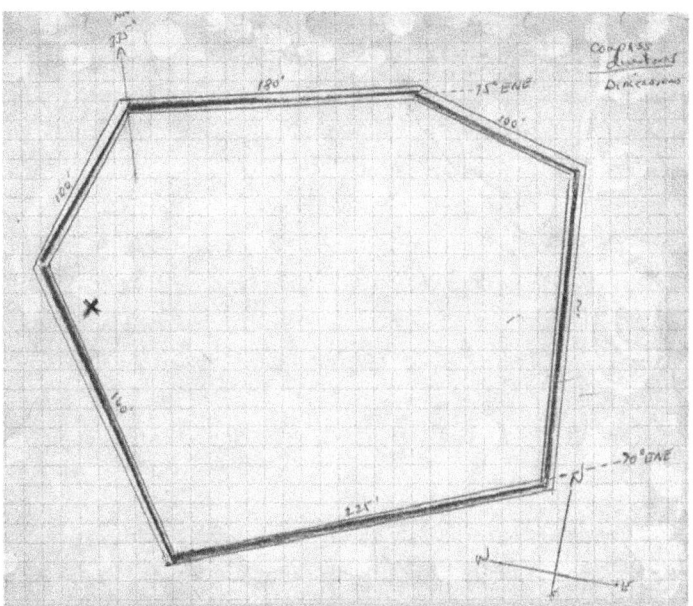
Bill Armistead survey of the perimeter rocks. The X marks the location of the recovered cannon

by the plans of the forts in the Mobile defenses. They were huge in scale, elaborate in detail and were actually built according to his plans.

The rocks and the plan are not necessarily inconsistent. The perimeter rocks and later the bulkhead simply protected the foundation upon which the fort was built. Von Sheliha's plans in his book are for only the fort and do not intend to show any portions of the Island foundation inside the perimeter rocks or bulkhead that are not within the footprint of his plan. Thus my conjectural or reconstructed "as built" plan shows some perimeter rocks which were back filled with sand outside the footprint of the Fort.

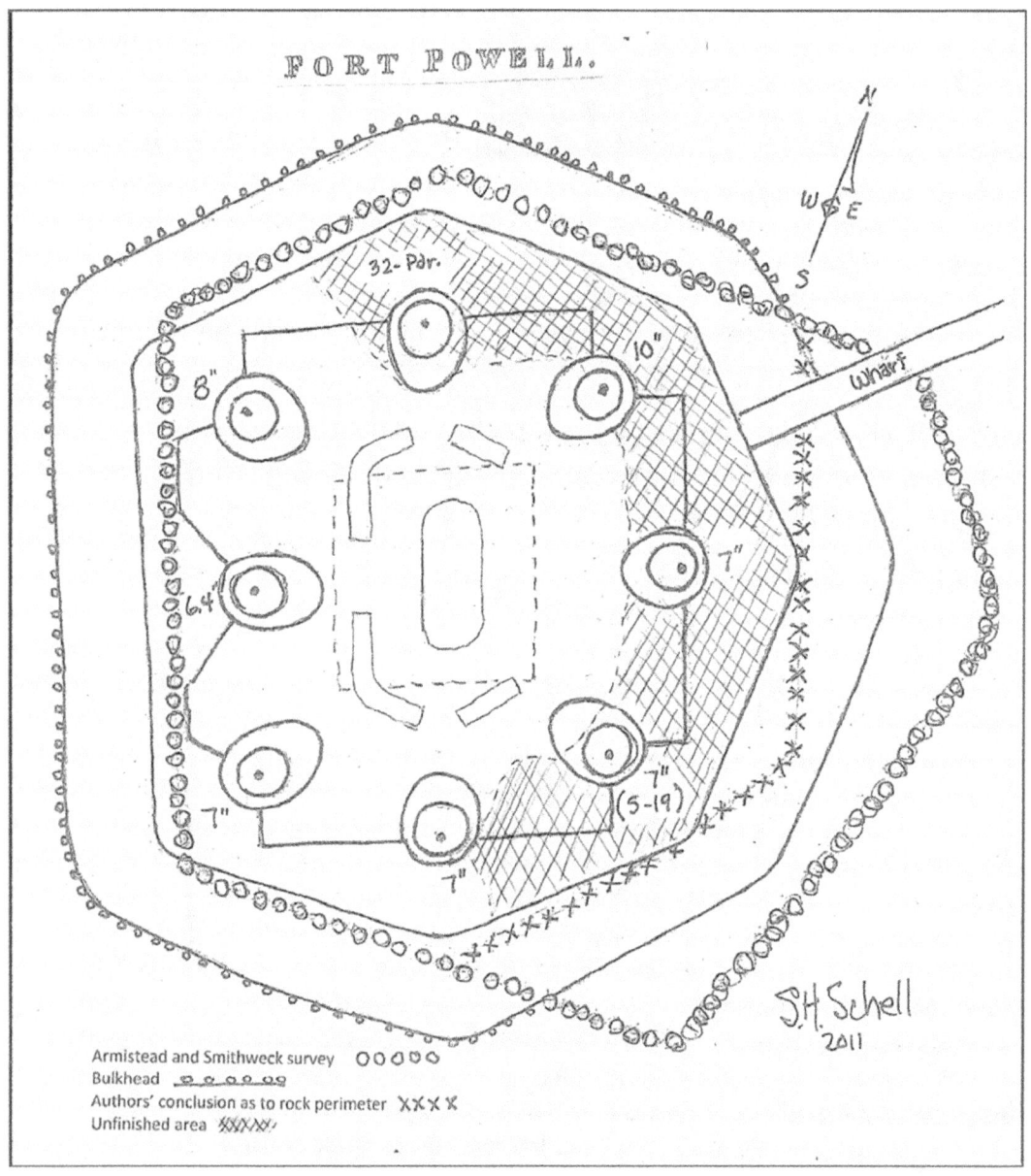

Conjectural "as built" plan of Fort Powell by Author

The east side of the fort was unfinished. The north side was unapproachable by ships, but an assault on Mobile was expected from Pascagoula which would have put Cedar Point within reach of Union troops. So the north side had to be built up to resist fire from any Federal battery that might have been established there. Thus the north side might have been completed. I do not think it was although there was apparently a 32-pounder mounted there.

Aerial View of perimeter rocks enhanced with markings

The "as built" drawing is based upon the dimensions of the Armistead and Smithweck survey modified to more accurately conform with photographs and some of my early on site drawings all overlaid to scale with Von Sheliha's plan.

The reports of Colonel Williams and others indicate which portions of the east face were unfinished in August 1864. My "as built" plan utilizes all of these reports while being mindful that Williams in explaining to his superiors why he evacuated the fort may have understated the readiness or completeness of the work.

Von Sheliha was a skilled experienced engineer and inventor. His post war book was crafted to exhibit his skill and experience. Fort Powell was the only one of his forts illustrated in his book so it is understandable that it would be shown as he had intended it to be completed.

Fort Powell was not Von Sheliha's strongest water battery. That would be battery Gladden, but only because there was more time to finish it and heavier 11-inch Brooke guns were available to arm it. If Von Sheliha had been given complete control, time and resources he would no doubt have built an impenetrable casemate work sheathed in iron surrounded by piles and torpedoes. He had no such luxury and sand was the best material he had available.

Sketch of the perimeter rocks by Author about 1978

Only iron could resist the heavy guns of the Union Navy. A sand fort offered better resistance to heavy projectiles than the brick forts in existence at the beginning of the war. But sand as a fort building material had its drawbacks.

Late in the war Rear Adm. David D. Porter was asked to provide his written views on seacoast fortifications. Porter obliged. His views are included in Von Sheliha's postwar book[371] pages 158 – 173. Porter noted that prior to the war it was thought that one gun on shore was worth 10 guns on a ship. That, he said, was probably true when it's one gun and one ship but when it's 100 shipboard guns versus ten shore side guns the 100 can generate such a sustained fire that even guns protected by parapets and well traversed become untenable.

Porter noted that sand itself as a fort building material had inherent drawbacks, even if the guns are spaced well apart with heavy intervening traverses. A heavy shell striking or exploding on the traverse, knocks the

---

[371] *Treatise on Coast Defense.*

sand into the muzzles of the guns, and disables them as effectively as if they were dismounted. Porter noted that happened at Fort Fisher, long before the guns were dismounted by Union shells. Secondly, sandbags and sods were thrown upon the circles, and prevented the training of the guns. They were also thrown upon the gunners. The sods used by Von Sheliha were probably more effective than the sandbags at Fort Fisher but it was obvious from the work of the *Chickasaw* that heavy shells did displace much sand.[372]

Powell was not intended to be a permanent work. Good enough was sufficient. The time, material and manpower, all of which was in short supply, expended to provide a neat geometrically correct structure paid no dividends. The fort was in essence simply a large sand covered bombproof, magazine, and workshop with guns surrounding at a minimal distance. Neatness does not count in a cannon fight. But its purpose was to prevent an incursion into Mobile Bay from the Mississippi Sound. It accomplished its design purpose.

---

[372] General Page in his Telegraph Book entry March 13, 1864 considered using hides on bomb proofs to keep sand from blowing off. It does not appear this method was used in this area.

CHAPTER 15

Artifacts

I am not a Civil War relic or artifact collector. I do have a few projectiles that have been given to me over the years and a few duplicates from Powell and from my previously described Fort Morgan expedition. I have never dug a minie' ball but what I do have is a large collection of books, maps, research notes and files. I have enjoyed the research and the occasional location of a site or vessel long since lost. Most of my Fort Morgan projectiles are in the Museum there and almost all of the artifacts that were recovered from Fort Powell are in the History Museum of Mobile. Two of the projectiles in the collection of the History Museum of Mobile are to me unique. Those are a 7-inch Brooke shell that tells a unique story and an 11-inch solid shot that should not have been there.

The log of the monitor *Chickasaw* shows that it fired 25 *shells* into the East face of Fort Powell. I find no record of any other 11-inch projectiles being fired at the fort. I assume that it was fired into the fort because the Confederates had no 11-inch smoothbore guns and the Union did not place any there after the fort was captured.[373] One plausible explanation is that the *Chickasaw* had been firing solid shot into the *Tennessee* and her guns were loaded with such when the order came to bombard Fort Powell with shell. The easiest way for the gunner to remove the solid shot was to simply pull the lanyard.

In the late 1970s I spent a number of days exploring the remains of Fort Powell. You brought your boat into the middle of the perimeter rocks between two PVC pipes on the east side that we called the "gate." The gate was placed by Armistead to mark a small gap, probably where the wharf would have prevented the laying of rocks.

---

[373] Following the war the Union Army collected all captured confederate artillery at warehouses and then transported it to points north where such was eventually displayed as trophies or melted as scrap.

David Smithweck and the Author on one of our many expeditions

At the time I had a 14 foot fiberglass skiff with a 33 horse power Evinrude motor. The motor was a Johnson until I lost the cover en route from Dauphin Island to Mobile and replaced it with a used cover of a sister brand. The boat had been given to me by Dick Boykin after a thief had turned it loose in the Lower Bay and its bottom was battered on the rocks at Fort Morgan. I patched it up and used it as an inshore diving boat until Hurricane Frederick dropped a tree on it in my backyard.

There is almost always a tidal current flowing over Fort Powell. Modern anchors simply do not dig in or hold on an oyster reef. Even with my 14 foot skiff I used an old-fashioned approximately 25 pound anchor with large flukes and a 6 foot chain between the anchor and rope.

To anchor on the site you must maneuver your boat through the gate, pick the point where you wish to set the anchor, throw the anchor overboard then immediately jump overboard and set the fluke in the reef with your foot. If you gaged the current and wind correctly and secured a correct amount of line to the boat then the current would not drift the boat onto the rocks or onto to the old iron boiler or water tank that was in the middle of the place. Anchoring was best done with two people, one to maneuver the boat off the rocks while the other set the anchor. My friend David Smithweck handled the anchor line on many of these expeditions.

One weekend I was alone at the site in my gift skiff when I picked up a large signal with a handheld underwater metal detector and started digging. You may ask; how does one dig a hole underwater in an oyster reef? It is not easy and takes some planning.

My usual kit for such a project was: in the fall a wetsuit or at least a wetsuit upper or vest. In the summer a bathing suit and an old T-shirt was sufficient. Always needed was a wetsuit hood to operate the underwater metal detector as the single flat earphone had to be tucked under the hood over the ear. I also wore sneakers, basketball player pull on kneepads and vinyl covered cotton gloves, yellow not black, as the black ones were too slippery.

For digging I used very simple tools. A long screwdriver to loosen the shells and a small three prong handheld gardeners rake to move them. I also had a 5 foot steel probe that could probe a foot or so into the shells. Shovels or trowels did not work. A water jet attached to a portable pump did not work as it would make a small hole until the shells starting falling right back into the hole. I also carried a knife, a length of cord and an inflatable float to mark locations.

Even though you may be only in three or 4 feet of water you still needed your dive mask, snorkel, scuba tank and regulator as well as a weight belt to hold you on the bottom. Oyster shells are like little knives. A medical kit containing a good antibiotic for the inevitable cuts and a meat tenderizer to treat jelly fish stings was a necessity.

Digging the target I found the top of an encrusted 11-inch 166 pound solid shot 18 inches deep in the reef. By the time I had the projectile uncovered so that I could jiggle it a bit I had dug a very large hole. Even though I was by myself I had plenty of sheepshead fish in the hole with me to keep me company. I could not roll the ball out of the hole and had no chance of lifting it into the boat. I left it, went home and called Bill Armistead who agreed to meet me the next day to see if we could get the shot in the boat.

The next day I returned with Bill and a wire milk carton basket, a heavy iron bar about 6 feet long and a rope. I rolled the ball into the carton at the bottom of the hole, turned it upright and lashed the bar to the carton. I took one end, Bill took the other and we stood up with the bar on our shoulders. We were about 6 inches short of being able to drop it into the boat. For the purpose of dropping a large cannonball 12 inches or so into the bottom of the boat, I had a wooden 24 count Coca-Cola carton to cushion the impact. We scoured the bottom and found some bricks and a half of a concrete block and with those and oyster shells built mounds to stand on. On our mounds we were able to drop the shot with several pounds of encrustation together with the milk carton into the boat. I brought it home, cleaned off the encrustation by tapping with a hammer, preserved it and in due course delivered it to the Museum where it is now in their collection.[374]

The other unusual Fort Powell projectile in the Museum collection is a 7-inch Brooke shell that was probably cast in Selma. It is not the projectile itself that is unusual. It is what was inside the shell that makes it unique.

I previously related the story of Brooke gun S-19 that was delivered untested to the Confederate Navy and loaned to the Army, who put it into immediate service at Fort Powell during Farragut's bombardment in February 1864. This is the gun where exploding shells blew off the end of the barrel. The barrel was trimmed up and the gun was put back into service and used against the monitor *Chickasaw*. When the gun was inspected after the explosion in February it was thought to have some defects in the barrel from the casting process. The officers considered it to be serviceable, but it appears that the crew of the gun did not trust it.

The projectile was found under a foot of oyster shells in the remnants of a shell box at or near the location of the service magazine for gun S-19. It is a percussion projectile with its fuse in place. After it was preserved and coated I had it sitting on my desk in my library.[375] All the lathe marks were clearly visible and the brass fuse threads appeared to be clean. I placed a cloth over the fuse to protect against marks and gave it a nudge with a large pair of pliers. To my surprise the fuse turned freely and I unscrewed it.

---

[374] Farragut's wooden fleet contained a total of about six 11-inch Dahlgren guns. Williams says that the only vessel that fired on the fort from the east was the monitor *Chickasaw*. None of the vessels in Mississippi sound had an 11-inch gun. Only the *Chickasaw* was ordered to bombard the fort. I find no record of any 11-inch projectiles fired into the fort other than from the *Chickasaw*.

[375] The Fort Powell projectiles were preserved at the University of South Alabama Archeology Laboratory on their Brookley Campus.

Since the fuse was screwed all the way in I expected that the striker safety pin had been removed and it was. The shell was ready to be fired. However, I found a buildup of white corrosion around the striker that prevented any movement. I laid out a piece of paper on my desk and upended the shell to pour out some of its contents. I expected to find black granular gunpowder. I found no such thing.

Instead of gunpowder the shell was filled with sand and enough red clay to give the sand mixture a reddish tint and with bits or flecks of oyster shells. This was the material from which the fort was built. I find no record that any red claylike material or red sand was used but I did find red clay embedded under the sabot of a Union projectile fired into the fort. Perhaps the red sand or clay came to the fort with the sods.

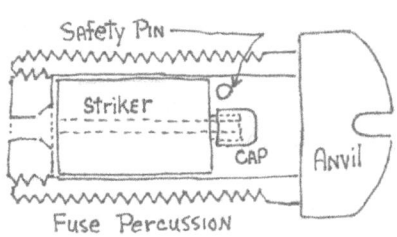

Sketch by Author

Why would the gunners fill a perfectly good percussion projectile with inert material? They had bolts (solid shot) available so there was no need to improvise. The only plausible answer appears to be that the crew of S-19 was fearful the gun would explode if shells were used in the weapon. They did not want more shells exploding in the barrel of the gun with the resultant risk of another explosion of the gun.

There were a few instances during the Civil War where gunners would fill hollow shot with sand to attack <u>forts</u> or ships. After the capture of the *C.S.S. Florida,* she had onboard no solid shot or bolts for her broadside 6-inch Blakely rifled guns. Instead she had 6-inch shells filled with sand.[376]

On March 5, 1862 the U.S.S. *Satellite* fired sand-filled shells from her Parrott gun at a Confederate battery on Aquia Creek, Virginia.[377] Fort McAllister, Georgia fired 10-inch mortar shells filled with sand at Union

---

[376] Official Records Navy, series 1, volume 3, page 261. The average weight of the powder filled 6 inch percussion shell from the *Florida* was 51.968 pounds while the average weight of a 6 inch shell filled with sand was 53.5 pounds.

[377] Official Records Navy, volume 5, page 610.

monitors in March 1863. They observed one such shell striking a monitors deck and "breaking to pieces."[378] That observation no doubt discouraged further use of sand filled projectiles, but the Union Navy saw it differently. They reported that the monitors' deck plating and planking were too weak and the sand filled shell would have gone clean through the deck had it not struck an iron beam.[379]

Another instance of a sand filled projectile striking a Union monitor occurred at Battery Gregg, Morris Island, South Carolina, on August 18, 1863. That shell filled with sand was "shivered to atoms, without affecting any material injury."[380] The U.S.S. *Mount Vernon* off New Inlet Bar near Fort Fisher, North Carolina, "Expended 10 pounds cannon powder, one 100-pound sand shot, firing at a schooner."[381]

No doubt there were other instances of sand filled projectiles used during the Civil War, but they were rare. I suspect that the Fort Powell specimen in the History Museum of Mobile may be the only remaining sand filled Civil War projectile. That would make it rare indeed. Each of the projectiles from Fort Powell has a story. I found these two to be the most interesting.

---

[378] Official Records Navy, volume 13, page 731.
[379] Official Records Navy, volume 13, page 727.
[380] Official Records Army, volume 46, page 533 and Official Records Navy, volume 14, page 487.
[381] Official Records Navy, volume 9, page 778, June 29, 1863.

Conclusion

If you are driving south on the Dauphin Island Bridge look to your right just before the bridge starts to climb to pass over the Intra-coastal Waterway. If there is a tidal flow and the sound is reasonably calm you will see a ripple of current caused by the perimeter rocks or if the tide is low you may actually see some of the rocks. You will be looking at the site of Fort Powell with Grants Pass immediately to the south of it.

Fort Powell survived one attack from the front but was not ready for the attack from the rear and was blown up by its own garrison. Yet it served its purpose for a time and its history, which includes the history of those that built, defended and attacked it, deserved to be told. I hope you enjoyed the telling.

APPENDIX NUMBER 1

The 21st Alabama Regiment and Lt. Colonel J.M. Williams

Timeline

1. October 1861 – the 21st Alabama formed at Mobile. J.M. Williams enlisted as first Sargent of Company A (Washington Light infantry). On October 13 the Mobile Cadets no. 2 mustered in and was assigned to the 21st as company K.

2. October 17, 1861 – sent to camp Hall's Mill (now Tillmans Corner) just west of Mobile.

3. November 16, 1861 – transferred to Fort Gaines.

4. December 13, 1861 – Williams resigned his rank of Sargent and joined the ranks as a private.

5. February 1, 1862 - with the "Army of Mobile" under General J.M. Withers at Gaines, Powell, Cedar Point and west along the Alabama coast.

6. February 1862 – Late in month returned to Hall's Mill and brigaded with 22nd and 25th Alabama and the first Louisiana Regiments under Brigadier General A. H. Gladden.

7. March 5, 1862 – Gladden's brigade transferred to the "Army of the West," commanded by General A. S. Johnston and ordered to Fort Pillow,

Tennessee where it remained for about two weeks when it removed to Corinth, Mississippi and was assigned to Withers division of Braggs Corps.

8. March 1862 – Williams was elected 2nd. Lieutenant of company A. Because of the absence of two senior officers he led the company at Shiloh.

9. April 6 – 7, 1862 – battle of Shiloh with General Gladdon's brigade.

10. April – following the battle and on return to Corinth the Regiment was reorganized and its enlistment extended to "for the war." Williams was elected Captain and the Regiment assigned to the brigade of General J. K. Jackson on picket duty at nearby Monterey, Mississippi. Williams appointed regimental adjutant.

11. May 8 – 28, 1862 – Regiment participated in skirmishes at and around Farmington, Mississippi.

12. May 30, 1862 – Corinth evacuated and Regiment fell back to Tupelo, Mississippi.

13. June 6, 1862 – Was at battle of "Blacklands" outside Tupelo.

14. July 26, 1862 – Regiment transferred to the "District of the Gulf," assigned to artillery at Fort Morgan. Williams commanded a battery.

15. October 1862 – Williams promoted to Major. Williams and four companies (first Battalion) transferred to Oven and Choctaw Bluffs, 2nd battalion under Colonel C.D. Anderson at Forts Morgan and Gaines.

16. June 1863 – Lieutenant Colonel C. S. Stewart was killed by the explosion of a gun at Fort Morgan. Williams was promoted to Lieutenant Colonel and ordered back to Fort Morgan to command the second Battalion.

17. Fall 1863 – to Pollard under Brigadier General James Canty.

18. January 1864 – the Regiment was assigned to General R. L. Page commanding defenses of lower Mobile Bay. Two companies to Fort Morgan, six companies to Fort Gaines and two companies (Mobile Cadets and Battle Guards) to Fort Powell. Colonel C. D. Anderson in command at Gaines, Williams at Powell and General Page at Fort Morgan.

19. February 1864 – defended Fort Powell against Farragut's fleet.

20. April 4—Regiment brigaded with 17th and 29th Alabama Regiments and ordered to Rome, Georgia but made it only to Pollard, Al.

21. April 17, 1864 – The regiment was ordered by General Garner to report to General Page. Williams and a section to Fort Powell. A detachment was at Cedar Point.

22. August 5, 1864 – Battle of Mobile Bay. Fort Powell evacuated. The Cadets and Battle Guards to Alabama Port. After the fall of Fort Morgan both removed to batteries Huger and Tracy under Captain B. Frank Dado. Williams was suspended pending court-martial for the loss of Fort Powell.

23. September 1864- Williams vindicated by Court Martial and placed in command of Redoubts 4, 5, 6 and Battery K in the Mobile defenses.

24. December7 1864-Williams placed in command of Batteries Huger and Tracy.

25. Winter 1864 – The Cadets and Battle Guards to Fort Blakely were they were joined by the six companies of their Regiment who had surrendered Fort Gaines. The other two companies, captured at Fort Morgan never rejoined as they were retained on Ship Island to the close of the war.

26. March 1865 – in Mid-March 8 Companies then comprising the 21st under Lt. Colonel Williams was sent to reinforce the Garrison at Spanish Fort under Brigadier General J. T. Holtzelaw.

27. March 21 – April 8, 1865 – siege of Spanish Fort.

28. April 8, 1865 – Garrison evacuated Spanish Fort through marsh to Blakely and took boats for Mobile. Six Cadets, part of rear guard were captured.

29. April 9, 1865 – after remaining in Mobile about 24 hours the Regiment was ordered to evacuate up the M&O railroad to Cuba station near York, Alabama.

30. May 4 – 21, 1865 soldiers of the Regiment surrendered at Cuba Station, Alabama in Sumter County.

31. May 10 1865 – the soldiers that surrendered at Cuba Station were paroled at Meridian, Mississippi. The war was over and they made their way back to Mobile.

APPENDIX NUMBER 2

Grants Pass Water Bottoms and Grants Island Possession and Ownership

Timeline

1. The State of Alabama, when admitted to the Union was placed in possession of to all the navigable waters and bottoms of the State not previously granted. The United States reserved title, for military purposes, to the several islands existing in 1842 between Dauphin Island and Cedar Point.
2. February 2, 1839 – the Alabama Legislature granted a franchise to John Grant for a period of 25 years to dredge a toll channel between Mobile Bay and Mississippi Sound. Grant completed the channel and built a small island on the North side of the channel from dredge spoil, went into possession of the island and began collecting tolls for the use of his channel.
3. 1861 – Confederate forces take possession of the island and channel. Fort Powell is built on Grants dredge spoil Island on the north side of the Pass.
4. February 2, 1864 – Grants permit set to expire but would have been extended by equity for the time of the war and in fact was extended by acquiescence of the State of Alabama.
5. August 1865 – U.S. forces captured Fort Powell and the Pass and retained possession thereof.
6. September 1865 – John Grant petitioned the United States by letter to President Johnson for reinstatement of his franchise. The United States military had occupied the island built by Grant from the dredge spoil and the fort built thereon as well as the channel as captured property. Grant alleged that he was the owner of Grants Pass an artificial channel which connects Mobile Bay with Mississippi Sound which work was constructed under a charter from the Alabama Legislature. He stated he also built an artificial island at the pass, that he was always a loyal

citizen of the U.S., voted against dissolution, never held Confederate office and never contributed voluntarily one dollar to any organized force of the rebellion against the U.S.

7. October 23, 1865 – U.S. puts Grant back in possession of pass and island: "Mr. John Grant is hereby reinstated in the possession of the artificial channel between Cedar Point and Dauphin island, in the County of Mobile, known as Grants Pass, and of the artificial shell bank island constructed by him at said pass, and in all the rights and privilege conferred on him and reference thereto, by and act of the Legislature of Alabama." Subject to free use by U.S. Government vessels

8. April 1866 – Grant successfully sues boat operators in an effort to collect tolls in the courts of Louisiana. Although the issue before the court was the right to collect tolls Grant maintained that his grant from the State of Alabama was not revoked, and was one that could not be revoked without remuneration for the expenditure incurred by him, citing numerous authorities in support of that position. The court found that the legislature had given Grant: "a license coupled with an interest." There are numerous Alabama Supreme Court cases, mostly relating to timber, mining and oil and gas leases that delineate the rights under such an interest. Grant made no claim in that lawsuit that his license had morphed into a fee simple ownership.

9. 1884 – Grant died.

10. September 1887 – Grants will probated in Mobile County. The inventory consisted of property known as "Grants' Pass" and the franchises appertaining thereto together with the island made by Captain Grant when he excavated the channel with all the tenements thereon. The property was appraised as "real estate" with a value of $15,000.

11. April 1887 – Petition by administrators to sell assets of Grants estate. The petition invoked the 4th section of the Alabama Legislative Act wherein power was given to Grant to sell or convey the "rights and privileges conferred on him by the act" indicating that the administrators considered that they held the property subject to the franchise granted Grant by the State of Alabama.

12. 1888 – The executors of the estate of John Grant filed an accounting for the period May 18, 1888 to December 24, 1889. The accounting showed revenues from the pass of $1498.25 and expenses from the

operation of $1119.80. Payments included keeper John Reeds salary, oil for the lamp, lumber, shingles, nails, caulking etc. for maintaining the keeper's house on the island.

13. December 16, 1889 – Date set for sale of the property. The advertisements for bids in newspapers referred to: "the following described property"***Grants Pass with the right to charge tolls, etc. – following the sale the court entered an order confirming the sale for $7400 to Felix McGill and Arthur McGill to all that land and property known as Grants Pass with the rights and benefits etc., together with all franchises, rights etc. as granted by the State of Alabama.
14. December 30, 1889 – Deed from the Estate of Grant to Felix and Arthur McGill conveying such land and franchise.
15. 1908 – Deed from the heirs of the McGills to the Catholic Bishop of Mobile conveying: "the land and the franchises known as Grants Pass and the island made by John Grant when he excavated the channel."
16. 1915 – No tolls were collected for the use of Grants Pass since about the time of World War I according to conversation with Vince Kilborn attorney for the Bishop.
17. 1915 to 1920 – The toll keeper's house was given by the Bishop of Mobile to Mr. Jimmy Mallon who demolished the house and used the materials to build a house on Dauphin Island.
18. 1955 – Deed from the Bishop of Mobile to the Mobile Chamber of Commerce conveying property with the same description as number 13.
19. 1974 – Deed from Chamber of Commerce to the University of South Alabama using the same description as above.
20. December 13, 1982 – Alabama attorney General Charles A. Graddick issued a finding to the Governor that the University of South Alabama through its predecessors in title had been in *adverse possession* of "Grants Pass" for more than 20 years prior to May 1, 1908 consisting of 7644 acres of water bottoms and islands.
21. December 13, 1982 – Alabama Governor Fob James, based upon Attorney General Graddick's findings, signed and issued to the University of South Alabama a patent for the same 7644 acres. Such patent is recorded in the land patents, volume 10, page, 889.
22. December 17, 1982 – The University of South Alabama by deed that stated that the University claimed 15,286 acres but settled with the State of Alabama for a patent for 7664 acres, granted to the State and the citizens of Alabama a permanent easement over the submerged real property for commercial and recreational navigation purposes and all

interest to the marine life covered in the patent including the oyster reefs. The deed pointed out that nothing restricted the University from entering into any future conveyances or leases in respect to the minerals, mineral rights and the right to lease. The University had or subsequently leased the minerals and is believed to have a received royalties for the natural gas produced from under the reef.

23. July 19, 1984 – The circuit court of Montgomery County, Alabama dismissed a lawsuit filed by the University of South Alabama against the State of Alabama in which the University tried to recover the remainder of the claimed 15,286 acres alleged to be a part of "Grants Pass" or water bottoms associated therewith on the basis of adverse possession. The court found that title was not vested with the University since the State could not lose its title the bottom lands by adverse possession. – As reported by Cumberland Law Review, volume 20, page 367, Montgomery County Cir. Ct. No. 83-1242, slip opinion at page 1.

24. Conclusion: a) Under Alabama law one cannot adverse possess against the State. b) Permissive use cannot ripen into adverse possession. To change permissive use status there must be a positive disclaimer – actual notice to the owner. c) Grants Island was filled land, not fast land. Filled land cannot ripen into title absent written consent or a permit from the State. d) Title to water bottoms under a man-made filled island that washed away by natural forces remains in the State. e) The licensees rights under a license coupled with an interest reverts to the grantor, or then fee owner when the purpose of the license is done, such as when a producing field is depleted and shut down under an oil and gas lease. f) Grants Island by 1950 had disappeared as a result of avulsion. g) Title to the site of Fort Powell rests in the University of South Alabama only as a result of the patent mentioned in 18 above. h) Unless there is some agreement between the University and the State of Alabama not apparent from the documents mentioned above, or unless Code of Ala. Sec. 41-3-1 is applicable then statutes regulating vessels or objects embedded in State water bottoms have no application to Fort Powell.

Bibliography

American Railroad Journal and Mechanics Magazine, Vol. 2, 1839.

Annual Report of the Chief of Engineers, United States Army, to the Secretary of War for the year 1895, part two. Washington: Government printing office, 1895.

Arnold, J. Barto lll -*The Denbigh's Civilian Imports.*

Bartleson, John D. Jr. -*Civil War Explosive Ordnance*, 1861 – 1865, U.S. Navy, 1972, Washington, US Government Printing Office.

Battles and Leaders of the Civil War, 1884-87.

Bearss, Edwin C - *Historic Structure Report, Administrative Data Sections, Fort on Ship Island (Fort Massachusetts) 1857-1935.*

Bell, Jack -*Civil War Heavy Explosive Ordinance, 2003.*

Bergeron, Arthur W. Jr. -*Confederate Mobile,* University Press of Mississippi, 1991.

Blackwood's Edinburgh Magazine, American Edition – volume 16, New York 1865, A Visit to the Cities and Camps of the Confederate States, 1863 – 64 , Part 3.

Borrensen,Thor - Simon Bernard and America's Coastal Forts, *The Regional Review*, February 1939, National Parks Service.

Boudousquie -1889 map by Paul C. Boudousquie, Alabama Department Archives and History map collection.

Brewer, Willis - *Alabama, Her History, Resources, War Record, and Public Men,* 1872.

Budiansky, Stephen - *Perilous Fight, America's Intrepid War with Britain on the High Seas, 1812 – 1815,* (2010).

Buchanan Letter Book, Southern Historical Society Collection, University of North Carolina, Chapel Hill.

Call, Lewis W. - *United States Military Reservations, National Cemeteries and Military Parks*, revised edition: 1910, Washington Government Printing Office.

Canny, Donald L. -*The Old Steam Navy*, volume 2, Naval Institute Press, 1993.

Civil War Naval Chronology, 1861 – 1865, Naval History Division, Washington, US Government Printing Office, 1971.

Clarke County Historical Society Quarterly, 1995-96.

Coker, William S. -*The Mobile Cadets 1845-1945*, an Anonymous Manuscript edited by William S. Coker, Patagonia Press, 1993.

Corps of Engineers Library map collection drawer number 1, maps 2-6, Grants Pass Railroad bridge location, 1893.

Cox, B.B.-*The Mobile Register*, Mobilian Tells of This City in Civil War, Nov. 1, 1915.

Davis, Jefferson --*Papers of Jefferson Davis*, Volume 2, June 1841-July 1846.

Davis, Virgil S.-*A History of the Mobile District*, U.S. Army Corps of Engineers 1815 to 1971, Mobile District, 1975.

Davis, William C., Editor - *The Images of War 1861-1865*, in six volumes, 1983.

Delaney, Caldwell - *Confederate Mobile a Pictorial History*; published by The Haunted Book Shop Mobile, Alabama, 1971.

Delaney, Caldwell- *The Story of Mobile*, 1981.

Dew, Charles B.- *Ironmaker to the Confederacy,* 1999.

Dickey- *Heavy Artillery Projectiles of the Civil War* by Sydney C. Kerksis and Thomas S. Dickey, Pheonix Press, 1972.

Dougherty, Kevin -*Sherman's Meridian Campaign a Practice Run for the March to the Sea*: at *Mississippi History Now*, an online publication of the Mississippi Historical Society.

Frazer, Mell A. - *Early History of Steamboats in Alabama,* Alabama Polytechnic Institute Historical Studies, 1907.

Friend, Jack -*West Wind, Flood Tide*, *The Battle of Mobile Bay,* 2004.

Folmer, John Kent, editor- *From That Terrible Field, Civil War letters of James W. Williams*, 21st Alabama Infantry Volunteers, 1981.

Folmer, John Kent- *The Alabama Review*, Lt. Col, James M. Williams and the Fort Powell Incident, April 1964.

Geary, Daniel - Geary Papers, Mobile Public Library.

Gilmer, Jeremy - Gilmer Collection, University of North Carolina.

Gorgas, Col J.-*The Ordnance Manual for the Use of the Officers of the Confederate States Army*, Charleston, 1863.

Gray, Edwyn-*19th Century Torpedoes and Their Inventors* , 2004.

Glenn, John-McMillan Collection, History Museum of Mobile, John Glenn Letters, November 29 and December 4, 1862.

Green, Arthur E. - *Mobile Confederates from Shiloh to Spanish Fort, the Story of the 21st Alabama Infantry Volunteers CSA*, Heritage Press, March 2012.

Higginbotham, Jay- *Pascagoula, Singing River City.* 1967.

Kerksis, Sydney C.- Heavy Artillery Projectiles of the Civil War by Sydney C. Kerksis and Thomas S. Dickey, Pheonix Press, 1972.

Lash, Jeffery N.-A Yankee in Gray: Danville Ledbetter and the Defense of Mobile Bay, 1861-1863, *Civil War History,* Vol. 37, number 3, Sept. 1991.

Latour, A. LaCarriere - Historical Memior of The War in West Florida and Louisiana 1814-1815, 1816.

Lonn, Ella - *Foreigners in the Confederacy*, 2001.

Mahan, Alfred T.- *The Gulf and Inland Waters, The Navy in the Civil War*, 1883.

Mahan, D. H. -*A Treatise on Field Fortification*, John Wilet, New York, 1852.

Manuel, Dale - *The Defenses of the Lower Mobile Bay,* 1999.

Maury, Dabney H.- *Recollections of a Virginian*, Charles Scribner's Sons, 1894.

McMillan collection - History Museum of Mobile.

Miller, Francis Trevelyan, Editor in Chief - *Photographic History of the Civil War*, in ten volumes, 1957.

Mobile City Directory - 1855.

Mobile Register and Advertiser

Mumford - *Diary of Lt. Mumford* found at the History Museum of Mobile.

National Archives - Mobile Squadron Papers.

National Archives - record group 109, Chapter 3, Volume 12, Engineer Department Records.

National Archives Cartographic Section - *Modified Plan on Tower at Grants Pass & Pass Heron, Mobile Bay,* approved by John B. Floyd Secretary of War, September 5, 1860.

O'Brien, Sean Michael -*Mobile 1865, Last Stand of the* Confederacy, Praeger, 2001.

Official Atlas of the Civil War - plate CVlll, Washington, US Government Printing Office.

Official Records Army- Washington, US Government Printing Office.

Official Records Army- Dyer's Compendium, US Government Printing Office.

Official Records Navy- Washington, US Government Printing Office.

Page, General Richard L.- Telegraph Book, Southern Historical Society Collection at University of North Carolina.

Parker, Foxall A. - *Battle of Mobile Bay,* 1878.

Perry, Milton F. -*Infernal Machines,* LSU Press, 1965.

Perkins-*Letters of Captain George H. Perkins*, published 1886.

Ray, Cyril William - *Captain Charles T. Liernur 1828-1893*, a genealogy compilation.

Report of the Secretary of the Interior, 1884, Washington, US Government Printing Office.

Reports of the Supreme Court of Louisiana, volume XX for the year 1868.

Reynolds, Bernard A. - *Sketches of Mobile,* published in Mobile 1868.

Ripley, Warren - *Artillery and Ammunition of the Civil War, 1970.*

Ross, Fitzgerald - *Cities and Camps of the Confederate States,* 1865.

Sheliha, Victor Von - *A Treatise on Coast Defense*, published in London in 1868 and reprinted by the Greenwood Press in 1971.

Stephen, Walter W. - The Brooke Guns from Selma, *Alabama Historical Quarterly,* volume 20, 1958.

Still, William N. Jr., editor - *Alabama Historical Quarterly*, The Civil War letters of Robert Tarleton.

Taylor, Richard - *Destruction and Reconstruction*, D. Appleton and Company, 1879.

Taylor, Richard - Letter book, Tulane University.

Taylor, Richard - telegraph book, Tulane University, New Orleans.

The Eutaw Whig -edition of May 18, 1862.

The Official Military Atlas of the Civil War plate XL.

U.S. District Court-Archives Branch, Federal Archives and Records Center, Waltham, Massachusetts, record group 21, Records of the U.S. District Court for the District of Massachusetts, December term 1865.

Williams, W.-*Traveller's and Tourist's Guide through the United States*, Lippencott., 1851.

Wood, Wales W.-*History of the 95th Regiment Illinois Volunteers,* by Wales W. Wood, Esquire, Chicago, 1865.

Young, Claiborne S. -*Cruising Guide to the Northern Gulf Coast: Florida, Alabama and Mississippi,* 2003.

Index

21st Alabama, 65
21st Alabama Infantry Regiment, 31
33rd Wisconsin, 140
44th Missouri, 140
72nd Illinois, 140
7-inch rifle marked S- 19, 67
95th Illinois, 140

Alabama Port, 157
Alabama, State of, Seizes the Forts, 19
Anderson, Colonel, 116
Armistead, William R. (Bill), 155
Arrow, C.S.S. gunboat, 25
Artifacts, 187

Bagaley, William, steamer, 24
Baker, Andrew, 159
Baltic,C.S.S., 37
Banks, Gen. N.P., 58
Banks, Jay, 159
Barrington, Frances, 159
Bernard, Simon, 1
Bizjack, Jim, 159
Blown Up, 124
Bombs Fly, 78
Bragg, Gen. Braxton, 27
Bridge, 151

Brooke rifles, 67
Brooke, John M., 85
Brooklyn, U.S.S., 114
Buchanan, Adm. Franklin, 41
Buchanan, Admiral, 117
Buckner, Gen. Simon Bolivar, 45
Building a Fort, 42

C. S. M, steamer, 49
Calhoun, U.S.S., 62
Canby, Gen. Edward R. S., 138
Capers,Maj. W.C., 88
Cedar Point, 79
Cedar Point battery, 91
Cedar Point Battery, 37
Cedar Point Occupied, 136
Cedar Point, Fortifying, 32
Centennial, 153
Charlie, Phillips, 159
Chase ,William H., 6
Chicago Board of Trade Regiment, 140
Chickasaw, U.S.S., 118
Choctaw and Oven Bluffs, 169
Choctaw Bluff, 37
Chugee Point, 89
Clifton,U.S.S., 51
Conemaugh, U.S.S., 111
Constitution, U.S.S., 92

Covert Construction, 59
Crutchfield, Col. S., 101
Cuba Station, 130
Cuba, steamer, 17

Dauphin Island Railroad and Dock Company, 149
Davis, Jerry, 159
DeKrafft Lt. Commander, 103
DeKrafft, Adm. J. C. P., 111
Delchamps community, 141
Demony, Sgt. William, 131
Denbigh, steamer, 97
Desport, Private, 124
Dorrance, steamer, 100
Duke, James, 56

Edward, Capt. James, 63
Erb, H. B., 160
Estrella, U.S.S., 127

Farragut Adm. David G., 30
Farragut Withdraws, 87
Final Preparations, 108
First Alabama Voluntary Infantry Regiment, 33
First Battle of Mobile Bay, 74
Fisheries, 93
Florida, C.S.S., 191
Florida, C.S.S. gunboat, 25
Fort Boyer, 3, 4
Fort Charlotte, 3, 4
Fort Clinch, 9
Fort Gaines, 7
Fort Grant, 23
Fort Morgan, 7
Fort Powell, 66

Fremaux, Capt. L. J., 99
Fretwell, J.R., 56

Gaines, C.S.S., 37
Gallimard, Capt. J.V., 107
Gallimard, Lt., 98
Gardner, General, 137
Gazzam, Lt. G. G., 35
Geary, Daniel, 91
Genesee, U.S.S., 60
Gilmer, Maj. Gen. Jeremy, 76
Glenn, Lt. John, 49
Grant ,John, 10, 13
Grant ,John, 198
Grant, John, 9, 10, 14, 18, 145, 147, 148, 197, 198, 199
Grant's ,Captain License, 12
Grants Battery, 51
Grants Pass, battery at, 54
Guns are Back, 40

Halleck, Gen. H.W., 58
Halls Mill Camp, 66
Hartford, U.S.S., 114
Hartford, U.S.S>, 30
Henry James, U.S.S., 70
Hermes, Sloop of War, 4
History Museum of Mobile, 162
Howard, Captain, 89
Huntsville, ironclad, 171
Huntsville,C.S.S., 87
Hurricane Frederick, 170

*Ingomar ,*barge, 51
Ingomar, barge, 123
Inspection, 101

J.P.Jackson, U.S.S., 111
Jackson,U.S.S., 51, 60
John Griffith, U.S.S., 70
Jones ,Catesby Ap R., 19
Jones ,Thomas Ap R., 19
Jones, Abner C. (A.C.), 155
Jones, Catesby Ap R., 67, 83

Kirkland, Roger Lee, 164

Leadbetter ,Gen. Danville, 21
Liernur, Capt. Charles T., 43
Little Dauphin Island, 90
Little Dauphin Island beach, 79
Lockett, Samuel, 53

Mackall, General, 93
Mader, Lt. G. W., 111
Madison, President James, 1
Manhattan, U.S.S., 120
Marshall I. Smith,schooner, 51
Martello Tower, 6
Miller, O. C., 159
Millington, Thomas H., 42
Mobile Battle Guards, 124
Mobile Cadets number 2, 124
Mobile Dragoons, 35
Mobile Steam Mail Line Company, 15
Moore, Col. J.B., 140
Morgan, A. L., 160
Morgan, C.S.S., 37
mortar boats, 69
mortar fleet, 34

Mount Vernon ,U.S.S., 192

Narcissus, U.S.S., 111
Nashville, C.S.S., 171
Nettles, John H. Sr., 159
New Orleans, Fall of, 36

O. H. Lee, U.S.S., 70
Octorara, **U.S.S.**, 70
Olde Fort Alabama Museum, 157
*Oregon,*C.S.S. gunboat, 25
*Orvetta,*U.S.S., 70
Oven Bluff, 37

Page, Gen. Richard Lucian, 92
Pamlico,C.S.S., 25
Pass aux Heron ,tower fort at, 6
Pensacola Evacuated, 40
Perkins, Capt. George H., 121
Perry, brig, 92
Phillips, Dr. Sidney, 159
Phillips, Tex, 159
Pipkins, Donald, 159
Pomeroy, Acting Master, Timothy, 133
Pontchartrain Railroad Company, 14
Porter, Rear Adm. David D., 185
Porter, Adm. David D., 39
Powell, Col. William Llewellyn, 27
Price, Jerry, 159
Prize money, 122
Purvis, Dan, 159

Railroad?, 148
Raines torpedoes, 113
Red River, 58
Researching Powell, 164
Rives, Col. A. L., 95
Robertson, Colonel, 59

Rodolph, U.S.S., 139
Ross, Fitzgerald, 95
Rousseau , Capt, Lawrence, 22
Run past Fort Morgan, 111
Running the Blockade, 96

S-19, 84
Sarah Bruen, U.S.S., 70
Saranthus, Woodrow, 159
Satellite, U.S.S., 191
Savage, Lt. Tom, 124
Schell, Pamela, 165
Schell, Roxie, 165
Schenkle shell, 128
Scott. Capt. C.C., 91
Sea Foam,U.S.S., 70
Seddon, Secretary of War, 88
Sheliha, Victor Von, 45
Sherman, General, 72
Skates and Company, 26
Skates/Read-Parrot projectiles, 102
Skirmish at Fowl River Narrows, 140
Slaughter, Brig. Gen., 55
Smallwood, J. C., 159
Smith, schooner, 43
Smithweck ,David, iv
Smithweck, David, 181, 184, 188
Stewart, Col. C. S., 85
Stowe, Read, 165
Sughee Point, 79

Sughee Point wharf, 90
Susquehanna, U.S.S., 40

Taylor, Gen. Richard, 97
Tecumseh, U.S.S., 114
Tennessee, C.S.S., 37, 82
Tennessee's hospital barge, 52
The Rocks, 180
third system of forts, 1
Todd, J. B., 16
Torpedo Problems, 81
Torpedoes, 55
Tritona, U.S.S., 139
Truehart, Maj. D., 88
Tuscaloosa, C.S.S., 87
Tuscaloosa, ironclad, 171

Venture, sloop, 35
Von Sheliha, Victor E.R.W.E., 45

Walker ,Percy, 11
Whitney, B. A., 56
Whitney, Donald, 159
Whitworth steel rifle, 96
Williams Lt. Col. James M., 60
Winnebago, U.S.S., 120
Withers, Gen. Jones M., 27

ABOUT THE AUTHOR

Sid Schell is a retired maritime lawyer in Mobile, Alabama. For more than 40 years he has been building research files on Mobile and Southwest Alabama. He has written articles on the Civil War submarines and secret weapons tested at Mobile, and the forts at Oven and Choctaw Bluffs in Choctaw County, Alabama. A scuba diver, he has located and surveyed numerous Civil War vessels including the C.S.S. *Huntsville* and *Tuscaloosa*. Sidney has served as a member of the Board of Directors of the History Museum of Mobile since the early 1980s with five terms as chairman. He was in 1985 appointed Adjunct Research Associate with the Department of Sociology/Anthropology with the University of South Alabama. He served on the Tecumseh commission, C.S.S. Alabama Commission and at one time chaired the Underwater Archaeology Committee for the Alabama Historic Commission. He is also an artist and ship model builder but primarily a grandfather trying to impart his love of history to his grandchildren.

www.ingramcontent.com/pod-product-compliance
Lightning Source LLC
Chambersburg PA
CBHW080411230426
43662CB00016B/2368